The Voyant and The Mark of Malice

Sadie Hewitt

Cover by Mayhem Cover Creations
Editing by Bailee Condie, Ink and Quill Publishing LLC
Beta Reading by Betti Nagy
Internal Art and Formatting by Sadie Hewitt

Paperback ISBN: 979-8-9876432-7-3
Ebook ISBN: 979-8-9876432-6-6

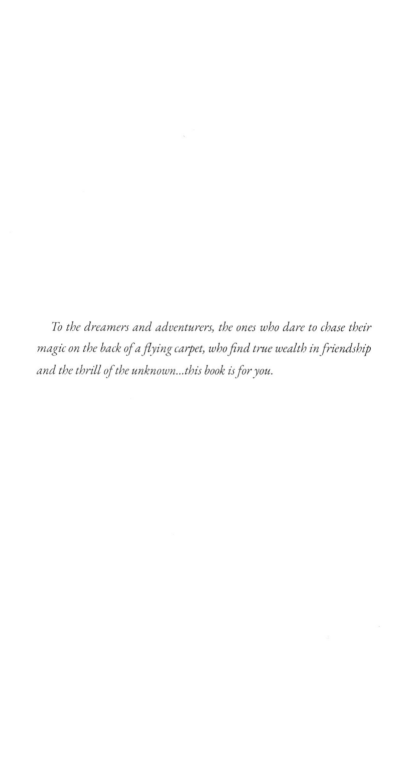

To the dreamers and adventurers, the ones who dare to chase their magic on the back of a flying carpet, who find true wealth in friendship and the thrill of the unknown...this book is for you.

The Voyant and The Mark of Malice is a pirate fantasy romance where all things wicked, dark, and dangerous collide.

This story contains elements of battle on a pirate ship, hand-to-hand combat involving pistols and blades, alcohol use, blood, brief mention of domestic violence, graphic violence, death/murder, profanity, on-page consensual sex, and a brief mention of a child's drowning.

Readers who may be sensitive to these, please continue with caution.

ONE YEAR AGO

"It's here, just here!"

Karim Fayez stumbled at the unexpected shout, catching his palm painfully on the sharp rocks that jutted from the stone at the cave entrance. Waves crashed against the shore behind them, tossing their small rowboat like a toy in bathwater. With a souring stomach, he watched an oar jostle loose from the mount and tumble into the sea, sinking into the blue depths.

That would certainly make the return trip more difficult.

"Are you looking at the map correctly, Soren?" an amused second voice called from behind Karim. "Captain won't be happy if we come back empty-handed again."

No, Captain *wouldn't* be happy if they came back empty-handed again. The sore thrashes on Karim's back from the flogging he took just weeks ago still stretched painfully with every step forward. Despite this, Karim could imagine Soren's dark face scowling as he looked down to scour the worn map for the twentieth time that day.

"Don't be ridiculous, Draven," Soren retorted, his echoing voice clearing as Karim navigated further from the cave's entrance. "I *know* how to read a map."

Karim jolted as Draven plopped a heavy hand on his shoulder. When Draven brushed past, the touch was both unwelcome and unanticipated. Karim didn't feel right in this cave. Though he was sure they were alone, he couldn't shake the feeling that he was being watched...and he was being watched closely. Was it the stone walls themselves? Perhaps the lichen that lined the rock or the uninhabited tide pools beneath his feet?

No, *that* was ridiculous.

Karim shook his head, surging into the darkness after Draven and Soren, following the dim flicker of light from the torch Soren held high above his head. The air grew increasingly stale as the minutes passed, the salty smell of the sea replaced by the stinging scent of mold and boggy water. It was quiet, too. Soren's heavy boot steps nearly drowned out the steady *drip, drip, drip* from the water leaking down the stone.

A chill went up Karim's spine, tenting the hairs on his neck. "I think we should return to the boat...?" he began slowly, and he hated the wavering tone his voice had taken on. He would gladly take another beating if it meant leaving the confines of the island at that very moment.

Unfortunately, the other two men also heard his trepidation.

"Where's your sense of adventure?" Draven boisterously asked. The question was followed by a snort that echoed off the wet walls.

"It left," Karim replied as he stepped into a puddle, water flooding the inside of his boot, "six caves ago." His sole squelched when he took another step forward, and the sound was like a cannon blast in the darkness. "I'm starting to have doubts this cave is even real."

The three men had been hunting for the cave on the map for over nine months. Nine months of sailing on *The Midnight Mariner* alongside Captain Nasir Al-Mahdi, the notoriously cruel corsair and one who reveled in laying down tar-covered leather straps on the backs of his men. Nine months of rationing food, guzzling bad *fion,* and working under the sun's heat, nearly going blind when it reflected off the cresting waves.

Karim hated it, hated every second of it. But Soren and Draven pushed him through, reminding him almost daily of the treasure at the end of it all. Captain Nasir wanted the *Luminaria*; they could take everything else.

"It's real," Draven clucked, ducking his head to avoid a low-hanging stalactite. "I overheard it from a merchant who overheard it from a—"

"A *concubine* who overheard it from a patron who overheard it from a priest at Liddros's temple in Sha'hadra," Karim finished for him. "And as I've said many times, that's not a promising start." He paused to sweep his black hair from his eyes, using his cold sweat to slick it back against the crown of his head. "We don't even know if that damn map is real."

"That," Soren interjected as he shifted to the side, shuffling through a crevice in the stone, "I *can* attest to. The map is as old as the temple priests say that it is. Its markings have not been used in the last five centuries."

Karim clamped his lips shut. Soren would know if the map was real, after all. He was the best cartographer on the continent, bought and paid for by the king. And Draven...well, Draven was the best thief on the continent. Soren bought and paid for *him* to steal said map.

Karim, on the other hand, was a friend of a friend who always wanted to go on an adventure and never thought that adventure would lead him to Captain Nasir Al-Mahdi— or his tarred leather whip. Draven was sure that the *Luminaria* required a virgin's hand to retrieve it, and while Karim never had the pleasure of sticking his cock in a woman, retrieving a magical gemstone was something he could do.

"Just think of all the cunts you'll be able to have once this is all over," Draven mused as they moved further into the cave. Karim glanced behind him, his muscles stiffening when he realized how far behind the entrance was. "You can flash your golden chalice or your ring made of pure silver at them and—"

"Quiet," Soren whispered, his tone suddenly throaty and harsh. He was louder now, and, in their bickering, Karim hadn't realized Soren had stopped walking. "Do you hear that?"

The three men were silent, waiting with bated breath for anything to make a noise. Karim watched the shadow from the torch's flame dance against the stone, casting long lines of black that reminded him of the fabled monsters his mother used to tell him about when he was a child. Just as he was about to open his mouth and ask what they were waiting for...he heard it.

It started as a whisper, a summoning, that skittered over his bones and pebbled his flesh. It was soft, cunning, and haunting, and...Karim had the sudden urge to flee, but his feet kept him rooted in place. The whispers were beckoning him, drawing him in, pleading for him to come closer, come see...

"It's here," Soren said with such finality that it snapped Karim from his thoughts. Soren swept the torch above his head, illuminating a crude serpent carving wrapped around a jagged staff. His head darted down and back up before dropping again, comparing the serpent to the one on the map. "Draven, dagger."

Draven didn't hesitate to yank his dagger from his belt and open his palm, sliding the sharpened blade against the curve of his hand.

His flesh split, a river of blood pooling in the seams of his fingers and spilling onto the rock beneath him. Karim's belly twisted at the sight.

A slap sounded, followed by a sickening wet drag against the stone as Draven wiped the blood from his hand onto the carved serpent. He tugged his scarf from his head, wrapping it around his palm and tying the knot closed with his teeth. Soren didn't bother looking at Draven; instead, he kept his stare on the wall.

A minute ticked by, then two, then three. Karim didn't know when he had started to wring his hands, only being alerted when his knuckles ground against one another. He let out a long, low breath that curled in a fog before his face.

That wasn't right. It was the middle of the warm season, and even in the cave's confines, he shouldn't have been able to see his breath. The temperature plummeted again, and the air suddenly became frigid, as though the rocks had turned to ice. Karim glanced toward the torch, the flame jarring violently against a phantom wind before it snuffed out, pitching them into complete darkness.

The three men went silent, breaths heavy against the black surrounding them.

The cave began to shake, the earth quaking so terribly beneath Karim's feet that his knees knocked together, and his teeth painfully chattered. He threw a hand out, attempting to steady himself against the wall, but only felt the cold, moist air against his fingers. Next to him, one of the men stumbled and fell, landing with a sharp *oof* and a *splash* into a pool of water. The shaking stopped just as suddenly as it started, and something small scrambled over the toe of Karim's boot. As if it, too, wanted to get away from what lived beyond the wall.

A grating of stone against stone sounded as a hidden door slid up, revealing a passage bathed in the moonlight shining through the deep cracks in the ceiling. Soren, who was the one to have fallen, pushed himself from the puddle and adjusted his spectacles back into place.

"This is—" Draven began, unabashedly staring at the sight before him.

Terrifying? Uneasy? Worrisome? Karim had a host of words to use instead of what Draven finished with.

"Unbelievable." Draven stepped over the threshold of the stone door, pushing past Soren to enter the passage. It was narrow enough that Draven's broad shoulders brushed each side. The smell wafting from inside of it was stagnant, as though the door had been sealed for a very long time. "What are you chaps waiting for?"

Soren entered the passage next, his slim figure fitting easily within the space, the map still clutched tightly in his hand. His head swiveled in every direction as he tried to take in every nook and cranny. Karim took a deep breath and swallowed hard, the act difficult against the dryness of his throat.

He could...wait here? No, they needed him if the *Luminaria* was indeed in this cave. Maybe they could call him when they found it? But what if they were too far away? The argument bobbed back and forth in his mind until he finally pitched forward and followed the other two men into the passage.

The air was heavy and eerily charged, and that feeling of being watched only intensified with every step Karim took. He glanced over his shoulder, half expecting to see someone standing there, but he was only met with darkness. Soren's torch lay haphazardly on the ground, half hidden in shadow. He shook it off despite the prickling over his skin.

The passage turned upward, leaving Karim short of breath and gasping when he reached the apex. Sweat dripped between his shoulder blades, sliding down his spine and settling uncomfortably into the waistband of his pants. *Concubines, fion, rings made of silver and gold, enough coin to last four generations...* He said the words like a mantra, thinking them repeatedly as they ventured further down.

And that mantra kept him going, enough that he ran directly into Soren's back when the man had stopped abruptly. Karim opened his mouth to inquire, but his words were lost as he peered around Draven's upper arm.

They had come to a chamber, the walls towering above them and curving in one smooth motion into the sweeping stone ceiling. The chamber was fit for the king's palace, large enough that Karim was sure one could fit an entire village inside...and then some. But that wasn't what caught his eye.

It was the treasure.

Piles of gold bars, coins made of silver and copper, and gemstones of all colors and sizes littered the ground. Treasure stacked in mounds taller than Draven, overflowing into the water pooling along the hall's edges. Marble statues, golden chests filled with crowns and pearls, necklaces embedded with sapphires. Karim drank it in, his eyes flitting over the piles and piles of riches.

It was here. It was real. Karim was *wealthy.* Wealthy didn't even begin to cover it. He could buy the whole fucking kingdom if he wanted to.

Draven let out a *whoop* and raced into the hall, skidding to a halt in front of the first pile of coins. He reached down and began to stuff handfuls into the pockets of his pants and the gaps of his boots. He laughed as he shuffled past, his breeches already weighed down under the amount he had taken, and picked up a necklace, slinging it over his head—the large emerald clunked against his chest.

Soren had also moved forward, kneeling to study the inscriptions on the coins at his feet. "This must be thousands of years old," he murmured, glancing over the rim of his spectacles for a better look. "Never in my studies..." He trailed off, his mouth remaining open as he fixed his stare on the coins.

"Fuck the *Luminaria,* and fuck the captain who wants it!" Draven said from the other end of the chamber.

Karim looked over to him. Draven had placed a crown on his head and threaded two more around each arm as bracelets. He then wound six more gleaming pieces of jewelry around his neck.

"And how would we return to shore?" Soren asked, not taking his eyes from the two coins he had lifted into the air, comparing them side by side. "We're in an archipelago at least a ten-day sail from the nearest port."

"There's no way *The Midnight Mariner* will be able to come any closer than where she's anchored," Draven replied, ignoring the question posed by Soren as he grabbed a chalice from the nearest mound, tossed it in the air, and then caught it. "We could slip from the island, use a stack of coins to hire our crew, and come back to claim the rest. Alerting the captain now will only alert the crew, which means we have to split this—" He paused to stretch his arms out wide. "—With fifty other men."

Karim had half a mind to agree. *They* had deciphered the map, spent months on board the ship with the insufferable Captain Nasir Al-Mahdi, and knew which gods-forsaken island this cave was on. Who were the crew to claim any of this?

"Let's give the *Luminaria* to the captain," Karim said, glancing between Draven and Soren. "We should bring just enough coins back to hire another ship upon our return to the nearest port. Tell the captain that there was no treasure, only the stone. The crew would be none the wiser, and the captain would be satisfied with our discovery."

Soren nodded as Draven heaved a sigh.

"Fine," Draven said, letting the crowns slide from his wrists and clatter to the stone floor. "But where will we find the *Luminaria* in all of this?"

Karim went quiet, looking around the chamber. Draven was right. It would take months, possibly years, to sift through everything here.

"There," Soren said, angling his head in gesture. "The doorway."

Karim slid his gaze toward Soren's head tilt, his eyes locking on the doorway at the other end. It was tiny, easily overlooked in the grand scheme of the chamber. Karim walked toward it, passing the seemingly never-ending mountains of coins as he went. He bent down and snagged a single one from the side of the nearest pile, pocketing it before continuing. Behind him, Draven chuckled.

"Couldn't help yourself, could you, boy?"

Karim ignored him.

His walk slowed as he approached the doorway. That feeling of being watched returned, ghosting over the back of his neck and boring like a plague into his spirit. *It's just Draven and Soren,* he told himself as he crossed the threshold. He couldn't quite bring himself to believe it.

The second room was dark, lit only by a single shaft of moonlight beaming down from the ceiling. That light, though narrow, was bright enough to illuminate the space and a set of torches. A deep pool of water bifurcated the room, splitting the floor into two peninsulas and conjoined by a slim walkway. There was nothing in the room— no piles of gold, coins, or jewels—except for a single pedestal made of jagged rock on the opposite peninsula. And there, on that pedestal, was a single ruby gemstone.

Karim felt a lightness in his chest that hadn't been there a moment prior, and a sudden rush of adrenaline flooded his body, spurring him on. He crossed the narrow path, one foot in front of the other, and didn't dare look into the inky black water on either side of him. It was still as glass, perfectly reflecting the ceiling far above him. He didn't pay too much attention to that either.

As he approached the pedestal, his breath caught in his throat, and his gaze fastened on the gemstone. It was smaller than he expected, one that could easily fit in the palm of his hand. It was also expertly cut, as though a professional jeweler had crafted it himself. Karim reached a hand forward, allowing it to float just above the ruby. He stopped just short of grabbing it, suddenly frozen in place.

There was an exhale behind him, and that breath tickled the back of Karim's head and up to the shell of his ear.

Do you believe yourself worthy? A ghostly voice asked. That same hauntingly eerie whisper that drew them deeper into the cave in the first place. Karim's extended hand trembled, and his legs tightened, readying for him to run, but he was rooted in place, unable to move. Fear churned his guts into water, his heartbeat loud in his ears.

"Aye, Karim!" Draven called from the chamber, his voice ricocheting in a sharp echo against the stone ceiling. "Is it there? Did you find the *Luminaria*?"

Draven's shout broke Karim from his stupor, and before he could change his mind, he reached down and grasped the stone.

For a long minute, nothing happened. Karim was about to place the stone in his pocket when an ear-piercing shriek had him whipping around to face the doorway to the hall. The once serene pools had begun to rumble, displacing the water onto the stone pathway and gurgling up to wash over his boots. In his shock, Karim dropped the stone, which was washed away by a sudden wave.

Karim rushed over the stone pathway, splashing through the water now nearing mid-calf, and waded toward the chamber. He slowed as he approached the threshold, gaping as he watched the water bounce against the doorway as though hitting a barrier. Lifting his eyes, he caught sight of something that made him stop in his tracks completely.

Using razor-sharp claws, humanoid corpses had clawed from the ground. Gray, weathered bodies with hollow eyes that seemed to glow despite the dim light. While each was in a different stage of decomposition, ranging from wholly emaciated and mummified to fleshy and rotten, they all had the same unsettling expression: hunger. And the shriek? That had been poor Soren, who was now laying wide-eyed and unseeing with his gut split open, two creatures covered in his blood as they feasted.

The map lay on the ground just at his fingertips.

The water had risen to Karim's waist in his delay to leave, and he realized he had two choices. He could stay in this room and drown, sooner rather than later, or face the creatures wandering the hall.

But Karim had one final secret in his pocket.

There was something Soren and Draven didn't know about Karim, something he had kept to himself. Karim had grown up in Sha'Hadra, the bustling desert city of the continent and the only major one that didn't connect directly to a seaport. Sha'Hadra was known for two things.

Well, three things.

One, they had the best spices on the continent. Spices that could be added to chicken or lamb, making any dish aromatic and decadent. The spices held up the infamous Sha'Hadra marketplace and were regularly exported to the capital, Mistral Bay.

Two, Sha'Hadra was rich in history and culture. Traditional art, music, and literature, each a distinct and vibrant form that drew tourists from every city on the continent.

The third, and the unofficial, was that Sha'Hadra had the highest number of guards out of all the cities on the continent. Guards dispatched from the capital on the king's orders spent their time targeting the native children of Sha'Hadra, chasing them away from the marketplace. The children who were fast enough were the ones to get away. The children who weren't...they didn't last long in Sha'Hadra.

Karim had been one of those children who got away.

Karim took off as the water crested over his shoulders, leaving the confines of the flooded room and entering the ring of creatures. To his right, he spotted Draven fighting for his life, his dagger drawn and swinging wildly. It caught the nearest creature in the chest, slicing the leathered skin open to reveal the ribcage underneath.

"Karim! Karim!" Draven shouted as he stepped back and tripped over the crown that had fallen off his head. One of the creatures lunged forward, pinning him to the pile of treasure beneath him.

"I'm sorry, Draven!" Karim called back, jostling to the side to slide past a creature who had lurched for him, claws outstretched. He locked his eyes on the map next to Soren's dismantled body. "Every *chap* for himself."

"You *traitor!*" Draven screamed, followed by a sharp cry as a creature dug its claws into his leg. "Karim! *Karim!*"

Karim sprinted, bending at the waist as he passed Soren to snatch the map. The two creatures didn't flinch as he fled, their faces still buried deep in the dead man's gut. He side-stepped around another creature, then another, their claws outstretched, and their yellowing teeth bared as he ran toward the passage back to the cave.

"Karim! Ka—" Draven's shout was cut silent, a wet, sickening garble in its place.

Karim crossed the threshold of the passageway, his shoulder knocking into the stone as he avoided the final creature in his way. It bounced off an invisible barrier, similar to the water in the *Luminaria's* chamber, and let out a monstrous roar at its loss for a fresh meal. The smell of its breath was stomach-turningly rancid.

He followed the moonlit passage back to the cave, relieved to find the open door. He kept up a brisk pace, using his left hand to follow the cave's wall to the entrance. Behind him, stone on stone ground together as the door to the chamber slid closed, trapping the bodies of his former colleagues inside.

But Karim had the map, the parchment still clutched in his hand, and he had a single coin. It might be enough to buy him passage aboard another ship. Now, he needed to find a captain willing to take him.

CHAPTER ONE

KALIA

Present Day

The man seated in the cushioned armchair wanted his cock sucked.

More specifically, Cranford Reed, the crooked-nosed and greasy-haired regular who liked to sit in the armchair next to the roaring fireplace, wanted his cock sucked by Nadine Booth. She was the best at it; everyone who worked or frequented *The Sand Glass Bordello* knew it.

Gods, even Kalia Salam knew it. And Kalia tried not to know anything about the ladies who worked at *The Sand Glass Bordello*. Not because the madam didn't allow for fraternizing— she preferred it, truth be told. Seeing the topless ladies laughing in the great room together gave the clientele something to consider. Kalia, however, had been employed long enough to know the likelihood of the ladies sticking around was low. They weren't *worth* fraternizing with...at least longer than it took Kalia to send visions of them to the men in the brothel, anyway.

That was Kalia's job. To manipulate the clientele who frequented the bordello into choosing a lady for the evening. To send them visions down the threads of her magic that would harden their cocks and make them lust for a woman who hadn't been booked yet. That kept the pockets of the madam's expensive silk dresses stuffed to the brim with coin.

It was the only reason Kalia was alive after the madam witnessed her wield her mind magic like a sharpened blade. The only reason she had been plucked off the streets of Sha'Hadra and dumped into Mistral Bay's most expensive bordello. She spent almost the first twelve years of her life alone, fighting to survive the harsh realities of the guarded alleys and running from the threat of the rope dangling above her head.

But that was fifteen years ago, and Kalia now knew better than to showcase her ability. Instead, she honed it to a subtlety. A flash of a woman peering through her lashes here, a vision of another moaning as her hips snapped over a cock there. Enough to twist the weak-willed minds of men into spending their hard-earned money.

Weak-willed minds like Cranford Reed, for example.

Unfortunately, Kalia also knew more about Cranford Reed than she ever wanted to. Because when she sent her threads racing down the bridges of these men, she more often than not caught glimpses of their violent visions barreling back down the bond she had created.

Kalia had inadvertently found out that Cranford Reed was the one who had beaten Mintie Lynk two weeks prior. Beaten her so severely that Mintie crawled, bloodied and broken, down the marbled stairs of the bordello to beg the madam for leave to seek a healer.

Of course, the madam denied that request before forcing Mintie to return to her room and await instructions for her next client.

Kalia bided her time, letting the vision of Cranford's fists slamming into the side of Mintie's head fester until he dared to show up like clockwork three days later. Mintie had been too afraid to rat Cranford out to the madam, mostly because he was a highly valued client and because Mintie knew the madam would fire her instantly. She wouldn't even bother to turn Cranford over to the capital guard but would surely welcome him back after things cooled down.

And *that* was something that didn't sit right with Kalia.

Kalia leaned against the marble pillar in the back of the great room, sweeping her green eyes through the cigar haze that settled over the patrons. The scent of stale sweat and sex seeped through the soft glow from the iron chandeliers, blanketing the plush cushions, the burgundy curtains, and the potted greenery that decorated the space.

Though clean and fairly well-regarded, the bordello was steeped in nothing but bad memories. Ones that Kalia was desperate to rid herself of. That was why she kept a small purse hidden under the floorboards of her bedroom, savings for the day she could buy her freedom from the madam. A year, maybe two at the most, and she would leave all of this behind.

And, *gods*, that day couldn't come soon enough.

It was busy tonight, busier than it should have been for a random day mid-week, and she had been watching Cranford through the gaps in the crowd for damn near an hour now. A moan elicited to her right, cutting through the sultry whine from the string instruments, and she slid her gaze over to spot one of the ladies straddling a man, her nipple clamped firmly between his teeth.

That day *really* couldn't come soon enough.

"Alright tonight, Kalia, love?" a husky voice sounded as it sidled up to her, the owner leaning a shoulder against the opposite round of the pillar.

Kalia hooked one sandaled foot over the other, feeling the thin satin of her high-slit dress brush against her leg. "Odion," she purred in return, shifting her stare to the handsome private guard who patrolled the great room. "You know she doesn't like it when we chat."

Odion smiled, his lips splitting wide to reveal a right-sided dimple. "I can't help it. You're a sight to behold this evening."

Kalia lifted a hand to tuck a strand of dark hair behind her ear, a move that adjusted the low-cut collar of her red dress enough that the top curves of her breasts peeked over the material. Odion gave a low whistle, turning his head to survey the room again. A coy smirk played on her lips. She knew what she did to him, what she *had* done to him. It was no secret.

"I'm still surprised that the madam doesn't let you become a lady," Odion said. He shifted on his feet, letting a casual hand rest on the pommel of his sword. "All the gods know that you would be the most sought-after one here." He cleared his throat. "I believe you are even now."

Kalia let out a humorless huff through her nose and darted out her tongue to lick her lips. Pleasure coiled in her belly when Odion's eyes dropped to her mouth, and she remembered the feeling of his muscled weight pinning her to her bed just days before. Gods, he was a good lay—one of the better ones she had recently. "Don't let the madam hear you say that. I've just been allowed to resume my duties in the great room."

Kalia had been sequestered to the second-floor balcony for nearly a month due to an *incident* involving one of the men, a rabid honey badger, and an ancient wine opener she found in the marketplace. An *incident* that the madam could not officially blame on Kalia but determined was her nonetheless.

And the madam would have been correct.

Odion chuckled, the sound skittering over her bones. That chuckle had been in Kalia's ear when she moaned his name, when she threw her hand up to keep him from thrusting her into the headboard. She wondered if she could convince him to come back later that evening. From the way he kept shifting his sword in front of his cock, she was sure she could make it worth his while.

"Maybe it's all for the best in the end. You wouldn't want to take away from the others who need to make a living." Odion paused to drink in her bronzed, high cheekbones, the delicate length of her nose, and the arrogant quirk of her brow. "When do you reckon the madam will allow me to take you to a tavern?"

Kalia's smile was genuine this time. "Never, I'm sure. Certainly, as long as I'm in her employment and I'm—"

"Honor bound to your debt," Odion finished with a dramatic sigh. "You've said that once or twice now. You know, to this day, I'm still unsure what you *do* for the madam."

Kalia opened her mouth to reply when Cranford rose from the armchair. His shuffling footsteps wound past two writhing female dancers, their hands teasing on waists and exposed hips. Kalia straightened, pushing herself from the pillar as he approached Nadine. There was a violent gleam to his stare, which she pinned with her own.

The image of Nadine's lips wrapped around his cock was funneling through his mind faster than the king's prized warships as they careened into the bay. He reached down to adjust himself, seemingly not caring that he did it in plain view of another lady, who scrunched her nose at the sight.

"Kalia," Odion said sharply, warning marring his once playful tone. "What are you—"

But his question was lost to the music and humming chatter as Kalia pushed through the crowd, following Cranford to where Nadine had perched on an overstuffed cushion.

"Kalia!" a whispering voice cracked through a sudden chasm in the crowd. "Kalia! I'm free for the next hour—" But the demand of the lady was swallowed just the same, and Kalia pressed on, not bothering to look back.

Kalia maneuvered toward Nadine, positioning herself against the red velvet curtain draped from the golden rods near the ceiling. She nearly blended in, slipping into the marbled room's background.

Just as the madam liked her.

"You're a pretty thing," Cranford rasped when he reached Nadine, lifting a dirt-crusted hand to caress his knuckle down her cheek. "I'm happy to see that you're available tonight."

Nadine smiled in response, flicking her blonde hair over her shoulder. Despite the sensual gaze she was sending Cranford, Kalia recognized the stiffening of her shoulders and the tick in her jaw as a suppressed shudder. Disgust was one thing many of the ladies had gotten quite good at covering up, something Kalia still couldn't manage to do. It was always written in the violent roll of her shoulders and how she clenched her knees together.

"Twelve coins for the half hour or twenty for the hour. Unless you've spent too much on your *fion* tonight," Nadine responded, pouting her lips into a sultry frown. She was good, one of the best in the bordello. She could play the men like clay, lightly tugging on their egos.

Cranford smirked, leaning down to set his empty goblet on the wooden table at his knees. "I certainly know how to pace myself for this."

Another flash of a vision erupted in Kalia's mind, one of his hands gripping Nadine's slim neck as he pistoned into her with rough thrusts. Kalia barely tempered her forming scowl—foul, disgusting man.

Nadine rose from her seat as Cranford dug into his pockets to extract twelve coins from the inside. He certainly wouldn't take that long...though Kalia was now aware of what he preferred to do with the other twenty-nine minutes of his time. Nadine's bare breasts shifted against her upper abdomen, the front panel of her skirt coming to rest between her pale thighs.

Cranford was bouncing with glee when he twisted on the toes of his boots to walk toward the sweeping marble staircase. Nadine made to brush past, her lips suddenly pressed into a hard line at what lay in store when Kalia reached out to clasp a hand around her wrist. Nadine stopped in her tracks, an expectant brow quirked in Kalia's direction.

At the silent, blank stare Kalia returned, Nadine looked to Cranford and said, "Go ahead darling, warm the bed. I'll be up in just a moment."

Cranford looked ready to argue but caught the glare Kalia sent his way. He hesitated, gaping for a beat, before crossing to the staircase and tromping to the second floor. Even his walk was foul with dried dirt falling to the stairs in clumps.

Nadine spun toward Kalia, her once honeyed voice now brimming with venom. "This better be important. I'm short on coin for the madam tonight."

Kalia turned a bored expression to Nadine. "Mintie Lynk." Nadine's eyes widened, shoulders dropping as her defenses waned. "Yeah, that's what I thought, too."

"How did you–" Nadine started, but Kalia cut her off with a curt shake of her head.

"No matter, but it was him." Kalia's gaze slid to the second-floor balcony, where Cranford had already disappeared behind a door just beyond the balustrade. From the corner of her eye, she saw Odion begin to navigate his way through the crowd.

Recognition flashed over Nadine's face, and she reeled her head back. "What did you do now?"

"What should have been done two weeks ago," Kalia flicked her gaze to Mintie, whose eye had finally turned a sickening shade of green and who still had to hide her limping gait. Revoltingly enough, plenty of men liked an injured woman, as shown by the concerningly large horde of extra clients Mintie had taken on in the past week.

"She's going to kill you for this," Nadine hissed. "She's going to—"

Whatever Nadine thought the madam was going to do was lost to the piercing, blood-curdling scream that ripped from the second floor. A hush fell over the crowd, furrowed brows and worried gazes turning upward when a second scream echoed over the domed ceiling.

A door flew open, and a very naked Cranford appeared at the threshold, his hands thrashing through the air as he tried to bat away the...

"Are those hornets?" Nadine asked, a frown curling the corners of her lips downward.

As Cranford stumbled down the marble staircase, in full view of the three dozen people whose attention was now fixed on him, Kalia saw at least fifty telltale red welts blooming on his skin. Perfect, just as she planned.

"They seem to be aggressive ones," Kalia responded with an air of shocked innocence as Odion steered toward Cranford to herd the man and the hornets through the front door.

Nadine tried and failed not to look impressed. "How does one get a nest of hornets..." she trailed off, glancing back toward Kalia.

"Under the mattress?" Kalia offered as she watched Odion stomp on a hornet that had landed on the marble floor before slamming the door shut behind Cranford. "Delicately." Small welts were still between her fingers where some of the hornets had stung her.

Silence descended, and no one moved, seemingly unsure of what to make of the sudden scene when a side door flew open with a crash that had the clientele jolting in surprise. It was a crash, however, that the ladies had grown used to. More often than not, it had to do with her.

"*Kalia!*"

Her name whipped through the room, and the voice managed to suck the oxygen from the air, sending even the most hardened sailors scrambling in the opposite direction. Kalia glanced to her left, eyes meeting the severe stare of the bordello's madam.

Nadine kept a small distance between herself and Kalia, her pretty face plastered with a knowing expression mixed with fearful pity.

"My office. *Now.*"

CHAPTER TWO

RAHMI

"That ship isn't *technically* sinking, captain," the quartermaster, Alaric Blackthorn, said, his voice raised over the gale. "I doubt anyone would be dying on it—"

"There are two," Captain Rahmi Abada corrected him, sliding his brown eyes from the ship back to his second-in-command, taking in the man's dark blonde hair and the crooked patch he wore over his missing right eye. "You cannot sense them, but I can. Their souls call to me." He stepped away from the helm, his boots landing heavily against the planks, and approached the staircase leading to the deck below.

Despite the storm raging around them, the crew halted their work to turn their gazes up to him. Out of respect? Perhaps. Out of fear? That was far more likely. And he reveled in it.

Captain Rahmi Abada wasn't just any captain who sailed the Aeglecian Seas; the jagged scar that ran down the center of his chest reminded him of that every day.

"Tether at her bow," Rahmi ordered over the winds, narrowing his eyes against the pelting rain. Thunder rumbled, closer than it had been only a few moments before. "Strip her of fresh water, rations, and anything of value you may find in the decks below." The crew jeered at that, their wicked smiles illuminated by the fork of lightning that flashed above them.

"And the ship's ammunition, captain?" Alaric asked, tilting his head toward the ship, bobbing with the churning waves. "It seems she isn't as keen on being taken as you seem to think she will be."

As if on cue, a *boom* echoed across the sea, the sound mixing with another crack of thunder. A cannonball fell short of *The Mark of Malice*'s port side, splashing into the rolling water. A flare of irritation heated Rahmi's gut, and he turned his glare on the ship as though it was all that was needed to get them to stop. He knew the captain of that ship wouldn't dare to fire on him if he knew *who* he was firing on.

It would only be considered a courtesy to let him know.

"Steer *The Mark of Malice* toward the bow," Rahmi repeated with an agitated sharpness. He wholly believed repetition was for captains who needed more control of their crew. He untied the cutlass strapped to his belt and caught the blade before it fell to the deck, pushing it into his quartermaster's unexpecting arms. "I'll meet you there."

"Captain, do you really—" Alaric began, fumbling to set down the cutlass with any semblance of dignity he believed Rahmi would accept, but Rahmi was already on the gunnel of his ship.

Rahmi placed a hand on the pommel of his dagger, the blade still sheathed on his other hip, and looked down into the water, rocking his ship. The waves blasted against the hull, and the wood creaked dangerously as though it threatened to give way at any moment. He knew it wouldn't; he knew his ship better than anything else. With that thought, Rahmi leaped from the gunnel, diving into the depths of the sea.

The cold water shocked his system, tightening his skin and seizing the air left in his lungs. If he were a lesser man or even a *mortal* man, Rahmi would have surely drowned from the drop alone. But Rahmi wasn't a lesser man or even a mortal man, and when he surfaced to take a breath, he locked his eyes on the merchant ship in the distance.

Rahmi ducked under the waves, the current tugging him one way and the next, but he kept an intense pace as he cut a path through the sea. The cannons blasted again; this time, he could smell the acrid scent of used gunpowder intermingling with the briny, charged air of the storm.

He made it to the merchant ship in a time that impressed even himself and grasped onto the rope ladder tethered to the side of the hull. Sticking one sodden boot into the first rung, he hauled himself upward. Water sluiced from his tunic and breeches, sliding into the already-flooded gaps of his boots. He took a moment to wipe his eyes before drawing the dagger from the sheath and sticking it between his teeth.

He didn't know how quickly he would need to use it, but merchant captains were never eager to have their ships boarded. Or, so was Rahmi's experience.

Rahmi scaled the side of the ship, his knuckles white under the pressure it took to grip the slick rope, and finally swung over the gunnel just a few moments later. The crew scrambled on the deck, men heaving their bodies against the strain of the lines to pull in the mainmast and mizzenmast sails against the roaring winds. They should have done that hours ago.

"Bare sails!" a man shouted, his body braced against the helm. "I said *bare sails, men*!"

Rahmi heaved a sigh and took the dagger from between his teeth while glancing around the deck again. The captain, or whom he assumed was the captain, was young. Rahmi had known the men were too inexperienced to realize that pulling the sails down amid the storm was futile, and the captain's smooth face merely confirmed it.

"She's coming in at full speed!" a sailor announced a few feet to Rahmi's left, drawing his attention away from the captain at the helm. "Sir, reload the cannons?"

"Aye, reload the cannons, you idiot!" another man shot back. From the whistle around his neck, Rahmi considered the man to be the bo'sun, or the petty officer who oversaw the sailors working the deck. "What are you standing there for? Are you afraid of your skirts getting wet?"

The bo'sun couldn't possibly be talking to Rahmi like *that*. He glanced around to see if the man had been speaking to someone else. "Me?" Rahmi finally responded, raising his brows as he pointed to himself. "Are you speaking to me?"

"Who else would I be speaking to, you fucking pool of bilge water?" His snarl was evident, even over the crack of thunder and the third *boom* from the cannons below. The ship rocked to the side, sending the bo'sun stumbling. Rahmi stayed sure-footed, a move that only seemed to stoke the man's anger further. "Man the ropes or be locked in the brig with the other ladies!" the bo'sun barked as soon as he regained his balance.

Rahmi shook his head, pressing his lips into a playful line. "I won't be doing that, but thank you for the opportunity. Where may I find your captain?"

"You will take a line," the bo'sun said as he took a menacing step forward, "or you will be keelhauled for insubordination as soon as this storm passes."

Rahmi's return smile was lethal. And he knew it, too, from the way the bo'sun's face slackened at the sight of it. "You will tell me where your captain is," he said slowly, running a finger over the sharp edge of his dagger. "Or you will find this shoved into a very inconvenient place of my choosing."

The bo'sun started, brows meeting in the middle as he took a small step back. Recognition flashed over his features. "You're— you're— *Specter*?" The last word came out as a squeak, almost drowned out by a roar of wind that caught the sails. Yells of shock and pain emanated from the crew as the ropes pulled, ripping at their hands.

"The captain previously known as *The Specter* has retired from his duties," Rahmi said, still running his pointer finger over the blade. "I won't ask again. Where is your captain?"

The bo'sun's muscular body grew rigid, puffing his chest out in a way that Rahmi felt was meant to be a show of force. "If you want to get to the captain, sir, you'll have to get through me first."

Rahmi stifled the instinct to roll his eyes. "Very well." He closed the distance between himself and the bo'sun in a flash, slicing the dagger through the air. It caught at the column of the bo'sun's throat, and blood began to spurt, melding with the rain and seawater that stained his tunic.

The bo'sun grappled at his open neck as though he could seal it back together if he pressed hard enough before falling with a loud *thunk* to the deck. Rahmi sniffed, wiping the rain from the tip of his nose with the back of his hand. It was too bad. He could have used the man aboard his ship.

The ship rocked again, and the river of blood coming from the bo'sun's body rerouted, now trailing to the nearest crew member's boot. Rahmi watched as the man glanced down briefly before looking back at the rope between his hands. He did a comical double-take to stare down at the blood gathering near the sole of his shoe. With a slow glide that almost made Rahmi chuckle, the sailor followed the trail of blood with his eyes, where his stare landed on Rahmi's boots, climbed up his breeches, and finally locked on the dagger still dripping crimson on the deck.

"*Spec*—" the sailor began to shout, but his voice dropped to a garble when a cutlass punched through his neck. Alaric withdrew the blade in the next moment, severing the man's head from the rest of his body.

Rahmi clicked his tongue against his teeth as his crew streamed onto the merchant ship, swinging on ropes and clambering over the gap using narrow planks connecting one gunnel to the other. "That's a shame. I rather liked the look of him, too."

Alaric wiped the blood from his cutlass on the back of the headless man's tunic. "Were those the two *souls* that called us to this ship?" he asked, pointing his cutlass toward the bo'sun at Rahmi's feet. "Because you could have said something before I killed him."

"Don't be ridiculous, Alaric. Did he look like he was dying *before* you stuck your blade into him?"

"What are you waiting for then?" Alaric asked in a haughty tone that would not have been acceptable from any other member of his crew.

This time, Rahmi did roll his eyes. "Patience." He paused to step over the bo'sun's body; the blood slowed from rushing to trickling. "Wasn't it you that was just saying the last few weeks had been—what was the phrase you used again? *Bloody fucking boring*?"

Alaric bristled. "I just thought we would have more *work* after taking over from *The Phantom Night*."

"And here we are," Rahmi retorted, sweeping his hands around the ship's deck. "Work. Go on, have some fun. I will speak with the captain, and then I'll find the men I'm looking for. They're somewhere below deck, I'm sure of it."

Alaric's single blue eye gleamed as he turned on the toes of his boots and clunked back toward the bow. He shoved his cutlass into the back of another merchant crewmember, who started in shock before falling to his knees. Rahmi shook his head again before navigating through the battle that had broken out, making a quick line toward the stairs that led to the helm.

Rahmi was slow to climb them, mostly because he needed to fight through the men defending the stern deck but also because his knee tweaked something awful from flinging himself off *The Mark of Malice.* He would consider looking at it later, though he suspected it would already be healed before the thought crossed his mind again. He reached the top of the stairs, threading along the deck to the other side of the wheel, and halted in his tracks when he lowered his gaze...

...To find the ship's captain huddled in a weeping mess against the helm.

"Come now," Rahmi said, wiping his dark hair from his brow before pulling the captain to his feet. He took a moment to dust the shoulders of the man's jacket, managing only to flick water from the front of it. "We die on our feet if we're going to man a ship, even one that may be for merchants. Show me a brave face before I gut you— that's a *sabie.*"

The captain's tanned face lifted in recognition of the word, though his nervous gulp still worked his Adam's apple. "S-sabie. That's a word I haven't heard in quite some time."

"You know it?" Rahmi was surprised. *Sabie* was a word in his native tongue that meant *boy* or *lad* in the common language used on the continent. He only met a few people who came from his part of the world. "Where are you from, captain?"

"Not a captain," the man responded through chattering teeth. "He— he fell ill not three days ago. I've been helping to man the helm ever since." He swallowed again. "Sha'Hadra. I'm from Sha'Hadra."

Rahmi considered him for a long minute. Sha'Hadra was the largest non-port city on the continent and was only half a day's walk from the village he grew up in. Of course, it had been nearly three hundred years since he set foot in a part of the world that wasn't a port. Most people born in Sha'Hadra didn't leave Sha'Hadra, preferring the radiance of the sun and the baking desert heat to the volatile weather that blanketed the coast. He sheathed his dagger, and the man visibly relaxed.

"What's your name, *sabie*?"

"K—Karim," he managed to stutter out as another resounding clap of thunder shuddered Rahmi's bones. "My name is Karim."

"What brings you to the sea, Karim?"

Karim flicked his gaze behind Rahmi, where Rahmi assumed a crew member had clambered up the stairs. "I—I wanted to find something different."

"And did you?" Rahmi asked with an amused smirk, chuckles sounding behind him. He glanced over his shoulder, unsurprised to see two of his men, Penley Byron and Tennant Bane, standing behind him. He turned back to Karim, who continued to watch the men warily. "Find something different?"

"I— I don't wish to say," Karim answered with a shake of his head that sent water droplets in every direction. "You'll kill me if I do."

"I'll kill you if you don't," Rahmi reasoned with ease, placing a confident hand on the pommel of his dagger. Penley and Tennant chuckled again, and Karim turned an unsettling shade of green. "But, you've intrigued me enough that you have a better chance if you just tell me."

Karim dropped a hand to his front pocket, protectively placing his palm over the opening. The movement seemed instinctual, and its oddness drew Rahmi's attention. He slid his fingers down the dagger's hilt, unsheathing it in the next breath. He settled the blade at Karim's throat, pressing the sharp edge into his flesh. Karim's eyes widened, but his hand only pressed more firmly to the front pocket.

Interesting. This would be fun to figure out.

"What's in your pocket, sailor?" Rahmi asked with a determined raise of his brow. Karim began to tremble, his shoulders shaking nearly uncontrollably as his green face turned ashen. "Remove your hand, *sabie*, or I will remove it for you." Karim's fear washed over Rahmi, and the man's wavering indecision forced Rahmi's expression into one that was tension-filled and strained. If there was something he hated more than anything else, it was indecision.

Karim hesitated at the new look but only long enough for Rahmi to move the dagger from the sailor's throat to his wrist.

"I've heard having your hand cut off is quite painful," Rahmi said in a voice that should have been used to comment on the weather. "But if you're willing to try it and let me know how it feels—"

Karim removed his hand from his pocket, letting it drop to his side.

"I'm impressed by your fortitude. Though I certainly was looking forward to our little experiment." Rahmi reached into Karim's front pocket and felt the edge of a thick piece of folded parchment. He began to pull it out, careful not to rip the sodden corners, when something solid clattered to the wooden planks at their feet.

Rahmi bent down to retrieve a copper coin, pinching it between his thumb and forefinger to hold in the air between them. Karim closed his eyes as he exhaled a long, defeated breath, one that wasn't lost on Rahmi.

"Now, where did you find this?" Rahmi asked, focusing his eyes on the coin. The detailing was old, and the copper used to make it even older. It wasn't engraved with a language he had seen in the last three hundred years.

Karim remained quiet, but Rahmi had already moved onto the parchment, gently unfolding it. The corners of the parchment flapped in the wind, and the rain pelted the smeared ink into a further blur, but he could tell by the outlines and the markings that the document was a map. Hundreds of blobs spanned the parchment, blobs that, at one time, may have been islands. In the corner, barely visible amidst the smudges of black ink, was the word *Luminaria.*

"*Luminaria*?" Rahmi asked, pinning Karim with a stare. "What's a *Luminaria*?" Karim was still silent, his shoulders sagging even further. The hand gripping the dagger shot upward, grasping Karim's cheeks and forcing his gaze. "That question was expecting an answer, and I would like one. Now."

A tremor rocked Karim's body as the ship dipped to one side, a wave crashing onto the quarterdeck below. "It— it's a map."

"Yes, I can see it's a map," Rahmi replied impatiently, gripping Karim's cheeks tighter. "What I want to know is what the map leads to."

Karim gulped for a third time, and his gaze slid toward the ship's side as though assessing whether it would be worth throwing himself over. Rahmi's smile turned wolfish.

"I don't think so. Penley, Tennant," Rahmi snapped to the two men still at his back. They stepped forward, flanking each side of him. Karim seemed to pale even further. "Take him to the brig." Rahmi unclenched his fist from around Karim's cheeks, and Karim flexed his jaw, lifting his hand to rub the sore spots where Rahmi's fingers had been. "Let me know when he's willing to speak freely."

"Wait, *wait—* " Karim yelped as Penley and Tennant took him under the arms and began to drag him toward the stairs. "I can talk. *I can talk*! Wait!"

Another rush of fear crested over Karim's face. But a second emotion moved like a shadow along with it, twisting underneath the fear as though attempting to stay hidden. That was one Rahmi knew well: guilt. It was nearly silent, riding like a deadly on the same wave.

Fascinating. Rahmi was eager to take the time to learn more about *that*.

But first, he needed to find his two souls and, quite possibly, pick a few more up on the way.

CHAPTER THREE

KALIA

T he madam was an intense woman.

She was taller than Kalia's average frame, towering at least six inches over her. Her expression always looked pinched, as though she were smelling a fillet of recently rotten fish. She wore her hair in a slicked bun, a single strand never out of place, and owned only the continent's finest silk dresses.

Kalia knew those silk dresses came directly from the sun-soaked marketplace in Sha'Hadra. As a child, she had seen them lying on the wooden counters and had run her hands along the smooth fabric, wishing that, one day, she would be rich enough to wear one.

While Kalia knew that dream wasn't worth dwelling on, she still worked to ensure that she would have enough money to walk the shop-lined alleys of her hometown.

As if that wasn't enough, the madam had also never given Kalia her name, only allowing anyone in her employ to address her as madam or ma'am, never anything else. Kalia had never even heard the madam say her actual name aloud, and, as a girl, she wondered if the madam's name was indeed just madam.

"Cranford Reed is a—" the madam had begun to say, her eyes narrowing into a glare that seemed to pierce through Kalia's soul.

"Disgusting brute?" Kalia offered as a response. She crossed her arms over her chest, the only defense she had. "He beat Mintie nearly to death and—"

"You thought it was in the best interest of *my* business to put hornets under the mattress of the room he happens to prefer?" The madam sneered, her sharp eyes sinking to scrutinize every inch of Kalia. "Like some desert filth vigilante?"

Kalia clamped her lips shut, returning the madam's glare with one of her own. She had been in the madam's office one too many times before and never for anything good. The dark wooden walls, complimented by crimson drapes that matched the ones in the brothel, held Kalia like a prison cell. The air was smoky, thanks to the thick plume of jasmine incense burning in the corner, and the iron-framed window on the opposite wall overlooked the grimy and unkempt streets of Mistral's Bay.

Even rooted in place, Kalia could see the faces of the homeless huddled tightly to the stone walls of the alley, grimacing against the devastating winds that used the city's corridors like a tunnel.

"You're quite lucky I haven't forgotten your *talent* yet, Kalia. You make me money, that's good. But you are never immune to being turned into the palace guards at the first sniff that you are becoming a nuisance to me."

Kalia couldn't help but notice the smirk that lifted her lips, the same smirk that tightened the corners of the madam's eyes. "*I make you good money* is an understatement," she bit out with a harsh laugh.

"If I remember, your bordello was on the verge of collapsing under the weight of the coin you owed to the palace. And I was the one who—"

The madam crossed the small room in three strides, her heeled boots tapping against the marble floor, and slapped Kalia hard enough that her head whipped to the side. Kalia gritted her teeth but refused to lift her hand to assess the swelling that she could feel along her jaw. The madam reached out, fingering the ends of Kalia's long, dark waves.

"You should be more mindful when you speak to me," the madam said, her voice soft and nurturing despite the warning. "And you should remember who saved who."

A memory roared to the forefront of Kalia's mind, one that began with a stolen loaf of bread and ended with her wrist being held down by a guard in Sha'Hadra as he lifted a cutlass high above her. Kalia shook her head but couldn't help the wince of pain that clouded her expression. The madam's lips curled in a triumphant grin.

"I knew we would agree." She withdrew her hand from Kalia's hair, letting her hand fall to her side. She stepped away, walking toward the window, where she paused to look at the gaslamp-lit streets. "I reflect on that day quite often, Kalia. I remember a little girl, starved and beaten. A devastatingly beautiful little girl, might I add, who had lost her mother seven years before. Such a tragedy." The madam turned to glance at Kalia over her shoulder. "One that we should never forget is your fault."

Grief clenched in Kalia's belly, but she only lifted her chin higher, refusing to give in. It would only satisfy the madam.

"Nothing to say now, hmm?" The madam goaded her further, clicking her tongue against the roof of her mouth. She looked back to the street, the glow from the lamps below bathing her face in gold. "You would be out there, you know, selling your body in a back alley for a scrap of meat or a stein of *fion*." She lifted a hand to tap a knuckle on the glass. "A single copper from a sailor to suck his disgusting dick dry before he went back out to sea. I saved you from that future, and this is how you thank me?"

The tension rose in the room, prickling the hair on the back of Kalia's neck.

"I stopped that guard from cutting off your hand when you were too afraid to summon your magic, even though I had seen you do it with the baker in the marketplace. I took you from Sha'Hadra, where other children had beaten you and were nearly too sick to carry on, and gave you a place here in my brothel. I helped you hone your *talent* into something that could bring me unimaginable wealth. And *this* is how you *thank me*?"

A jingle followed a heavy thunk, and Kalia glanced down, her mouth drying when she saw her coin-filled purse on the floor between them. No, no, no, no. She couldn't breathe; her lungs refused to draw in any air.

"I know all about your stash," the madam continued, her lips pressed into a tight, white line. "You can thank the maids for finding it for me. Did you truly think you could buy your freedom from me? Did you think I wouldn't notice my safe's missing coins or jewels? You are *mine*, Kalia."

If Kalia had a heart, it would have crumbled to the ground next to that bag of coins. Instead, she further reinforced that wall around it and steeled it in place so that nothing would escape. She couldn't allow *anything* to escape.

The madam grabbed the lash from where it hung next to the window and whirled around, striking Kalia in the arm with the tarred leather strips. Kalia let out an involuntary shriek as the skin split open, blood bubbling to the surface. The madam reeled back and came down with the lash again, this time catching Kalia on the shoulder.

The dress tore, revealing a welt that puckered near her collarbone. Kalia didn't make another sound, stoking the madam's fury. She reeled back again and again, bringing the lash down on Kalia's back, chest, and legs. And she didn't stop until Kalia's red, satin dress was hanging from her body in ribbons, blood dripping onto the marble floor beneath them.

"Get out of my sight," the madam hissed, dropping the lash to the floor with a *clunk*. "And get Mintie in here to clean up this mess. I don't want to look at it a second longer."

Kalia's throat burned with the lump that formed there as she limped to the door, wrapping her tattered hand around the knob. Despite her fresh injuries, ones that opened her already scarred back from the madam's previous lashings, the onslaught of tears was for her hard-earned well of coins. Money she had saved for years was taken from her in the blink of an eye.

There would be no end, and she would be here until her dying day. The madam made damn sure of that. The ladies of the bordello may come and go, but Kalia Salam would remain, battered and broken by the sands of time.

The cool air of Mistral's Bay felt good against the swollen welts on Kalia's skin. It had taken her only a moment to change her dress before she headed into the alleys, her familiar dagger strapped tightly to her waist. The one thing the maid had yet to find. Gutting her sounded like the right option. It would cost her life, but the executioner's block was looking more inviting every day.

The path Kalia took was grimy. The cracks in the stone were filled with waste from humans and horses alike, and the smell was sour enough to turn even the strongest of stomachs.

And it was nothing like Sha'Hadra, where the various spices wafted from the barrels, subtly mixing with the scents of drying leather and freshly pressed oils. Gods, she missed the sandy streets, the mud-bricked houses, and the view of the sun rising over the dunes. She would scramble to the rooftop of whatever building she slept in that night, eager to set her chin on her knees and watch as the navy sky turned blood-red, then orange, before finally splitting into bright blue, the rays spilling onto the golden sand far beyond the city walls.

She yearned to return to the desert city, where the people would smile at her, the culture was wonderful, and she could visit her mother's grave marker whenever she felt the urge. She hadn't returned to Sha'Hadra since she had been loaded into the madam's carriage, grateful to the woman for being kind enough to step in front of the guard and pay for a baked pastry she had been dying to try for years.

But now...the capital city was a foul pit of dark, winding alleys, spilled waste flung from the windows above, and the king's gleaming white palace seated high on the hill overlooking it all. The only place of reprieve was a beach just before the bustling port, but that space could get crowded with those seeking similar respite. Even then, the smells of old fish from the docks and garbage from the anchored ships cracked any resolve lingering there.

Kalia passed a beggar on the corner, the man wrapped in a thin, ragged blanket, his lips chapped and bleeding from the unrelenting wind. He held a stein in his hand, which Kalia was sure would be filled with *fion* before the night's end, but she gave him a single copper coin anyway. He nodded in thanks as she walked on, turning onto the next street, where an unencumbered view of the palace's white dome rose above the tops of the trees.

She could see the gardened walls from where she stood, large torches burning brightly against the star-speckled night sky. The brilliance of the white looked sorely out of place amongst the dingy, brick buildings that made up the city—a not-so-subtle reminder of where the king stood in relation to his people. The intricate iron gates rarely opened these days, but Kalia knew from passing them on her weekly walks that a carved white fountain to match the palace stood in the center of an ornately decorated courtyard. The opulence was sickening.

The only times Kalia had ever seen the king leave the confines of his palace were to attend executions of highly sought-after criminals. ..most of them pirates. And he always appeared youthful and glowing every time she had seen him in the last fifteen years. He hadn't seemed to age, not in the nearly two decades she had been in the capital city.

A woman bumped into Kalia's shoulder, pulling her from her thoughts. The woman mumbled an apology as she pressed on, her hood pulled tightly over her head and her chin tucked against her chest. It was dangerous to be in the city alone as a woman; the guards would do nothing to stop an attack, but Kalia was out on urgent business.

She walked further down the street, her sandals slapping against the stone, mudding the tips of her toes, until she came across a wooden sign labeled *Nectar of the Woods Apothecary*. The sign knocked against the glass panes of the fogged window, and as Kalia pushed the door open, a bell above tinkled to signal her arrival.

The apothecary was one of the city's smaller ones, meaning it was frequented less than the others. But the owner was an expert at mixing healing salves and pain potions, something the other shopkeepers could only dream of doing. He also never positioned himself as something he wasn't, as many others pretended to read divination cards or would give you a *premonition* for the right price.

Magic was strictly outlawed in the continent, from the villages surrounding Sha'Hadra to the islands littering the coast. If you were caught, the penalty was death. But that didn't stop the underground users from practicing, though it certainly gave Kalia thought when she was wielding her power outside of the bordello. She had seen an underground user or two get carted off in the last few years, regardless of whether they could perform magic.

Most couldn't, and those who could did not dare tout it publicly.

But the apothecaries were different. All of them only created what could be grown from the earth, and while this could be considered a simpler form of magic, Kalia had heard the king was afraid of a revolt if he made them illegal. So, here they stayed.

Nectar of the Woods Apothecary was lined from floor to ceiling with wooden shelves, each neatly displaying glass jars with assortments of roots, dried herbs, powders, and spices. Drawers filled some of the spaces, all meticulously labeled with symbols Kalia couldn't read, and bundles of herbs hung from the rafters of the ceiling, every so often sprinkling the floor with leaves that released from the stalks. Behind the narrow counter stood a small table, just wide enough for one chair, where a pestle and mortar were placed prominently in the middle, a half-filled jar nestled beside it.

It was one of the only places in the city where the smell of waste from the streets didn't seep under the door, and Kalia had often found herself wandering here as a child, the owner taking pity over her fresh bruises and welts.

"I wondered when you would grace my doorstep again," a soft voice floated from the shadows of the shop. An older man stepped from behind a curtained doorframe, his wispy gray hair matted against the crown of his head. "It has been quite a few days since—" He paused, and despite half of his face still being cast in darkness, Kalia could feel his gaze roaming her body. "Again, Kalia?"

Kalia followed the woodgrain pattern on the counter, tracing the tips of her fingers along the grooves. "There was a customer, Pete, one who—"

"There is *always* a customer, my darling. That doesn't mean you *always* need to involve yourself." A sigh escaped the man's thin lips as he hobbled toward the nearest wall and plucked jars from the shelves above his head. "But I would just be beating a dead siren if I repeated it, so I will make you the salve and pray to the gods that you heal quickly."

"Thank you, Pete," Kalia replied, roving her eyes along the man's knobby knees and hunched back. It had become more pronounced in the last three years, and her chest tightened at the thought of him aging. "How is Marta these days?"

"Marta," Pete grunted as he turned to set the armful of jars on the counter, where they softly clinked together. He began to uncork the tops, his thickened knuckles struggling to grip the lids, and Kalia reached forward to help him despite the glare she knew he would send her. She ignored it when it came. "Marta is proving to be a further thorn in my side than I anticipated."

Marta was Pete's old cat. She was missing patches of fur, had only three legs, and had, at some point, burnt half of her whiskers off as she lay near the hearth in the back room. Pete had her for the entirety of the fifteen years Kalia had been coming to see him, and though the cat was cranky and only preferred the company of Pete, Kalia always liked to ask about her.

"When is Marta *not* a thorn in your side?" Kalia teased as Pete hobbled to the table to retrieve the pestle and mortar before hobbling back to the counter.

"When are you *both* not a thorn in my side?" Pete retorted as he pinched the powders and herbs from the various jars into the mortar. He never seemed to measure or look at a recipe, but somehow, he always knew how much of each to use.

The apothecary was the only place Kalia found peace, and even after all of these years, she loved to watch him work. He glanced up for a moment, staring at the deepest gouge mark—the one that split open the top of her left shoulder. He grunted as he turned to pluck one more jar from the shelf, thumb it open, and pour the liquid into the mortar. Then, he picked up the pestle and began to grind everything together.

"It was Mintie this time," Kalia continued, watching Pete's brows pinched together. "Cranford Reed was the one who beat her."

"Cranford Reed." A single drop of sweat worked its way down his temple, settling in the fuzz of his mustache. "Cranford Reed was a foul child, and he turned into an equally foul man."

"That's what I told the madam when she asked about the hornets."

"Hornets?" Pete lifted his eyes to connect with hers before he shook his head. "You have a dangerous mind, Kalia Salam, one that I fear to be on the wrong side of." He paused to grab a pitcher of water from under the counter, pouring enough into the mortar to thin the paste. "How is Mintie, then? Would she be the one you sent into my shop a few weeks ago?"

"Yes, she was."

"For someone who claims not to want friends, you certainly go out of your way to protect the women in that bordello."

Kalia froze, the nail of her pinky finger wedging into the groove of the wood. "There's a difference."

Pete was quiet for a moment before he finally said, "Just getting to know them won't—"

"People have a way of betraying you if you know them well enough," Kalia interjected with a finality that, she hoped, would further deter Pete.

It didn't.

"You've been off the streets of Sha'Hadra for fifteen years, my darling," he replied softly, glancing up at her with enough kindness that it tugged at her heart.

"People are the same everywhere, Pete. It doesn't matter if they're here or in Sha'Hadra." Kalia didn't have the strength to mention what else the madam had done.

Pete sighed, shaking his head. "How is sweet Mintie? I trust she's feeling better?"

Kalia seized on the subject change. "Better enough to go back to work, though the madam still required her to finish the night bloodied and broken, so I doubt she would have done any less."

Pete's lips thinned into a tight line as he worked the pestle even harder. "I was never a fan of the madam, you know this well. I still don't understand why you wouldn't be my apprentice. I've requested it many times from you."

Kalia sighed as Pete picked up an empty jar and scraped the salve into it. "She would never let me go. I make her too much money." She knew that even more now.

"Ah, yes. Your magic. It certainly would be a shame if her bordello went under. How many *undesirable* men would go to other areas of town when their ships were docked in the harbor?"

Pete was the only other person in the capital to know of Kalia's talents, having guessed what she was the moment she attempted to use them to steal a salve in her early days in the city. *A Voyant*, that's what he had whispered to her. A person who could project visions into other people's minds or steal those visions from their minds entirely. Pete had kept her secret for fifteen years; he was the only one she still trusted.

That trust had managed to wane in recent months through no fault of his own. Kalia couldn't quite bring herself to admit to him how much money the madam had stolen from her. She didn't want him to know how much she had access to, just in case he betrayed her, just as the maid had. She would need to start from scratch, and soon.

"Probably the same number of men who come across your apothecary in need of herbs for rope burns and seasickness."

Pete grunted again as he pushed a cork into the top of the jar, sealing the fresh salve inside. He took her hand, pressing the jar into her palm. "You may be right, my darling, but I would give up the coin from the men in the port to see you to safety. Now, how about we not stoke the anger of the madam for the next week or so, hmm? I need to restock my *Melaleuca alternifolia*. Between you and Mintie, I'm afraid I've used it all."

Kalia closed her fingers around the jar and sent him a small smile. "I'll do my best."

"And that is all I know that I can ask for."

CHAPTER FOUR

RAHMI

"We've got seven souls, captain," Alaric announced as he leaned against his cutlass, the tip digging into the deck. A triumphant nod dipped his chin to his chest. "Tied them all up right here."

"And the eighth?" Rahmi asked, sweeping his eyes along the shivering and trembling men restrained to the main mast, the sharp edges of daggers and swords pinning them further in place.

"Already below, as are the rations and barrels of fresh water."

Rahmi made a noise of interest from the back of his throat as he began to walk toward the captives. His boots fell heavy against the deck, the *clunk* menacing amongst the otherwise silent crew and captured. He could almost taste their fear. Seven souls— eight total if he counted Karim— and he doubted he would take more than two.

Pity.

He halted before the first sailor, a stout, redheaded man with a pallid face and tight shoulders. His crew member, Thomas Kennedy, removed the dagger tip from the man's chest and took a step back, a jeer curling his lip. The captured man didn't look up at Rahmi; instead, he kept his head bent forward and his eyes fixed on his feet.

One of Rahmi's favorite pastimes was guessing the emotions of the captured crew. He reveled in being right and had taught himself the art of reading people through it. This man? *Fear*— that was a given. They were always afraid. *Sadness*— perhaps a bit from the sag of his chest, though still unexpected. *Anxiety*— indeed unavoidable considering the man's current circumstances.

Rahmi shook his head. He didn't take men who died bowing to others. He had no need on his ship for that. "Thomas? Return him to Samael. Death requires a soul." He had already stepped in front of the second man by the time the first let out a cry of panic, followed by a shriek of pain, then nothing.

The man's body hung limp against the ropes binding him to the mast, blood steadily dripping from the slit in his neck, dousing the air with a tang of metallic.

Rahmi turned his attention to the second man, who was still eyeing the dead one with wide-eyed horror, his brow slick and clammy. *Fear*— well, that seemed to be the theme. *Dread*— his downward gaze was a giveaway. He did watch his crewmate die, after all. *Guilt*— ah, there it was. There was always a telltale sign of guilt. Sometimes, it was in flustered stuttering; other times, it was in the unnatural stillness of the body. All had the pain of it mirrored in their eyes—a pain they desperately wanted handled before they died.

It was like a shadow hanging over them, one that Rahmi could spot a league away.

The second man let out an involuntary whimper as Rahmi leered, hinging at the waist to lean toward him. "What's your name, sailor?"

"C-Cobden, s-sir," he managed to stutter.

"Are you ready to join a ship crewed by the guilty and captained by the cursed, Cobden?" Rahmi asked, wrapping a hand around the hilt of his dagger and unsheathing it. The clouds, lit from below by the setting sun, were shifting from soft pink to golden orange, and those colors were reflected off the metal.

"I—I—" Cobden began, his gaze drifting to the dagger now positioned at the rope around his wrists.

Rahmi slipped the sharp edge of the dagger underneath the knot and snapped the rope in two with a quick tug upward, where it fell to the deck between their feet. Cobden lifted his hands to brush his fingers over the area where the rope had rubbed his skin red and raw. Rahmi flicked his dark locks from his forehead, surveying Cobden's calloused palms, strapped muscles, and freckled face.

"Do you work the sails?" Rahmi kicked the ropes to the side, and they collided with the dead man's ankle. "I need men who can work the rigging."

Cobden opened his mouth to speak, and the mast's shadow lengthened with the new set of clouds, casting half of his face in darkness.

"Don't do it, Cobden."

Rahmi's head tilted with interest as his eyes snapped three men to the left. A challenge? It had been quite some time since he had one of those. He was keen to see if the man would keep his vigor in the face of death. Rahmi began a slow, calculated walk down his line of prisoners, dragging the tip of his dagger along the bellies of the men as he went. The one who spoke out gulped when Rahmi halted directly before him but still squared his shoulders.

"Something to say?" Rahmi asked, placing the dagger under the man's chin and forcing it to lift. There, in the spot behind his navel, a shiver of pleasure began to coil. He wouldn't give himself over to the joy of fear, not yet.

"Don't join his crew," the man said, doing his best to side-eye in Cobden's direction without turning his head. "He can't take us without our permission. I've heard of him. *The Specter—*"

Behind him, Rahmi heard Alaric snort. He couldn't wait until the likes of Devlin *fucking* Cato was long forgotten. He sent an irritated glance over his shoulder, locking eyes with his quartermaster. "When do you think they'll realize I'm not Captain Devlin Cato, and this isn't *The Phantom Night*?"

Alaric shrugged, a humored grin tugging at his mouth. "Couldn't begin to tell you, captain. They'll learn soon enough, I suppose."

Rahmi turned back to look down at the man, the top of his balding head meeting just under Rahmi's nose. *Disdain. Hatred. Determination.* An interesting trio of emotions were echoed in the man's blue eyes. Rahmi let out a huff of amusement just before removing the dagger from the man's chin and thrusting it into his side. The blade scraped against his ribcage, the hum of metal scraping against bone reverberating up Rahmi's forearm.

"If it needed repeating, and I will not do so again, I am not *The Specter,* and this isn't *The Phantom Night*," Rahmi murmured in the dying man's ear as he yanked his dagger back, feeling the flow of warm blood coat his fingers. "And men on my ship don't get a choice."

The man grunted, blood bubbling in the corner of his mouth. He took a wet breath, and death rode on the gurgle that escaped with his exhale. "At least...I won't...live long...enough to...see." He chuckled before coughing, and a spray of red dotted the front of Rahmi's tunic. "You won't...be able to...take me...not if I'm...dead."

Rahmi contemplated the man for a moment, his focus narrowing onto the stream of blood that trickled from the curve of the man's bottom lip to his pointed chin. Letting this man die would be easy, and he didn't fuck with things that came easy. "I don't normally take sailors like you—" he said, sheathing the dagger into the leather belt at his waist.

"Captain—" Alaric started, and warning marred his tone. Rahmi ignored him.

"Elman!" Cobden cried out, attempting to wrestle past Thomas but coming to a grinding halt when three more cutlasses crisscrossed in front of him.

"I prefer ones who are hurting," Rahmi went on, lifting his hand to thumb the blood away from the man's lip. "You aren't in pain, Elman, not in the way I like them to be." His hand shot forward, fingers wrapping in a fist around Elman's neck. Elman tried to swallow, his throat bobbing beneath Rahmi's grasp, but Rahmi only closed his grip further. "I think you'll learn today that I'm not a man who steps away from a challenge."

Power pulsed from within Rahmi, a thrum deep in his chest…a place where he knew his shrunken heart lay. That power bloomed, hot and greedy, against his sternum. It beat like a drum up his shoulder and ricocheted down to his elbow before blasting like a cannon through his hand and into the man. The air crackled around them as the man let out a gasping shout.

"What did you do?" Elman cried out, his voice growing stronger as his leaning hunch straightened. The blood from his side slowed to a stop as the skin that peeked out from beneath the torn tunic began to knit together. "What did you—"

"I'm Captain Rahmi Abada, collector of souls and proprietor of power from Liddros, God of the Sea," Rahmi seethed through gritted teeth as he began to withdraw the magic that had latched onto Elman's soul, tearing away pieces of it as though it were an owed pound of flesh. "Many would consider it a curse, and perhaps it is." Elman let out a scream as Rahmi let go of his throat, and he collapsed against the ropes still binding him to the mast. "But let me tell you a secret, Elman. It's not a curse to me."

Rahmi stepped back to survey Elman, the newest member of his crew.

"I've found my two," Rahmi said. "Send the rest to Samael."

Rahmi whistled a song he faintly remembered learning as a child, aiming his walk toward the hatch leading to the underbelly of *The Mark of Malice.* The remaining men pleaded for mercy as the crew lifted their cutlasses and daggers, but none received it.

The path leading to the brig was one Rahmi took a fair few times a month, as many of the people he forced aboard his ship needed time to process. It wasn't uncommon that they needed to process more than once. There was no better place to sit with one's thoughts than behind the iron cell doors, surrounded by nothing save for the lantern fixed to the far wall and the sound of wood creaking as *The Mark of Malice* carved her way through the sea.

It was dark and musty, and the stale air did not help those with mold issues. Pooled water slipped into the cracks between the floorboards. If one yelled loud enough, which they often did, they might be heard in the berth if the water was calm and the sails weren't snapping in the wind.

Rahmi paused at the doorframe of the brig, surprised to see that Karim was quiet as he sat on the dirty floor, his legs bent and his forearms resting on his knees. His head was tilted back to rest against the wall, eyes closed. He almost looked peaceful. It was unnerving enough that Rahmi briefly considered sending Tennant in if only to rough him up further. He needed to get this over with. He had other things to tend to.

Rahmi crossed the threshold, the wooden planks squeaking beneath his boots. Karim opened his eyes at the sound and took a deep breath before lifting his head from the wall to plant his sight on the captain. Rahmi stopped at the door to the cell, leaning a shoulder against the cool metal bars.

"I've been told you're ready to talk," Rahmi said, glancing at Karim, who had stood and was busy brushing the dirt from the back of his breeches. Rahmi reached into his pocket and pulled out the parchment, unfolding it carefully. The map crinkled between his fingers, and the ink had dried where it smeared. "It's interesting you've been carrying this around, even amid a storm."

"I couldn't risk it falling into the wrong hands," Karim replied, though his gaze dropped to the map. "I could use it as leverage if I held onto it."

"And now?" Rahmi asked as he quirked a brow.

Karim darted forward, thrusting his hand through the cell bars to snatch the map. Rahmi was quicker. He grasped Karim's arm, pinning it against the crossbar and putting just enough pressure on the elbow that Karim let out a yelp of pain.

"Tell me where you found that coin," Rahmi said as the ship rocked against a wave. Karim stumbled, though his arm remained hooked through the door.

There was a *pop* followed by a scream as Karim's elbow dislocated. Rahmi only leaned further on the arm, bending the joint to an excruciatingly impossible angle.

"I can't...tell you..." Karim rasped through a clenched jaw, his lips whitening as they pressed together. Rahmi watched with interest as Karim's nostrils flared with his next breath. "If...you don't...let me...go."

Rahmi stepped back, and Karim fell to the floor, cradling his arm to his chest. Impatience tore through Rahmi, igniting a tightness that tugged at his chest. He *could* do this all day, but did he *want* to? Not particularly. Pure interest kept him fixated on Karim, and that alone made him change tactics. He crouched next to the cell, draping his forearms over his thighs and letting the map dangle between his knees. "You talk, and I'll find you a healer. You remain silent, and I'll unlock this cell door and find more ways to injure you until you do."

Karim whimpered, a trickle of sweat dripping down his temple. He swallowed thickly as though trying to bypass a large lump in his throat and took one more inhale before leveling Rahmi with a murderous stare. Rahmi almost grinned.

"I'll tell you...as much as I can..." Karim breathed out. "But...I'm going...to need...that healer."

Rahmi said nothing and merely waited for Karim to continue. The ship rolled again, and the framing of the hull groaned. Down the passageway, the new barrels of fresh water from the merchant ship pulled against the ropes holding them in place, the sound echoing down the narrow hall.

Karim took another steadying breath. "Almost two years ago, I was in Sha'Hadra, living in the alleyways of the marketplace. I was looking for a way to get to the coast when I was approached by a thief named Draven, who needed help stealing that map—" He paused to tilt his head in gesture toward the parchment. "From a temple in Sha'Hadra. He heard through a string of friends that I knew intimately about the city's layout."

"That certainly doesn't explain this..." Rahmi trailed off to tuck his hand into the pocket of his tunic and retrieve the coin. Karim's face paled, if possible, even further at the sight of it.

"The third man I was with," Karim pressed on as Rahmi rose, planting his shoulder against the iron bars and hooking one ankle over the other. "He was a scholar during his prime...a map reader for the king. He interpreted it for us, and we used some extra funds Draven and I stole to hire a ship."

Rahmi flicked the coin into the air and caught it as it began to fall. "And the map led you to this single coin?"

Karim scoffed as he shifted from his knees, grimacing when the movement jostled his elbow. "Not a single coin. An entire cave filled with them. It was a— a hall fit for the king's palace in Mistral's Bay. Treasure beyond your wildest imagination." He leaned forward, grimacing again. "The map is a set of islands nearly a ten-day sail from the coast. Hundreds of islands. We searched for *months* and—"

Rahmi was quiet for a long minute as he stared at the map. A set of gentle footsteps passed the threshold of the brig, and he looked over his shoulder to see Elodie, one of the galley workers, breeze by with a crate of root vegetables in her arms. He held his gaze on the empty doorframe, focusing on the steady beat of his heart, before finally turning back to Karim.

"You expect me to believe that?" Rahmi asked, a slow smile splitting his mouth. He lifted the parchment, shaking it in the air. "You expect me to believe *this map* leads to a cave filled with treasure beyond my— what did you say? My wildest imagination?" He snorted, letting his hand fall to his side. "I've been sailing the Aeglecian Seas for three hundred years—"

"The islands aren't there all of the time—"

"Well, isn't *that* convenient?"

"They appear with the light of the crescent moon," Karim said, shuffling backward as Rahmi approached the cell door. He reached toward the set of keys he had tethered to his belt. "I'm not lying to you! The *Luminaria*!"

Rahmi paused at the door, the iron key floating just above the level of the lock.

"You asked me about the *Luminaria*," Karim rushed out, tightening his grip on his injured elbow. Rahmi could see it had begun to swell, the sleeve of Karim's tunic tighter than it had been a few minutes previously. "Soren, he was the scholar. He came across a legend when he was doing his research on the map. It was a legend that had been associated with the *Luminaria*. He convinced the ship's captain that we would allow him to have it if he gave us passage."

"My patience is wearing thin," Rahmi said, his knuckles whitening as he tightened his grip on the key. Stifling the urge to break Karim's other arm was becoming much harder.

"There's a legend that the *Luminaria* was a gift from the gods, but it was lost, along with the treasure we found in the hall. It's a gemstone—a ruby, almost, but...more refined." Karim's gaze dropped to a pool of water on the floor of his cell. His eyes went distant, faded, as though he were lost in a memory.

The glazed expression gave Rahmi pause, and he leaned to the side to better peer at Karim through the bars. "And what does this gemstone do?" He would entertain it. The story might give him something to ponder before dinner, anyway.

"Its powers are rumored to be unlimited. The captain who gave us passage, Captain Nasir Al-Mahdi, was interested in it when we told him. He had gotten in a bad way with the king. He allowed Nasir to stay out of prison as long as we found him the stone. We drew up an accord with the king himself."

Rahmi narrowed his eyes and, in a sudden flash, shoved the key into the lock and pushed the cell door open. Karim shuffled back, seemingly torn between protecting his injured arm and getting as far away from Rahmi as quickly as possible. Rahmi crouched in front of him, reaching out a hand to grasp Karim's elbow. "Why does the king seek the gem?"

"I—" Karim said, but he clamped his lips shut, and Rahmi watched as his face turned a shade of green usually only reserved for extreme seasickness. Rahmi tightened his grip. "I don't know! *For the love of the gods, I don't know!*"

Rahmi released him, and Karim collapsed against the framing of the hull, chest heaving as he sucked in deep breaths. In the next moment, he leaned to the side and emptied his stomach onto the floor. It splashed back up, coating the front of Karim's tunic and the toes of Rahmi's boots.

"You will lead me to this *Luminaria*," Rahmi said, the statement not posed as a question. He stood, lifting his boot to wipe the vomit onto Karim's breeches.

Karim shuddered as he wiped his mouth with the back of his hand. "I—I've spent the last year trying to find it again."

"You said you found it with your associates," Rahmi pressed him, crossing his arms over his chest and tucking the map between his arm and ribcage. "Where can we find them?"

Karim shook his head, and, for a moment, Rahmi thought he would be sick again. "Dead. They...they died at the cave. I was the only one to get out alive." Rahmi raised his brows, but his expression alone must have been enough to intimidate Karim because he flinched back again. "I'm telling the truth, captain. That is all I know."

Rahmi surveyed the man huddled in the corner of the cell, covered in his own sick, pale, and clammy. He nodded once before pivoting and exiting the cell, locking the door behind him.

"Wait! I need a healer!" Karim began to scoot himself forward, accidentally smearing his pile of vomit across the floor with his hip. "Please! A healer! Please!"

Rahmi clicked his tongue against his teeth as he reached up and snuffed out the lamp with a quick pinch of his fingers, pitching the brig into black. "I'll get you a healer," he said as he began the familiar walk toward the passage, quickly navigating the room despite the darkness. "I just didn't say when. Maybe your time down here will help you remember further."

"No! *No!*" Karim screamed as Rahmi stepped into the hallway, shutting the thick door of the brig behind him. The screams dulled to a muffle.

Rahmi turned toward the stairs at the ship's bow and was un-surprised to see Alaric leaning against the wall. Alaric's one blue eye studied Rahmi as the captain pushed past his quartermaster.

"Pennley and Elodie caught enough fish that they are making fresh stew for supper," Alaric said, following Rahmi down the passage. By Alaric's tone, Rahmi knew that he was skirting around what he wanted to say.

Rahmi shot him a look over his shoulder, marching up the stairs as the ship surged forward with a sudden gust of wind that caught the sails. "Speak plainly, Alaric. From the look on your face, you overheard, at least, some of that."

"We have to inquire about it further, captain," Alaric replied as though he had never mentioned fish stew. "A gemstone with unlim-ited abilities? We can—"

"It's a farce, Alaric," Rahmi said with a shake of his head.

They passed through the berth, half of the swinging hammocks filled with softly snoring men scheduled to crew overnight. The stench was acrid and eye-watering. From Alaric's rapid blinks and the curl of his lip, he must have smelled it, too. They would have the men wash out their hammocks and clothes during the next rain.

"You are a pirate captain cursed to a ship for over three hundred years, and you can only go on land once every seven years," Alaric replied, logic threading his tone in a condescendingly slow way that made Rami want to throttle him. "And you don't believe in a gemstone that could potentially break that curse?" He sighed as they climbed another set of stairs, exiting onto the quarterdeck. "If only there were a way to verify it."

Rahmi stopped in his tracks, and Alaric ran straight into his back. "Maybe—" He lifted a hand to stroke the stubbled beard on his jawline. "Alaric, set course for the ice caves north of the capital. There is one person we can ask— one person who studied the curse long enough to break it."

Alaric's brows knitted together. "Who?"

"Devlin Cato. The captain of *The Phantom Night.*"

CHAPTER FIVE

KALIA

A side from the small beach nestled by the port, Willow Row was the one place in Mistral's Bay that Kalia could stand. It was the main thoroughfare that split the city in two. The northern end was where the palace and the subsequent white-stoned mansions of the obscenely wealthy sat. It was known for luxury, and they didn't bother trying to hide that they turned their nose up at anyone who didn't wear at least three pieces of gold jewelry on just a casual stroll around the gardens. Even its smell screamed opulence, with notes of amber, vanilla, and rose flowers.

The southern end, on the other hand, was known for its brothels, gambling dens, and common houses where sailors or the impoverished could rent a moldy, straw-stuffed mattress for the night—that is if they didn't pass out in the filth-soaked alleyways first. Every so often, a wealthy lord or business owner would wander into the brothels to have a bit of fun, but the different sides of the city kept to themselves for the most part.

Kalia exited the apothecary, holding the jar of salve tightly, and crossed the cobblestone street before taking a left onto Willow Row. At the heart of it was a cheap marketplace compared to the vibrant one of Sha'Hadra, selling stale and damaged goods that made the voyage from the bustling desert city. Still, the barrels of powdered spices and walls full of dyed leather bags reminded her of home, something she had been missing as of late. Sometimes, she would sneak onto the roof of the stone buildings that bracketed the market like a prison to watch the stars blink into existence as the sky darkened into navy.

Pushing through a gap in the crowd, Kalia made her way to a stall where a sweet, aromatic steam rose from the pots on the hearths behind the counter. The owners shouted at the customers strolling the market to entice someone to buy their food. The sizzling meats and baking bread seemed only to call the attention of the stray dogs that wandered the streets, most people deterred by the barrage of yells. To Kalia, it was just another piece of home. She handed over two coins Pete had slipped into her palm on the way from the apothecary, and the shopkeeper gave her a bag of roasted nuts in return.

Kalia snacked on them as she wandered the street, watching as vendors haggled over prices and armed guards stood in the shadows of the wooden awnings that stretched over the shop entrances, their eyes sweeping over the heads of the visitors. Wind chimes twinkled their songs in the light breeze, one that carried the scent of musty rolls of fabric, pipe smoke, and stale sweat. There was a delicate hum of chatter, pierced by the peals of giggles from children running through the crowds.

Kalia's wounds were beginning to rub uncomfortably against the fabric of her dress, and the sore stiffness that accompanied the lash marks barreled to the forefront of her mind. Still, she couldn't stand the thought of re-entering the brothel to face the madam, not right

now, and she knew that she would have some reprieve when she lathered the salve on later that night. At least, she hoped to get some decent
rest.

"Thief! *Thief!*"

The words rang out like a cannon blast, and a small elbow caught
Kalia in the hip as a child rushed past. Her gaze locked on the back of
the girl's head, her long braids bouncing against her back as she ran
with half a loaf of bread tucked under her arm. At that moment, Kalia
was seven years old and sprinting down the back alleys of Sha'Hadra.
Now, it was her being chased through the streets, a triumphant grin on
her face as she made off with an entire roasted chicken. The memory
struck fast, briefly leaving Kalia lost in her thoughts.

The girl wove through the crowd, ducking under outstretched arms
meaning to catch her, and shoving through a gathering of dirty-faced
boys who jeered at her as she went.

Kalia lifted her stare and looked to the nearest guard. He unsheathed his sword and began to navigate the crowded street easily
after the girl. The shoppers parted as the guard approached, trying
their best to avoid getting sliced by the blade held in his hand. Kalia
knew that he wouldn't think twice about cutting down someone who
got in his way.

The girl looked over her shoulder, her eyes widening and lips parting as he quickly closed the space between them. Kalia had seen this
dance play out a time or two. If the guard could catch the girl, she
would lose her hand, if not her life. If by a miracle she could get away,
she would be forced into hiding as the guards hunted her down, at
least until they found someone else to pass the time torturing.

Kalia dropped into the shadows of the nearest alleyway, tripping
over a bent leg. She glanced down to see a man fast asleep while
propped against the stone wall, the sour stench of his dirty clothes

filling the air of the narrow passage. She ignored him the best she could, instead focusing on the guard.

Opening her mind, Kalia shot a thread of magic into the square, focusing it entirely on his back. She imagined it piercing his skull, wriggling into the layers of his mind like a worm and hooking into the core of his subconscious. The air crackled around her, raising the hair on her arms as though an intense lightning storm was readying to batter the port. The guard stretched out a hand, coming within inches of the young girl's tunic before he froze.

To anyone else, it may have looked like the guard merely halted in his tracks. Kalia knew by the thrashing and gnashing his mind was doing in a sore attempt to dislodge her that the man was fighting for his life. She glimpsed flashes of memories— a boy running in a field as an older man, perhaps his father, chased him through the wildflowers. A first kiss with a freckle-faced girl. A fist slammed into his temple during a training session.

Kalia hated diving like this. She preferred the light, superficial impressions that she had become accustomed to. Sorting through old memories and distant thoughts made her prickle with discomfort and made her *know* the person she was connecting herself to. And that was the absolute last thing she wanted to do. Any sympathy would only lead to pity, an avenue for weakness that ultimately leads to betrayal.

Desperate times called for desperate measures, though, and Kalia instantly decided that she would save that child's life as no one would have done for her.

A pounding headache began to nestle at the base of her neck, and her clammy brow furrowed as she struggled to remain tethered to the man's mind. She inhaled deeply and sent a vision down their new bond, transporting him somewhere else entirely.

They were at the port, and the guard's cheeks blistered red from the whipping winds. Kalia made it as believable as possible, down to the salty scent of the water and the sound of the chains rattling against the masts as the ships bobbed in the waves. The guard blinked, confusion etching into the soft lines of his face. Kalia watched as he gazed over the barnacles latching to the docks near the waterline and the birds gliding over the crates of fish being carried across the narrow wooden ramps.

Because of this, her magic at the end of it all was what the king feared most. With her in his mind, showing him something that only existed to them, she could make him do nearly anything. She could force him to walk off a roof, thinking he was walking along a beach. She could have him eat a poisoned berry while he thought it was a sweet pastry from the market.

Kalia pulled back on the connection just enough to see that a woman had stepped in front of the guard, lifted a hand, and was waving it in front of his dulled, lifeless face. Another man snickered as the woman began to snap her fingers. The young girl was lost to the crowd.

Kalia released the threads of her power, and they whipped back into place. She grimaced as jarring pain shot through the split of her brain and settled into her skull. The aftermath of using the entirety of her magic was always uncomfortable, but it was worth it to see the child keep both of her hands for another day.

The guard woke, a slack expression loosening his jaw when he stumbled forward. His chin flinched back as though he were trying to remember where he was, and he rubbed his forehead with the tips of his fingers.

"Come back to the present, did ya?" A man shouted from the opposite side of the street. He let out a low chuckle as he shook his head. "Couldn't even collect a street girl. Waste of the guard, you are."

Waves of laughter followed at the quip, and a fierce blush crept up the back of the guard's neck. Unease crawled through Kalia's belly. Taunting a guard was almost as bad as taunting the king, and the punishments were nearly the same.

Cries of protest rose from the crowd as the woman assisting the guard was suddenly hit in the face by the pommel of his sword. Her basket of fresh oranges spilled onto the cobblestone path while a nauseating *crack* sounded through the market. A few people rushed forward to survey her nose, blood now gushing from both nostrils, while others helped to gather the fruit. A small boy with an ash-smeared face collected one that had rolled to his feet and took off down the nearest alleyway.

"Back to your cart, sir, or I'll have you arrested," the guard said as he approached the man who had spoken out, settling the tip of his sword near the vendor's chest.

"Arrested for what?" the man responded in outrage, but he clamped his lips together when the guard pressed the sword into his flesh just enough for a droplet of blood to stain his tunic.

"Disturbing the peace," the guard spat in reply. "Whatever I would like. I'm sure I can come up with something." The vendor's nostrils flared, but he remained silent. "That's what I thought. Does anyone have anything else to add?"

The same jingle of windchimes was eerie now that an unsettled silence blanketed the market. The guard sheathed his sword, that flush of red still curling over the shell of his ear. He would undoubtedly be looking for retribution soon, for nothing except to soothe his embarrassment, and Kalia had no interest in seeing who he would level that attention on.

There weren't many in the capital who could pinpoint her as the culprit, as magic users didn't dare to practice in public, but she had stayed too long nonetheless. Without a second look at the man still snoring behind her, Kalia slid from the alleyway and skirted the shoppers of Willow Row.

Kalia slinked through the bordello, taking the door from the back alley. The path brought her through the hot, overcrowded kitchen and up the rickety staircase only used by the servants, ending in the narrow hallway that led to her room.

It was the bedroom Kalia had been assigned since her arrival at the bordello, one that she tried to spend as little time in as possible. The small window overlooked the same back alley and housed four panes of glass that were all cracked in one spot or another. If she glanced down in the daylight, she could easily spot the rust-pitted garbage bins, puddles of dried vomit, and grease-covered pools of water that sunk between the cobblestones. At night, drunken brawls and howling stray cats could be heard above the noise from the street.

No matter how often Kalia cleaned the surface of the end table or the simple wooden chair in the corner of the room, they both somehow ended up grimy and slick by the end of the week. She attributed it to the near-constant stream of cigar smoke that wafted through the window from below, but the rotting garbage and mildew weren't helpful either. She kept the room neat, much to the madam's expectations, but aside from the trunk at the foot of her bed or the loose floorboard where she once stashed her coins, she didn't bother keeping any personal effects there.

When Kalia opened the door, the room was washed in a glow of golden candlelight. She was unsurprised to see Odion seated on the mattress and his sword untethered from his belt resting against the far wall. She stifled a sigh and closed the door with a soft *click*, drowning out the music and raucous laughter from the main room of the bordello.

"I could have guessed you would have made it to the apothecary," Odion started when his eyes dropped to the jar in Kalia's hand. "Mintie had all sorts of things to say about the state of the madam's office after you were dismissed."

"I'm sure she did." Kalia crossed the room and sat at the vanity, gazing at her reflection in the cracked mirror. She leaned forward to inspect the split flesh on the top of her shoulder, ignoring Odion's stare that she could feel boring into the center of her back. "Mintie always has things to say."

Odion was silent as Kalia unscrewed the jar and dipped two fingers into the salve. Sucking in a breath through her nose, she began to smear the concoction onto her shoulder and her chest, swallowing back the hisses of pain that clawed up her throat. Behind her, the bedframe groaned as Odion stood, and his boots fell heavy against the wooden floorboards. He reached over her shoulder to pluck the jar from the vanity before sweeping her hair over her right shoulder.

"You shouldn't anger her," Odion said as he untied the satin ribbons that held the back of her dress together, letting the straps fall onto her bare shoulders. He dipped his finger into the salve and lightly painted it across the lashes on her back. "If you want to stay in the bordello—"

"The madam isn't going to let me go, no matter what I do," Kalia interrupted. She lifted her hands to pin the front of her dress against her chest, keeping the swells of her breasts covered. She glanced up to look into the mirror again, only to see that his intense stare was studying her. "I make her too much coin. Plus—" She trailed off as she let out an involuntary moan when he smeared the salve over a particularly sore welt near the base of her shoulder blade. "Despite what you may think, I'm only trying to help."

"By setting loose a nest of angry hornets for Cranford Reed to find? I don't think anyone asked you to do that. Especially not Mintie or Nadine."

"No one had to. Cranford Reed, he—"

"Kalia," Odion cut her off as he leaned forward to set the jar back onto the vanity. It clunked a little too hard against the surface. "Everyone knows Cranford Reed is a disgusting man. Gods, half of the men who frequent this bordello are disgusting men, but you can't just—"

"Are you seriously reprimanding me?" Kalia shot back, a surge of anger overtaking the burning pain from her wounds. She stood quickly, sending the stool from the vanity skirting harshly across the floor. "I don't believe I *asked* for your opinion, Odion."

Odion's lips parted as he stared at her, and tension clouded the space between them. "I care for you; don't you see that?" he finally returned. He stepped forward to close the gap, his leather armor brushing against the skin on the back of her wrist. "If you would just let me in—"

"I think we're done here, Odion," Kalia interjected, side-stepping him to sweep toward the door. "What we had the last couple of weeks was fun, but it certainly wasn't something that would last. I'm not here to be cared for or looked after. I can do that myself."

Odion scoffed as he lifted a hand to run it through his hair. Kalia knew the feeling of her fingers curling into his locks, and, for a brief moment, she imagined herself apologizing before taking him to her bed. She held steady against his scrutinizing gaze, which lasted far too long for her liking. Instead, she reached for the knob and yanked the door open, flooding the room with the humming chatter from below. The silence seemed endless, but Odion finally lurched forward to grab his sword from the far wall.

"Just because you *can* look after yourself doesn't mean you *have* to."

"Please just leave. We don't need this to be difficult."

Odion paused at the door long enough to tether his sword to his belt. "I'll ask the madam for a transfer then?"

Kalia glanced into the narrow hallway, where two servant girls were now perched on the staircase, no doubt listening to their argument. She was sure they hoped to overhear something they could take to the madam for additional compensation. They giggled as they turned away. She looked back up at Odion. "You can do what you wish. I'm not your keeper."

Odion pursed his lips, his gaze roving her face for another minute before he curtly nodded. He was barely over the threshold before Kalia snapped the door shut behind him. She closed her eyes, letting her forehead rest against the cool wood. The pain in her back was creeping up her spine, and the welted laceration on her shoulder had begun to leak again. She would take care of those later.

She wanted to lay on her bed and stare at the ceiling. There was no use in getting close to the guard, no matter how handsome or kind she found him. At the end of it all, he would betray her, or she would betray him. It wasn't worth the heartbreak. No, it was better this way. It was better to cut all contact and be done with it before either fell into a heap of feelings they could no longer control.

CHAPTER SIX

RAHMI

*T*he *Phantom Night* was once a sister ship to *The Mark of Malice.* Both were used to collect dying souls from the sea, though that was where the captains' similarities ended. Devlin Cato, captain of *The Phantom Night,* gave his sailors a choice to sell their souls to Liddros. He offered them time and allowed them to barter for more once it was over.

Rahmi, on the other hand, did no such thing. He picked the sailors wracked with guilt using telltale signs from body language. Some called it intuitive, but he knew it was nothing more than skilled observation—something he had honed over the past three hundred years. If a man or woman displayed said guilt, Rahmi gave them twenty years to remedy their regret. Rahmi allowed them to pass peacefully into the next life if they did. If they didn't, they were delivered to Liddros.

The most glaring difference between the two ships was that *The Phantom Night* was no longer a cursed crew. Devlin Cato had seen to that two years previously, thanks to the woman he had taken as a wife. It hadn't surprised Rahmi in the least bit that Devlin had found a way out of his agreement with Liddros. Knowing the other captain as well as he did, Rahmi figured it was only a matter of time. Devlin had always been a slippery fuck.

This is precisely why Rahmi wanted to sail straight for *The Phantom Night* and Captain Devlin Cato. If there were anyone who would have heard of a gemstone with innumerable magical abilities, it would be him.

Luckily, *The Phantom Night* was easy enough to track down. Devlin was a creature of habit, after all. From the waterways he preferred to sail down to where he set his goblet at the dinner table. It was summer. Therefore, Devlin would sail his ship to the northern end of the continent to escape the oppressive humidity and constant rains of the jungles to the south. It had been that way for over a century now.

And that was precisely where Rahmi found him.

"Captain Rahmi Abada, as I live and breathe," Devlin said, his mouth splitting into a grin that crinkled the corners of his eyes. "I certainly didn't think I would see the likes of you again."

Rahmi stepped from the gunnel, landing heavily on the wooden floorboards of the deck. His crew bustled behind him to stabilize the dropped anchor and tether the two ships to one another, though the warm, salty wind flapped under the sails tied tightly to the masts.

"Captain Devlin Cato," Rahmi retorted as he held out his hand, which Devlin took in a firm shake. "I hope my presence comes at an appropriate time."

"Aye." Devlin nodded, squinting his eyes against the sun's brilliant rays that bounded off the tops of the cresting waves. "We were readying to make sail for the ice caves. It's the only time of year my wife and I agree to explore the northernmost islands of the continent. Have you met Fenna?"

As though summoned by an invisible wind, an auburn-haired woman appeared at Devlin's elbow. Rahmi glanced down to look at her. She was of average height, the crown of her head lined with the top of Devlin's shoulder, and freckles smattered her cheeks and the bridge of her nose. The book tucked under her right arm made her seem naively young, though her hazel-eyed gaze pierced Rahmi in a way that made him highly uncomfortable. He couldn't help shifting on his feet as he lifted his eyes back to Devlin.

"I don't believe that I have, and I won't keep you long," Rahmi replied, reaching toward his belt to pull the crinkled map from where he had tucked it near the cutlass. He carefully unfolded it, pinching it between two fingers to ensure it didn't rip at the creases. "In your studies to break your curse, did you ever encounter something called a *Luminaria*?"

Devlin stilled, the action nearly imperceptible amongst the rocking and rolling of the ship. "No, I've never heard of it."

Rahmi narrowed his eyes, pinning Devlin in place. "No one likes a liar, and you've always been terrible."

Waves slapped against the hull, the rigging high above them creaking in the breeze. Rahmi remained silent. From the corner of his eye, he saw Fenna's gaze dart back and forth between the two men.

"Using the *Luminaria* comes with a price," Devlin said, though Rahmi was forced to lean forward to hear him. "I've heard...tales of it." His seafoam green eyes darkened like a storm brewing on the dawn horizon. "You're best to leave it be. Find another way to break your curse—"

Rahmi had never been good at leaving things be. "I have no interest in breaking my curse. At least, in the way you think."

Devlin seemed torn, his cheek bowing in slightly as he chewed on the inside of it. "Come to my cabin then. I'll give you the information

I have." He pivoted on the toes of his boots, navigating through a crew of sun-kissed and tanned faces. Fenna sent Rahmi a wary glance before following Devlin to the ship's stern, her cotton skirts billowing in the wind. She reached over to squeeze the forearm of a tawny-skinned woman, who only set eyes on Rahmi long enough to glare.

"It's been almost fifty years since I first heard of the *Luminaria*," Devlin said as Rahmi crossed the threshold, closing the cabin door behind him. The whistling wind and shouts from both crews snuffed out immediately. "I researched as much of it as I could for almost three decades, sifting through scrolls in the temples of the capital city when I was allowed to go ashore." He wove around the desk laden with journals and brass instruments, stopping in front of a bookcase settled neatly into the far wall. "There wasn't much there, but I found what I could."

Devlin plucked a book from the top shelf and cracked it open, settling it on top of an unfurled map on the wooden surface. He began to rifle through the old pages, running a finger down the lines as he quickly scanned each one. Rahmi leaned a hip against the corner of the desk before reaching into his pocket and pulling out the single coin.

"Does it have anything to do with this?" Rahmi asked, holding up the copper between his forefinger and his thumb.

Fenna's hazel eyes narrowed as she reached up a hand and took the coin, laying it flat in her palm. She surveyed it for a long moment before finally saying, "Is this language *Ubarian*?"

"I can't be sure. It certainly isn't one that I recognize," Rahmi replied. He watched as Fenna turned away and walked toward the bookcase, pulling an old journal from the lower shelf. He swallowed the instinct to snatch back the coin, not appreciating that it was out of his hand.

Fenna returned to the desk, opened the book, and settled it across from Devlin's. She scanned the pages twice as quickly as her husband, her eyes flitting from the pages to the coin still in her palm. "It is *Ubarian,*" she said, gesturing for Rahmi to move closer. "I've heard of this. I remember reading it in a book I found at the shop I once worked at."

Rahmi stepped forward and dropped his gaze down to the open journal, the page littered with drawings of old coins and ancient markings. One drawing in particular caught his eye. From how Fenna was staring at it, he knew it had caught her eye, too. He was just glad that the assessing gaze was turned away from him.

Fenna leaned forward to pick up Devlin's book and set it, still open, on top of her own.

"What are you—?" Devlin started, but the small woman at his front quickly shushed him. Rahmi bit his tongue to keep from chuckling.

"I know *exactly* where I've seen this before," Fenna said, flicking through the pages so quickly that Rahmi was sure the parchment would rip. They never did. "The City of Pillars." She halted on a page toward the middle of the book, pointing triumphantly down with a finger tipped with black ink. When neither man moved to congratulate her, she clucked her tongue against the roof of her mouth, the sound as condescending as she certainly meant it. "The ancient city, fabled to be lost to the sands? Rumored to be bracketed by pillars so tall the tops could kiss the clouds? Pillars that were so ornate that thieves *still* excavate the desert in hopes of finding even a shard of the golden casting?"

Devlin and Rahmi glanced at one another. Rahmi finally shrugged his shoulder. "There were stories in my village," he said slowly, shaking his head as he read the page over Fenna's shoulder. "There was once a city completely entrenched in magic, thanks to the beings that raised it from the ground. The gods were unhappy with the amount of power given to those beings, and a war was fought. The desert swallowed the city, and the gods vowed never to allow the power to surface again." He paused to straighten from his lean. "Those are children's stories, though, ones that my mother told me, and her mother told her to keep us in our beds at night."

Fenna bustled over to the bookshelf one final time, pulling a third book from the shelf. "The City of Pillars," she started, flicking the book open with a quick turn of her wrist, "was once in the desert region of Ubar, thought to be not far from where the city of Sha'Hadra stands today." She placed the book on the growing stack on the desk, tucking a lock of auburn hair behind her ear. "The legend goes that a powerful djinn once ruled over the city, guiding his citizens to pray in the temples dedicated to the gods that created him. But as the city grew and trade routes were established, the djinn became greedy with his newfound riches. He forced the temples to begin to praise him instead, angering the gods. There was a war, one that finally buried the city beneath the sands."

A frown pulled down the corners of Rahmi's lips. "And the *Luminaria*? How does the gemstone play into the story?"

Fenna tilted her head as her eyes roved over the page. "This passage doesn't mention that name, but it does mention that the djinn created a red gemstone as a final attempt to win the war. He poured his power into it, hoping to use it to banish the gods from this world."

"A gemstone with innumerable abilities indeed," Rahmi muttered. He glanced toward the small circular window on the other side of the cabin, taking in the sandbars' descending slopes just below the shimmering waves' surface. "And the riches? Does it say what happened to them?"

Fenna shook her head.

"Trade routes," Devlin said suddenly. He leaned onto his knuckles, surveying the open pages of the book. "You said that Ubar made its wealth through trade. Is it possible the djinn knew of the impending war and decided to clear out his stores? That's certainly what I would have done." He glanced from the journal to the copper coin in his wife's hand. "Will you retrieve Loma for me, my love? And tell her to set our courses north."

Fenna nodded, moving toward the door, but Rahmi stopped her with an outstretched hand. She blinked before a scowl darkened her features. Her eyes dropped to his upturned palm before lifting to connect with his expectant stare.

"Do you expect me to make off with your copper?" she asked, her nostrils flaring with irritation. "Perhaps purchase a bottle of *fion* from the market that will surely be established in the ice caves? I just wanted to run it by another crew member, one who has some working knowledge of old legends."

"What you will or won't do with it is none of my concern," Rahmi retorted, watching with caution as Devlin straightened from his hunched position over the book and glided a hand to rest on the pommel of his cutlass. "My concern is that you don't make off with it at all."

There was a charged silence between the three of them before Fenna let out a huffed chuckle, slapping the coin into his hand. "*You* sought us out," she added, as though he needed reminding. "It might do *you* some good to place some trust in those you—"

"I'm here for a specific purpose," Rahmi retorted, readying to wrap his hand around his blade's hilt at any moment. It had been decades since he and Devlin last drew swords against one another, but he had no hesitancy to do it again. "Information doesn't require trust." He dropped back to let her pass, smirking at the flash of disbelief that momentarily lit up her eyes.

Fenna wrapped her hand around the knob, yanking the door open with a quick tug. The sounds of gulls squawking and the clanking of metal rigging flooded the cabin before it went quiet again with the snap of the door closing.

"I like her," Rahmi announced, flipping the coin into the air before catching it deftly in his other hand. "I see why you made her your wife. She's smarter than you could ever hope to be."

"I appreciate your deduction," Devlin responded dryly as he removed his hand from his cutlass. "Though, as usual, she does remain correct." He gave Rahmi an assessing look. "What do you want the *Luminaria* for?"

Rahmi was quiet for a series of heartbeats, running the tip of his forefinger over his bottom lip as he thought. "Tell me what you know about the djinn," he replied instead.

Devlin's muttered curse cut through the cabin, a pointed annoyance pinching his lips into a tight slash. "The *Luminaria* is dangerous, Rahmi. That's why it takes a djinn to use it—"

"So there *is* a way to use it?" Rahmi interjected, crossing his arms over his chest.

"Power comes with a price," Devlin seethed through gritted teeth. "Power that you don't know how to deal with. It's suicide to trap one. It's suicide to find the *Luminaria*. And it's suicide to use it." He tented a hand on the stack of books. "I studied it for decades and did as much research as I could find. It isn't *worth* your time, and it isn't *worth* your life."

Rahmi sucked in a breath, rocking from the toes of his boots to his heels. "Why don't you let me judge what is *worth* my time and my life, Captain Cato?"

At the use of his formal title, Devlin stiffened. He shrugged as he sat in the chair behind his desk, the wood groaning beneath the sudden introduction of his weight. "You're right," he said as he retrieved a bottle of ink, a quill, and a roll of parchment from the top drawer. "I'll write down what I know most about the djinn. They're harder to find than a cognizant, but the temples in the capital city are the best place to start. The priests have been known to hide magic wielders from the king."

Rahmi didn't stop Devlin to inquire what a cognizant was, knowing the captain wouldn't get back on course if he asked. Devlin dipped the quill's tip into the ink bottle and began to write, a rhythmic scratching against the parchment filling the cabin.

"They're capricious creatures," Devlin finally said after a few minutes, fanning his hand over the wet ink to help it dry faster. "Unpredictable, fickle, and easy to anger. They'll kill you faster than you even begin to *think* about drawing your blade." He carefully rolled up the parchment, handing it over the desk to Rahmi. "And that's if you can find one."

Rahmi took the scroll, tucking it into a belt loop at his waist. "It's always a pleasure, Devlin."

Devlin leaned back in his seat, crossing his arms over his chest. "I let you live solely because of the duty we once shared. But threaten my wife again, Captain Abada, and I'll take more than your life. I'll take your crew. I'll take your ship. And I'll ensure that every person still living in the village you crawled out of pays for your sins."

Rahmi merely grinned.

CHAPTER SEVEN

RAHMI

Not many things truly frightened Rahmi, but Liddros was one of them. Ruthless and cunning were the only words Rahmi could use to describe the god of the sea; even those seemed to light a sentence.

Additionally, there was only one way to summon a god, something Rahmi hadn't done in years—centuries. He tried to keep to himself, to bring on just enough souls that Liddros had no reason to hunt him down. The king was demanding, and it was taking far more souls these days to keep him young, but the number of callous and guilted men sailing the seas never dwindled. It was easy enough work.

Rahmi struck a match, murmured the incantation he knew from heart, and lit the corner of the parchment on which he had scribbled the runes. It went up in flame, the orange glow licking the parchment to cinder. It reached the runes, where a black shimmer that matched the markings covering his arms swallowed the light. He let the ashes fall to his desk, only allowing the moon's silver light to penetrate the darkness of his quarters.

Then, he waited. Two minutes. Five minutes. Ten minutes. Each second felt longer than the last, ticking by with a guttering slowness that made Rahmi want to fidget in his seat. He managed to stay still, to coolly survey the brass instruments at the edge of his desk, and listen to the calm waves lap against the side of his ship.

"I'm surprised to hear from you," a man drawled from the shadows of the cabin, his low voice filled with enough authority that Rahmi had to stifle a primal instinct to sit up straighter. He actively fought against it, hating the control it took from him. "I thought we concluded our *last* visit that you would not contact me again."

Rahmi remembered the argument well. He had been raging at the short leash that tethered him to Liddros. He hadn't bothered to understand the fine print regarding his job. He hadn't realized what it meant to be a cursed captain when he cut the heart from the previous one before tossing it into the waves when he took command of *The Mark of Malice* and set her on a course that would forever change the lives of the crew onboard. Not to mention his own.

And he had thrown a fist at Liddros in retaliation, who easily dodged the blow and caught Rahmi in the gut in return, shattering three ribs that took weeks to heal. They hadn't spoken since, but Rahmi ensured that he kept a steady flow of souls to the god, if only to keep him far away from his ship.

"Things have changed in two hundred years," Rahmi retorted, letting a hand rest on the dagger he had laid on the desk in front of him. "And I have questions that require answering."

Liddros waved a hand, lighting the three lanterns that hung in various places around the cabin. The flames flickered in his wake, even the fire coming to bow at his power. It illuminated the cabin, basking just enough light in the darkness that Rahmi saw the god's face for the first time in centuries.

He was tall, his broad shoulders taking up nearly an entire corner of the cabin. His hair was dark, tied back in the same bun as Rahmi's, though his locks were straight and smooth. His curious quirk to his lips promised mischief, and his unnatural stone-colored eyes danced with that same promise. He wore pristine fighting leathers with a sword hitched tightly to his back, and Rahmi knew he would use it if provoked. Dark markings encircled his neck and upper arms, chains of his own, and those markings seemed to absorb any light that dared grace his tanned skin.

A warrior. A god. One who Rahmi had known for a long time not to fuck with.

"Are we readying for another battle?" Liddros asked lightly, a chuckle gracing his tone. There was an unsaid *don't you fucking dare* attached to the end of his question. He dropped his eyes to the dagger, quirking an amused brow.

Rahmi merely slid the dagger away from him, letting it rest at the edge of the desk. "I wasn't sure how I would be received," he responded in just as light of a tone. "I wanted to be prepared." *Just in case you came in, swords drawn.*

Liddros's smirk was devastating. "We both know that dagger would do nothing to me."

Rahmi knew that to be true, but he wouldn't allow the god to kill him without a fight. Instead of countering that, he silently reached into his pocket, pulled out the folded map, and tossed it on the desk between them. He gestured to it, not taking his gaze away from Liddros. "I saw Devlin today. He seems to be doing well." The words were meant in jest, though Rahmi couldn't help the bitterness that rode on them.

Liddros stepped forward, his brows pinned high on his forehead. "Is there something you wish to tell me before we begin this dance?

One that I'll inevitably win, might I add." Irritation flared within Rahmi. Liddros reached down and picked up the parchment, unfolding it carefully. "Devlin was a terrible captain, both you and I know this well. He felt too much for the people he was reaping. He was on the verge of—" Liddros trailed off, his eyes gliding over the map.

"I wondered how interesting you would find that," Rahmi said, leaning back in his seat to survey the god. That sudden irritation was replaced with something much sweeter. "It seems that I found my answer."

Liddros cleared his throat. "And where did you find this?" His eyes flashed up to meet Rahmi, who swallowed back the fear taking root in the recesses of his chest. "The *Luminaria*. That is a name I have not heard in a long time."

Rahmi sat forward at this, resting his forearms on the edge of his desk. "So, have you heard of it, then?"

Liddros was quiet for a moment, quiet enough that Rahmi was sure he was going to disappear into the cabin's shadows. Instead, he waved a hand, conjured a chair—no, an embossed, cushioned *throne*—and sank into it. All the while, he never took his eyes off the map.

Rahmi waited the appropriate amount to speak again, watching with caution as the god roved his eyes over the map. "Devlin's wife, Fenna, mentioned the *Luminaria* was created by djinn and could only be used by—"

"Stories sure do like to change over time," Liddros said, finally looking up from the map. His piercing gaze sunk into the depths of Rahmi's soul, an iciness again sliding through his chest. "It's ridiculous to imagine that djinn would have enough power to..." He paused again, cocking his head as rain began to plunk against the panes of the window behind Rahmi. "The *Luminaria* was the name given to a gemstone that fell from my brother's sword during the War of the

Sixteen. It was a war that ended in a treaty between two factions of gods and one that sent my brothers and me into different corners of the universe."

"I've never heard of it," Rahmi responded, running a finger over his bottom lip in thought. "It's not something that's ever been taught in the learning houses around here."

Liddros rolled his eyes. "Of course, it hasn't. Your world is *old*. And it was already here when the War of the Sixteen broke out." He glanced back down at the map. "There was another world created from the war, where most of my brothers rest. Thanks to a betrayal from my twin that is. The gemstone comes from the hilt of my younger brother's dagger. Maher is his name, and he used it to bind the power of the djinn. Make them slaves to its whim."

"The God of War?" It was Rahmi's turn to raise his brows. "The gods have long disappeared from this world. As far as I know, you're the only one left."

A smile curled Liddros's lips, and it wasn't one bought out of amusement. "The djinn were infused with magic directly from a god; that's what made them so powerful compared to other creatures. Due to their power, the gemstone could be used to control a djinn. But make no mistake, they did not create it."

"Can the *Luminaria* do what it has been rumored to do?" Rahmi asked, threading his fingers together to prevent himself from tapping against the desk in thought. "Can it truly break all magical bonds?"

Liddros narrowed his eyes, his body coming to a preternatural stillness that sent an uneasiness blooming in Rahmi's gut. "Why?" The question was a command, a tone that Rahmi frequently employed. Even though Rahmi hated the god sitting in front of him, he also knew better than to lie.

"You know why," Rahmi said carefully, his eyes flickered back to the map. A movement that was, unfortunately, not lost on the god in front of him. "The ability to break my bond to *you* while remaining an immortal captain on the seas is..." It was tempting, to say the least. It was more than tempting. It was a gods-damned miracle.

Liddros scrutinized Rahmi, his lips pressed into a tight, white line. "Picking up men and women who have guilt in their hearts, allowing them to work through it before my twin, Samael, takes them beyond...that's a nice touch. How long before you realized you could work around your curse that way?"

"Too long," Rahmi replied, sliding his eyes toward the rain that now lashed heavily against the sea, blurring the horizon and the water together. He angled his head. "I rather enjoy my job now. Makes it easier when I know the people on my ship deserve to be here."

Liddros let out a huff of a laugh. "And who says you should have that kind of power?"

"You did when you gave me this curse and set me loose like a rabid dog on the Aeglecian Seas," Rahmi retorted. "Just like you're going to tell me where I can find the *Luminaria*." He unthreaded his fingers, delicately sliding his left hand toward the dagger, letting it stop next to the sheath. Liddros caught that, too.

"Don't you think," the god seethed from between his teeth, his eyes darkening, "that I would have found it long ago if I knew it was still here?" His leather armor creaked as he lifted his hand to gesture toward the markings that still seemed to swallow the light. "That I would willingly keep myself bound to that fool of a king if I knew of a way to end it? He and I have come to an understanding these last one thousand years, but not one that includes setting me free. I think he knows what will happen to him if I am."

One thousand? Rahmi knew the king was old, but he didn't realize... "Do you know where to start? Do you know where the *Luminaria* could have gone after it left the City of Pillars?"

Liddros seemed impressed. "The old djinn city. Fenna has a propensity for knowledge that surprises even me. Some may call it nosy, but I find her curiosity endearing. The city is long gone, leveled by the War of the Sixteen and buried when the djinn rose against the gods a few hundred years later. It no longer exists, not to the extent you need it to. Though the magic still lingers..." He tapped a finger against the chair's armrest, his eyes darting across the map in thought. "I can't tell you where it is, nor can I say where it could be, but there are still three djinn who survived the uprising on this continent. All three are hidden, but I assure you are trapped here. You find one, you convince them to help you, and you can find the *Luminaria*. It won't be easy. The djinn won't be eager to be told what to do after this long."

"Why are you helping me?" Rahmi knew the god didn't do anything for free.

"Because you are going to find the gemstone for *me*."

Rahmi was silent for a long minute before a harsh, barking laugh burst out of him. "You truly think I summoned you to my ship to ask you about a gemstone I'm now going to steal for *you*?"

"No," Liddros corrected him, his tone a touch too condescending for Rahmi's liking. "My powers are dulled thanks to these chains given to me by the king. And that limits what I'm able to do otherwise. I cannot make the gemstone work on my own. This might be my only chance to break my bonds, too. And how do you think a god would repay the man, the captain, who found the way to do it?"

Rahmi's heart thundered against his chest. Was he willing to make a deal with a god? To give up possession of the gemstone to Liddros in return for...what, exactly? He asked just that.

"What you desire most of all," Liddros responded, steepling his fingers as he leaned back in his seat. "I could give you true immortality, not something tethered to a curse. I could allow you to sail the seas for the remainder of this world's existence. That's what you want, isn't it?"

That was precisely what Rahmi wanted. There was no hesitation in his decision as he braced his forearms on the edge of his desk. "Let's come to an accord then, shall we?"

CHAPTER EIGHT

KALIA

Two weeks had passed since the incident with the hornets, and Kalia had not seen a hair on Cranford Reed's head. While Nadine was grateful for the intervention, even though she didn't quite understand how Kalia figured it out, Mintie had been embarrassed. News of the ordeal spread like wildfire in a dry forest, kindling with the regulars before exploding in a spell of rumors and made-up stories. Each one was more outlandish than the next, and each one fueled a want from certain men that Mintie was having a hard time keeping up with.

Kalia had been sequestered to the upper balcony of the bordello as she healed, much as she often was when the madam didn't want her answering questions about her split flesh or bruised skin. But Pete's salve's healing power, accompanied by the madam's itching desire to return Kalia to her full employment, permitted her to the main room as long as an armed guard was kept by her side.

And luckily for Kalia, that guard was not Odion.

The privateer had fulfilled his promise to find a new position, leaving his lucrative job at the bordello only hours after their argument. She didn't know where he had been transferred to, nor did she care to find out, but she was grateful that his replacement had the sexual prowess of a dying toad and was no closer to sticking his cock in her than Cranford Reed was.

As grateful as she was that the new guard was decidedly not Odion, she was equally displeased that he was there at all. He made stealing coins from the drunken men passed out against the cushions much harder. She still managed a coin or two, but only when the crowd was so heavy that he couldn't spot her hands pickpocketing the men as she made her way to and from her station.

Kalia leaned against the red curtain that graced the marble wall, the stone smooth beneath her bare feet. She had opted for golden anklets in place of her usual strappy sandals, the heat from the summer weather pouring into the stale-aired brothel making her skin sticky. The string quartet in the opposite corner played a sultry song that the ladies used to grind against the laps of the men seated in the cushioned poufs. Aromatic smoke from the incense burning at the end tables curled high above the heads of the patrons.

It was stifling, and, not for the first time that night, Kalia was forced to take deep breaths to calm her rapidly racing heart. The heat only constricted in her lungs, tightening her throat into a narrow passage that made it difficult to swallow. She cleared it, shifting on her feet slowly enough that the guard sent her a long look.

"I'm not going anywhere," Kalia snapped in return, adjusting her satin dress to cover the tops of her breasts. She felt raw. And, despite the dress having a slit that showed off the majority of her tanned left leg, she wanted to take it off. The fabric rubbed against her skin, flaying an unknown nerve open. She needed out of this bordello, out of this city. And having him right fucking there all night long was an obstacle that she couldn't figure out how to cross. "I can move without your permission."

The guard scoffed, and his response earned him an eye roll. She bit back the additional retort on the tip of her tongue, instead sweeping her gaze over the new throng of clients who had waltzed through the door.

Five men, each clad in tunics and breeches that had certainly seen better days, crossed the threshold of the bordello, their eyes widening at the sight of the women dancing to the whine of the strings. Sailors. Kalia *hated* it when the sailors came into port. Loud, brash, and bringing the smell of rotting fish with them, the sailors weren't nearly as enticing as the brothel ladies led them to believe. Something that Kalia liked to remind them of, and often.

Kalia lifted her chin to survey them over the growing crowd, scanning their tunics and frock coats for the telltale ship emblem that typically graced their left chest pockets. They didn't have any pins or patches designating them to the navy or mercenary group. That meant they were more than likely pirates... and that was even worse.

"Come on, lads," a man pushed to the front of the group, clapping one hand on the shoulder of another as he passed. "We've been to six temples already. I think it's time to take a break while we're on land, don't you?" He lifted a hand to tighten the strap of his eye patch, the motion kinking his blonde hair at the back of his head. "We've got enough coin to satisfy ourselves a few times over."

Grunts of laughter rose over the crowd as the five men walked past the marble staircase that led to the private bedrooms on the second floor.

Gods, Kalia hoped they would be quick. At the very least, she hoped their smell wouldn't saturate the main room as the pirates' smell usually did. Her eyes followed the five men as they squeezed past a man on a barstool, his fingers digging into the hips of one of the women. Kalia glanced at the cracked door, nodding toward the madam who had stuck her nose from her office. The door clicked shut, and Kalia knew what she needed to do, what she had been brought from Sha'Hadra to do.

The first two men of the group didn't require Kalia's intervention; their minds were already set on Iris and Calliope at the back of the main room. The ladies lounged on their poufs, their legs spread wide, as they beckoned the two men toward them with gesturing fingers. The two pirates scuttled forward, pushing straight through the gap that had split in the crowd.

The third man swept his eyes over the iron chandeliers that hung from the ceilings, taking in the gold that adorned the end tables and bar counter. Kalia began to wonder if he was trying to figure out how to steal them when his gaze finally landed on Nadine, who was descending the stairs as she fluffed her hair and blotted at the lipstick smeared near the corners of her mouth. A vision collided in Kalia's mind, barreling down the bond she had bridged. He wanted her, wanted her mouth around his cock, and the feeling of her moans vibrating down to his balls.

Kalia sent another vision down the bond, changing his initial one just enough that Nadine glanced up at him through her lashes, her cheeks hollowed as she took him. Kalia knew how to manipulate these men and knew what they wanted, even if they didn't know themselves.

And it seemed to work, as the third man nearly tripped over the edge of the area rug while hurrying to meet her at the bottom of the stairs, pulling out a handful of copper coins as he went. Nadine's brows rose as she glanced at Kalia, but she only sent a nod of confirmation before turning back to the final two men.

The fourth had sidled up to the bar, a stein of *fion* clenched tightly in his fist. That was good enough for now. *Fion* was the remedy for an anxious man, and Kalia knew better than to push someone who wasn't ready to dive into the world of women. She had made that mistake before, which usually resulted in a disastrous encounter with losing a potential return customer. Though from the visions flicking through his mind, he had no limit to his imagination, and the liquid courage would be minimal. Perfect.

Kalia turned to the fifth man, the blonde with the eye patch, and focused on him. He shuffled on his feet, glancing uncomfortably around the bordello with his single eye. Hand on the pommel of his cutlass, hand back to his side. Shoulders squared toward the door, shoulders swiveled to face the bartender. He moved as though he were trying to find a position that looked natural and realized that he was failing. And she was bored enough to be intrigued by it.

She pushed her magic forward, infiltrating his mind with ease.

Well, *that* was certainly peculiar. Instead of the usual visions of dancing women and sultry stares, his thoughts were fraught with old maps, ruby gemstones, and the guard who stood at Kalia's side. Kalia furrowed her brow, glancing inconspicuously toward the man at her right.

Him? Kalia returned her stare to the one-eyed man. She wasn't one to judge, having had her fair share of dalliances with both men and women herself, but *him*. The man kept sliding his gaze toward the guard, attempting to keep his single eye low to the ground. Kalia made another pass at the guard, narrowing her attention onto him once more. She couldn't see it. The thin lips, the wide-set eyes, the high

nasal bridge, the curled sneer as though someone had run a crate of
bad oysters under his pointed chin.

The guard turned to Kalia, leveling her with a glare that would
have melted any of the younger women to a puddle of nerves. Kalia
merely returned it, deciding to reach out to brush an antagonizing
hand down his forearm. His knuckles whitened as he curved his fingers
into fists, crossing his arms over his chest in warning. Kalia watched
from her periphery as the one-eyed man looked away, the tips of his
ears reddening.

"Sir, how much time do we have?" One of the other men called from
across the room, his voice rising above the noise.

Kalia grimaced. *Pirates*. His bold tone drew the attention of those
seated at the bar counter.

The one-eyed man spun on the heel of his boots, putting his back
to the guard as though he had been caught red-handed trying to
steal a fresh loaf of bread from a Sha'Hadra market. Twenty minutes,
Thomas. Long enough to bury your face between a pair of thighs." His
laugh was gruff. "I don't think you'll need much longer than that."

Thomas grinned, and Kalia noticed that a top front tooth was
missing. "Maybe I'll have time for two." He paused, tilting his head
toward Mintie, who had just finished with her third man of the night.
"Get yourself one, aye, Alaric? I heard that one is popular."

Kalia wrinkled her nose in disgust. *Gods*, fucking pirates. She
glanced through the stained window, staring at the cool moonlight
slicing across the cobblestone. It cast the darkened gaslamps in silver
as they awaited lighting. She spotted the men with the flamed torches
making their way down the street, and, in the best case, the lamps
would be lit by the time it was time for these men to return to their
ship.

Kalia could hardly wait.

"Gotta keep my wits for the captain," Alaric responded with a sly smile that Kalia knew covered his lie. That man had no interest in the ladies of the bordello. Kalia thought he didn't have much interest in women at all. "I don't want to be smelling like cunt when we deliver the bad news to the captain."

That seemed to sober Thomas. "Should we be..." He trailed off, looking over his shoulder as though this captain might burst through the front door of the bordello in the next moment. "I mean, should we get back then?"

Alaric swept his gaze through the haze of incense smoke, the hilt of his cutlass glinting in the firelight. "Give them a few minutes. We're all dead men anyways."

Kalia tilted her head toward the two men, perking her left ear to better hear over the string instruments.

"Did the captain even tell you who we were looking for?" Thomas asked, crossing his arms over his chest. Mintie came up behind him, caressing the top of his shoulder with a gentle hand. He ignored her, fixing his expectant stare on Alaric. "Maybe we should double back and revisit one of the temples to see if we missed something?"

Alaric shook his head, leaning an elbow on the wooden surface of the bar. The bartender slid a stein of *fion* next to Alaric's arm before grabbing the stained rag from his apron to wipe a spill. Alaric nodded, wrapping his hand around the stein and taking a large gulp. He wiped his mouth with the back of his hand before answering. "Captain gave me strict instructions. One pass to not draw attention. If we don't find anything today, we'll return in a few months." There was a clink of metal against wood as he set the stein down. "We'll still be flayed within an inch of our lives, hence—" He gestured vaguely toward the two men in the corner, both locked in a tight embrace with Iris and Calliope.

Kalia watched as Thomas bit his lip, contemplation blanketing his features. "Do *you* know what we're looking for?" He finally asked, ignoring Mintie for a second time as she pressed her bare breasts into the side of his arm. Her expression downturned into a scowl when she realized he had lost interest.

"I was given an idea," Alaric responded as he took another sip from his stein. A drunken man wobbled forward, jostling Alaric's arm and sending a wave of *fion* cresting over the rim of the pewter tankard. Alaric snarled as he pushed the man away, who merely stumbled further into the crowd. "Captain heard the stories from a woman aboard *The Phantom Night* and wanted to learn. He said that I would know when I saw it." His snort echoed into the half-filled stein, and he shook his head and took another gulp.

"What is it, then?" Thomas pressed on, leaning into Alaric enough that Kalia was forced to adjust. The guard gave her another long glance before shifting his focus to the crowd. "What are we looking for?"

A sudden shout swallowed Alaric's answer as the drunken man stumbled into Mintie, who had found another client to keep her company. Fists flew through the air as the shouting intensified. The guard at Kalia's side pushed back his shoulders as he walked into the throng, separating the two men with relative ease.

Irritation pinched at the spot behind Kalia's navel. She wanted to *know* things whether or not she was involved in them, and a vague mission by a pirate captain was the precise thing she *needed* to know. The madam called her nosy, but she preferred the term *curious*. There wasn't much for her to live for. This was something.

Leaning back against the marble wall, Kalia sent another curl of her power toward Alaric. She navigated through the first layers of his mind, pushing past the visions of old maps and ruby gemstones. An aching settled into the base of her skull, but she ignored that, too. She needled through the small spaces of his thoughts, rummaging through old memories of childhood and lovers from long ago.

It was certainly interesting, though. His memories, the ones she had brought to the forefront, were...old. The clothing style, how their hair was worn, and the shops on the main artery that ran through the capital city were not recognizable, especially in the last fifteen years.

Kalia wiped the sweat that had formed on her brow, the thin sheen collecting into droplets that ran down her temple. Alaric's mind was more complex to wade through than that of most sailors or pirates she had encountered. His memories and visions clamped tightly to his subconscious as though he were afraid to let them go. She picked at them, attempting to peel them from his grasp.

Alaric grimaced, slapping a palm against his forehead.

"What is it, boss?" Thomas asked as Alaric fell against the counter, tipping his stein over, where it clattered to the marble floor. "Alaric?"

Kalia's power wedged into his memories like hooks, pushing and shoving as she wrangled with him. He pulled her under, and the shout he let out as he collapsed to his knees was muffled as though they had both been submerged in the bay. But it was there she finally glimpsed what she was looking for.

She saw flashes of parchment and the roll spread wide on a wooden desk. *Djinn. Magic. Luminaria.* The words inked on the parchment were slightly smeared. She took in a breath, smelling wood shavings and mint leaves. There was a muscled forearm, and the shirt's sleeve rolled to the elbow to reveal tanned skin covered in dark markings—a sweep of brown hair, a firm hand gliding down the parchment.

Kalia was shoved from Alaric's mind, and she stumbled back, slamming her shoulder against the marble column. She let out a hiss of pain as the guard rushed over, holding out his hands to help her stand. She pushed him away, chest still heaving as she struggled to take in a breath.

"I'm fine, I'm *fine*," she rasped, straightening her red satin dress. The tightness of the straps smarted against her shoulder, still sore from the lashes and now threatening to bruise from her fall against the column. He reached for her a final time, and she pushed him away again. "Do not touch me."

The guard held up his hands and stepped away, scoffing. "It must be hot in here," he said, placing his hand on the pommel of his cutlass once more. "More than one of you is dropping."

Kalia swept her hair over her shoulder and glanced around, settling back into her nonchalant lean against the marble wall. *Djinn*? *Luminaria*? Going through Alaric's mind didn't put hers at ease. Instead, it only fueled her curiosity further.

Her gaze slid over the crowd, landing on the blonde-haired, one-eyed man. Her heart lurched in her chest, thunking uncomfortably against her ribs. Alaric, it seemed, had recovered from her probing. His face, though pale and clammy, was turned toward her, his one eye narrowed as it roamed her face. Their eyes connected, and his stare darkened as it bored into her own.

The sounds around them muffled once more. It all ceased to exist for that moment, time stopping just long enough that the garbled hum of chattering and moaning came to a silent pause. It was a long minute before Alaric broke the contact and turned to shake off Thomas, who had busied himself with wiping the spilled *fion* from Alaric's stained tunic.

There was no way...he couldn't have...he didn't...Kalia swallowed past the brick that had formed in her throat and looked away to watch Mintie drag a client up the staircase. The whine of the string band returned at full force, a loud blast to her already sensitive head.

Though the group of pirates had seemed to move on, stumbling from the bordello only minutes later, Kalia couldn't help the unsettled feeling that nestled in the pit of her belly. She shook it off. She was being ridiculous.

But as Alaric eyed her one last time through the fogged glass windows, she wondered if she had finally taken her magic a step too far.

CHAPTER NINE

KALIA

A dense fog had settled over the city, its tendrils snaking around the sharp inclines of the roofs and chimney columns. Thanks to the fight and the unexpected appearance of the pirates, the brothel closed earlier than usual that evening. But still, Kalia found herself pacing the floor of her tiny bedroom late into the night, the dark shadows arcing across the wall as the moon reached its apex.

She couldn't shake the dread that settled like a bucket of ice water in her chest. More than once, she hadn't realized she'd been rubbing at her sternum as she paced, her eyes glued to the wood-grained patterns in the floorboards. She thought of the one-eyed man, his resolve to fight her off, and the look of pure disdain when his stare finally landed on her.

It had been years— decades even— since someone had pointedly figured out her magic. And the last time...the last time...Kalia couldn't quite manage to suppress the shudder that built, and a shock of pimpled flesh broke out over her skin. She didn't want to remember the last time. She actively tried to forget it. Maybe, just maybe, she got it wrong. Perhaps the man had no idea who or *what* she was, and she was merely projecting her uneasiness onto him.

Yet the familiar flicker of knowledge that darkened Alaric's gaze put the fear of the gods into Kalia, something she wasn't bound to forget easily. She hoped the man and his bandy group of pirates were already aboard their ship, readying to set sail at the earliest hint of dawn. She glanced out the window to find the black, star-speckled sky still blanketing the city, no hues of orange or gold streaking through the clouds.

Kalia sighed, soothing her bare arms as she turned toward her bed. At the very least, she could try to get some sleep and visit Pete in the morning for a calming draft. It was okay. She was fine. She was reading into everything. It was ridiculous to think a pirate who lacked the fortitude to keep both of his eyes figured out what she was. She lifted her hands to press the heels of her palms into her eyes, taking in a deep, slow breath that smelled faintly of rotting garbage and heavily of floral perfume that wafted from the main room.

A damp chill rose from the cracked panes, rustling the torn curtain and skittering along the floor. Kalia sighed again as she pivoted on the balls of her bare feet, grabbed her cloak from the back of the old chair, and marched toward the window. She hated this city. She hated this room. She hated this view. She hated that she always felt wet in the year's cooler months. She reached the window and began to stuff the corners of the cloak into the cracked crevices of the glass, careful not to cut herself on the jagged pieces.

But movement caught the corner of her eye, and Kalia lifted her gaze to peer down to the alley below. She drew her head back as a sudden cold that had nothing to do with the draft expanded in her belly.

Alaric, the one-eyed, blonde man, leaned against the brick wall opposite her window. He watched her through the grimy, stain-riddled panes that separated Kalia from the outside world. He exhaled, the air curling around him in a misty cloud. He nodded into the shadows to his right and left. The four other men stepped forward, drawing their blades as they crossed the grease-slickened stones.

Kalia stepped back, the cloak slipping from her fingers and tumbling to her feet. A memory floated to the forefront of her mind, one of flashing swords and screams of terror only met with mirthless smiles. It couldn't end this way. *She* wouldn't let it end this way. And she was prepared to fight to the death before being taken to the king.

The glass shattered in the hallway beneath Kalia's bedroom, ripping her from her thoughts. The following screech of surprise had her whipping her head toward the door. She waited silently on bated breath, listening intently. A second scream echoed through the hall, and three sets of feet hurried past the door.

Muffled voices rose, and Kalia strained her ears further, trying to make out anything being said below.

"Guards!" The first discernible voice finally shouted. "*Guards!* Hel–" The voice cut out, replaced by a smattering of coarse laughter and the unmistakable zing of metal blades against...

Gods, she hoped it wasn't what she thought it was.

Kalia lunged toward her bed, the satin of her dress clinging to her legs in a tangle of fabric. She reached down, retrieving two daggers wedged between the frame and the mattress. One she quickly strapped beneath her skirt, tightening the leather belt around her thigh. The second she kept in her hand, and she focused on the feeling of the smooth hilt against her palm to steady her jarring heart.

The bordello had awoken in a panic by the time Kalia yanked the door of her bedroom open. Servants scuttled by, running away from the staircase that led to the kitchens and the quarters near the back alley, forcing her to press against the wall as they went. She kept to the outer edge of the hallway when she finally lurched forward, deftly moving toward the narrow, wooden staircase.

A pistol went off as Kalia stormed down the stairs. She didn't bother to be quiet now. Just as her bare foot touched the landing, she entered the fray, the acrid smell of used gunpowder heavy on the air.

"Kalia!" A servant cried out, grabbing her forearm like Kalia was a life raft in a winter sea storm. "Pirates. It's *pirates*!"

Something was warm and sticky beneath the servant's hand, smeared onto Kalia's skin. She glanced down that coldness in her chest growing when she noticed the bloody handprint stamped against her arm. She swallowed and leveled the servant with a steady gaze.

"What do they want?" Kalia asked as she attempted to pull her arm from the servant's grasp. She hadn't learned this one's name and didn't think she needed to until now. The woman tightened her grip, and half-moon indentations bit into Kalia's wrist from the servant's fingernails.

"Coin? One of the ladies? The madam? Take your pick." The woman used her free hand to wipe the sweat from her brow. More blood smeared there. "We have to go. The guards, they–"

Kalia jostled forward when someone shoved past her to clamber up the stairs. She couldn't see who it was, only catching the end of their cloak whipping around the corner when she looked up. She darted to the kitchen and spotted a group of servants huddled beneath the bundled herbs hanging from the ceiling.

She steeled her resolve, swallowing through the rawness of her throat from the slowly increasing smoke and dust.

"In the kitchens, under the far counter, there is a hidden door barred by an iron lock," Kalia started, gripping the servant's shoulders and twisting her around to face the entrance where the group was huddled. "The madam keeps the keys hanging by the door in her office. Get as many people as you can to—"

"What about you?" The servant asked, her eyes wide as she frantically glanced over her shoulder. "Aren't you—" She trailed off, her gaze falling to the blade in Kalia's hand. "No, Kalia, you can't. Come with us, please. Come with—"

Before the servant could finish, another pistol shot rang from the threshold of the main room. The servant let out a pained grunt as she fell to her knees, the crack of bone against wood a sharp *thwack* over the surrounding battle. She swayed for a long moment, her breathing falling shallow as blood stained the apron still tied around her waist. And when the nameless woman finally crumpled over, Kalia stumbled back while covering her mouth with the back of her hand.

"Hello, lovely."

The voice was amused, the coarse rasp tone hinting toward someone whose vocals had long been affected by the briny, open-sea air. Kalia dropped her hand and lifted her gaze to scrutinize the man who had appeared, fixing her unblinking stare on him.

"You were here before," Kalia said as she tilted her chin, tightening her grip on the blade. She wasn't pleasant. There was no reason for that. He would undoubtedly kill her either way. "What do you want?"

Alaric stepped toward her, but she stood her ground, refusing to shift even an inch. He paused, regarding her with wary, narrowed eyes. "I know what you are," he finally replied. "I felt you. In here." He tapped his knuckle against the side of his head.

"I don't know what you're talking about."

Alaric's yellowing, toothy grin vanished as his lip curled in disgust. "Playing ignorant isn't going to work." He spat to the side— she hated pirates, the foul creatures— though his eyes never left Kalia. "I *saw* you in my memory. I *felt* you."

"Imagining things, are we?" Kalia shot back. She prayed to the gods that it would buy the other servants time to escape. "Even for a pirate, that's—"

Alaric took another demanding step toward her, but Kalia was ready. Her power webbed from her like a fishing net, ensnaring him in a binding trap she knew he couldn't escape. It plunged them into mindless darkness, surrounding them in a never-ending black. If she died while the battle raged around them, at least she would take him with her.

The sound of rushing water filled her ears, drowning out Alaric's muffled yells of anger. Sunlight suddenly bloomed around them, illuminating the scene Kalia had dropped them in.

Alaric blinked, reeling his head back as he looked around. Confusion blanketed his features, making him appear even more brainless than she already knew he was. "Where...?" He paused, and Kalia knew he was taking in the ship's deck that appeared around them. It could have been real—from the boat's dip in the waves to the gulls squawking as they landed on the masts to the faceless men pulling at the rigging. "What did you—?"

"I could make you do anything, you know," Kalia said quietly, reveling in the powerlessness that erratically flickered over his face. He may have had no clue what she was, but she would ensure he regretted finding out. "They say the mind is a powerful thing. I could make you think you were drowning."

The scene switched in a snap, and the two of them were underwater. Fish darted past, their shadows tinged a bluish-green. Kalia's hair rippled in the current, and she watched as he clutched his throat, thrashing in the cool water.

"Or you could be falling."

The vision flipped again. This time, moisture dampened their skin as they careened through a wispy cloud. Shafts of light pierced through, casting shadows on the earth far below them. Alaric let out a gasping yell, his chest heaving as he struggled to catch his breath.

The ground came closer and closer, the rocky shore sharpening into view. Alaric squeezed his eyes closed just as the speckled coloring on the stones could be picked apart, and suddenly, his vision shifted for a third time.

Alaric trembled, his knees knocking together as he cowered into himself, still anticipating an impact. When it didn't come, Kalia watched as he peeked his eyes open to glance around.

They were in a meadow now. Tall, dry grass swished as it bent in the warm breeze, and Kalia ran her hands over the bristles that grew on the end of it. Alaric seemed to realize he was safe. His shoulders dropped in relief, and his spine straightened as he stood to full height. She wanted to make sure he never felt relief again.

"I could make you feel so much pain that you wished you were dead."

Dark clouds gathered on the horizon as a vicious wind built, blowing away the light wisps slowly tracking across the blue sky. The once swaying grass now bowed to the incoming storm. The clouds obscured the sun, drawing the meadow into shadow. Thunder cracked, shuddering the ground beneath their feet, and lightning forked across the gray.

Her fury rose as it collided with Alaric's fear, and it swelled inside Kalia with such intention that she thought her chest would crack from the pressure. There was nowhere for it to go—nowhere for her to go. So she poured that white-hot rage into the storm, clenching her hands into tight fists at her side.

Alaric came into the bordello and assisted in killing all of those people. How *dare* he smirk at her as he stood there over the servant's dead body? If it were up to her, and with Kalia in control here, she knew it would be, Alaric would get swept up in this game. In her game.

She was a Voyant, and she would ensure he felt every bit of her power.

A maelstrom formed in the clouds above, swirling air and debris that ripped the distant trees from the ground, splaying their roots toward the sky. Hailstones began to fall, pelting Alaric until red welts bubbled on his flesh. And, still, he held firm. That only spurred Kalia's anger further.

"I've known of your power, djinn," he yelled over the roar of gale. He ducked down as a loose branch flew by, narrowly missing the crown of his head. "I know what you can do. But there's one thing you've overlooked."

Djinn? What the fuck was a djinn?

Kalia quirked her brow, crossing her arms over her chest. "Oh?" She asked instead, sending him a challenging stare. A saccharine smile pulled the corners of her lips. "And what's that?"

"My men are looking for you, too. If you're in here with me," Alaric said, his eye lighting with a sparkle that made Kalia's belly twist. "Then who is protecting you out there?"

Before Kalia could respond, there was a sharp *whack* at the base of her skull that ripped her from Alaric's mind. The smoke of the bordello came clear, as did the servant's body at her feet. Her vision blurred as she doubled over, and then everything went black.

"Excuse me, gents. What are you doing with her?" A man called out in veiled disinterest, though his hurried footsteps behind them still sloshed in a grease-stricken puddle.

Kalia groaned, cracking her eyes open. She was looking up, the smattering of stars nearly buried by the thick plumes of smoke shrouding the night. It smelled awful, like burnt fabric and charcoal wood that had smoked for too long. Someone was screaming—more than one someone.

And, *gods*, her head fucking *hurt*.

She was cradled in a pair of strong arms, the scent of sour body odor and salt flooding her nose as they left the thick smoke clouds. A roll of nausea and a cold clamminess crested through her. It took everything in her to swallow back the bile that sat heavy in her throat, though she had enough grit left in her to consider unleashing the vomit *onto* the man carrying her. Then she imagined how hard she would hit the cobblestone street, and her head throbbed further.

"You should consider removing your hands—" the voice continued, though this time it was closer. A hand brushed against her ankle, and the person carrying her halted in their tracks. There was a thump and a groan, followed by another splash.

"Do not touch her," a second voice commanded. "She's going to Captain Rahmi Abada aboard *The Mark of Malice*. I'll slit your throat if you try that again."

They began to move, the rocking akin to a ship bobbing in the port. She was going to be sick. *Gods*, her head hurt. She went to lift her hand

and inspect the tender bump she knew was there but found her arm was too heavy. It flopped back to her side, dangling precariously over the man's forearm.

"You cannot take her," the first man called out. His voice ebbed with anger now, and heavy boots over slick stone echoed again through a narrow passage. "She's *unconscious,* that's *vile,* you–"

They must have been in an alley. Where *were* they taking her? Could she attempt a swift knee to her captor's temple? Perhaps if she aimed it right. She tried to pry her eyes open further, but the gas lamps above her doubled with her blurred vision. She closed them tightly, moaning as her stomach overturned.

"What are you going to– Oi! He's got a blade!"

A zing of metal on metal sliced through the air: *clash, clash, clash.*

"You're better than I thought you would be," another voice purred, carnal brutality dancing in his tone. Kalia knew that purr well enough from the ladies in the bordello. And she knew it came from Alaric. "But now, you're between us and our way to the port. I wouldn't want to damage that pretty face of yours–"

Clash, clash, clash.

The sharp tick of the blades rang between her ears, clattering against the side of her skull.

"Take her to the ship!" Alaric ordered. The strain was audible from his effort to hold off the man following them. "Now! Take her now!"

Kalia groaned as she tried to dislodge herself from her captor's arms, but he only held her tighter to his chest. The man started to run, jarring her against him. He wasn't careful, and her bare feet scraped against the brick walls as they turned one corner and then another. She wanted to pull her magic forward, but the pain in her head revolted at the very thought. The narrow passages of the back alleys acted like a funnel for the wind. She shivered against the cold air instead.

Footsteps pounded behind her, followed by a grunt and a final splash of water.

"He tried chasing after us," Alaric rasped. Metal against leather sounded— a sword being sheathed. "I finally got him, I think. One cut in the back of the knee."

There was a quiet pause as the man holding Kalia swung around, and she felt her stomach flip again. Dizziness overtook her, and despite her eyes being tightly clamped shut, stars broke out beneath her lids. She was definitely going to be sick. Her captor was definitely going to be unhappy about it.

"What are you thinking, boss?"

Kalia felt the rumble of his words vibrate against her shoulder. The shift of his tunic only worsened the sour stench of his sweat. That only worsened her nausea.

"Take him with us," Alaric finally said. He snapped his fingers. A pair of boots shuffled forward. "Captain needs more men. And we can't have him report us to any guards before we return to the ship."

"You don't want to kill him?"

There was another pregnant silence.

"No," Alaric replied, though his hesitation was noted. "Let the captain decide."

The darkness Kalia had been combatting finally overtook her and she succumbed to the pain in her head once more.

CHAPTER TEN

KALIA

K alia didn't know what roused her first— the scent of old fish and wet rope, the sound of the rigging clinking together and the unfurled sails, or how she had been unceremoniously dumped onto the deck. She blinked, groaning as she lifted her hand to the back of her head, finally prodding at the lump that had grown there.

What happened? Why was she cold to the bone? And why was she not wearing shoes?

It all came flooding back in a jolt that shot pain through her tender head: the bordello, the pirates, the attack. Rage simmered in Kalia's belly as she swept her eyes along the puddles of water that filled the crevices between the wooden planks before finally taking in the dozens of worn leather boots circling the deck. She had watched men in the bordello long enough to know that the owners of those boots were currently studying every inch of her. The feeling of exposure that only came from nakedness brimmed over. She subtly swiped her hand along her side to ensure she was still dressed, only satisfied when she felt the satin cloth still intact beneath her palm.

Kalia curled her fingers into fists, slowly pushing herself to a wobbly stand. Her hand reached out to grasp the side of the...*ship*. Lifting her head, she scanned the crowd of unfamiliar faces, each dirtier than the next, before finally sweeping her gaze to the horizon in confirmation. She was indeed on a ship—the city's sprawling coast spread before her. The view was almost pretty.

At least they were still in the harbor, and the crown's navy had yet to be deployed. Though, for how long Kalia wasn't sure. The palace glittered from its perch on the hill in the distance, the white dome still bright despite the night sky. The king had certainly ensured his opulence could be felt from every angle and light. Plumes of smoke rose from the left side of the city just beyond the port, and there was an unmistakable orange glow of fire that illuminated the underside of the haze.

The bordello. She wondered how many of the ladies had made it out. A weight sunk in her chest when she thought of what little she had been able to pilfer from the madam. The beginnings of her second stash were hidden in a hollowed leg of her bedframe. By now, it would certainly be molten copper in the blaze.

Kalia steeled her expression into fearless disdain and turned to face the crew. They regarded her with wary excitement, their eyes roving her face, her breasts, and the high slit in her dress. She tempered back the instinct to tug it together, not wanting to draw even more attention. Their foul stares, reminiscent of Cranford Reed staring from his place near the hearth, kindled a rage inside her.

She *hated* pirates.

Kalia rolled her shoulders and tapped into her mind, ready to send her magic flinging in every direction. Maybe she would drown them, much like she had threatened Alaric. Force them to jump into the sea or hold their breath until they were blue in the face. Perhaps hang themselves from the masts with the coils of rope that littered the deck. The men were always the easiest to toy with—their minds unfiltered and simple. These ones certainly wouldn't be any different.

Her power crackled beneath her skull, surfacing in her mind for merely a heartbeat before it winked into nothing. *What?* Her panic built. *Fuck.* Her pulse rattled down to her fingertips, something she focused on instead of succumbing to the fact that she was utterly defenseless. She reached for it again and again, each time coming up short. It had been nearly ten years since she had burned through her magic, always careful not to reach the bottom of that well.

She shouldn't have goaded Alaric like she did.

A chuckle started near the front of the crowd, and it morphed as it caught on until it became a blazing inferno of humiliation. Roars of laughter cut into her, deeply splicing against the hardened exterior she had built for herself. Kalia felt like a trapped animal that had been cornered in a cage by a fire, and she did the only thing she thought of doing.

Pivoting toward the nearest set of ropes, Kalia hauled herself onto the gunnel, her bare toes wrapping around the edge of it. She knew what men like them did to women like her. And she would rather jump from the ship to face the frigid, dirty water of the bay than find out exactly what the crew had planned.

There was a barking order that Kalia couldn't quite make out, but the crew immediately fell silent. Her dress whipped in the sea breeze, forming the curve of her hips, and she tightened her grip on the rope when the ship dipped with a wave. She glanced over her shoulder, doubling back when she realized the crowd had split into two. Their faces downturned away from the gap, and they each busied themselves with scrubbing the deck, working the sails, or hurrying to the ship's underbelly.

A man walked up the newly formed path, his steps a casual arrogance against the deck. Kalia narrowed her gaze on him. He was handsome enough, she supposed, with tanned skin and brown, oval eyes that reminded her of Sha'Hadra. She knew of a woman or two who would do many questionable things just to get lost in the depths of him. In any other circumstance, she may have been one of them. Locks of his dark hair were pulled up in a bun near the back of his head. He looked up at her, his scrutinizing stare boring into her.

This was a man who commanded control at all times and who reveled in it. He must be the captain. And this was the one whom she needed to bargain with? The thought made Kalia hate him even more than she hated his crew. She hadn't bargained before, and she certainly wouldn't start now.

A knowing smirk pulled on his lips as he rested his hand on the pommel of his cutlass, the blade still strapped to the belt at his hip. That casual arrogance made a second appearance in how his eyes gleamed when he took her in. It was the first time Kalia wondered if this was how it felt for two territorial predators to circle one another.

"*Ruehi*," the man amusedly drawled, his gaze snapping to connect with hers. "It's time to come down from there."

Kalia scoffed, shaking her head. The movement shifted the hair cascading down her back. "There's been a mistake. Your mongrels brought me onto your ship," she said, tilting her chin toward the men pretending to work behind him. They jeered at her, showing their yellowing, crooked teeth. "You're going to take me back to shore— don't come any closer."

The man halted his progression, and Kalia didn't miss the agitated muscle that ticked in the corner of his jaw. Satisfaction swelled within her, something he didn't seem to miss either.

"Captain Rahmi Abada," the man said, leaning a hip against the nearest stack of crates. "I've been looking for you, but you aren't what I expected."

The clocktower near the city's center let out a single *gong* that echoed across the bay. Kalia carefully pivoted on her toes, spinning to face the captain instead of staring over her shoulder. The tips of his fingers danced along the hilt, tracing the stitching of the leather. Another tell that he was unhappy with her bold disrespect. She was just pleased he caught on.

"Oh?" Kalia replied, quirking a brow. "I've never even heard of you. But considering you're a pirate captain..." She paused, making a show of trailing her gaze down his tunic, narrowing on the groin of his breeches before dragging it back up again. "You're exactly what I expected."

Rahmi took in a slow breath that forced his shoulders to rise and blew it back out. In his commanding silence, Kalia calculated her next move. Her well of magic was still too low, and she knew from past experiences that it would take days to fill back up. She could kill him, she supposed. At least she might be able to catch him off guard long enough that she could grab his cutlass. The crew might chop her to pieces, but that was still better than any alternative.

She swept her eyes toward Rahmi's right, where Alaric had appeared at his elbow.

"You should speak to him with more consideration," Alaric snapped at her, and this time, she couldn't help the lethal grin that stole from her mouth. "He's the captain—"

"Does your captain always order his men to brothels?" Kalia purred, watching with sharp precision as his shoulders sagged just enough to be noticed. "Or was this a special occasion?"

From how a flush crept up the sides of Alaric's neck and how Rahmi's knuckles whitened when his fingers curled around the pommel of his cutlass, Kalia knew she had struck a nerve. An unknown, lying-right-hand-man nerve.

"He didn't tell you where he found me?" Kalia went on, *tsking* her tongue against the roof of her mouth. "For shame, captain. A crew of men who hide things from you? That's—"

"Hold your tongue, woman," Alaric interjected, the flush still crawling up the curves of his ears, but he had already shown his hand. Kalia's return smile was knowing. Alaric glanced up at Rahmi. "Captain, I—"

"Quiet, Alaric," Rahmi managed to say through gritted teeth, and he appeared half-ready to run Alaric through with his cutlass right then.

Kalia pounced on the new development, wrestling away the control that Rahmi seemed to hold onto so tightly. "We can chalk this all up to a terrible misunderstanding. You can return me to the port, where I can find my way to the bordello and assist in rebuilding what your men burned to the ground." Alaric glared up at her, but she ignored him. "And, if the crown doesn't arrest us all on our return, perhaps I can convince some ladies to service your men out of gratitude."

Rahmi remained silent, and Kalia took a moment to regard Alaric with a triumphant and vindictive smirk, challenging him to say anything. He only sneered back. She settled her lips into a tight line that she hoped conveyed forgiveness as the captain studied the port behind her. Blistering shouts sounded from the shore, and the muffled boots fell against the wooden gangway, splitting apart the fog that had begun to resettle on the bay.

The king's navy was boarding the warship, and Kalia knew they were running out of time. Her impatience flared, burning the coolness of the night away from her bare flesh. She swallowed back the instinct to tap her foot or massage her temples, not wanting to show her frustration by fidgeting.

Rahmi's eyes darted from the shore, landing on Kalia's face, and she held his intense gaze. From how he blinked, she was sure that didn't happen as often as it should. She boarded her expression to an expectant understanding as though to say she wouldn't cause any more trouble. And in a sudden and unnerving shift, his mouth tugged into a dazzling, heart-stopping grin.

"No," Rahmi said, pushing his hip from the crates to stand straight. He took three steps forward, stopping when he was in front of her, and his smile turned overly saccharine. "I think you'll stay with me here on this ship."

Kalia's eyes widened, and the fibers of the rope bit into her palm when she tightened her hand around it. With that one sentence, she felt the control eddying away from her, the bulk of it slinking into the void that was Rahmi-*fucking*-Abada. It was a game to him, she realized—a cat-and-mouse play that she wanted no part of.

"Why?" Kalia demanded through gritted teeth, her honeyed tone taking on something colder, more sinister. "What do you want from me?"

Rahmi took another step forward, and Kalia felt a second shift, one of a predator transforming into prey. And she was, unarguably, the prey. It was not a sensation she was fond of growing used to.

"Alaric, despite his flaws, told me what you did, how you broke into his mind. How you sunk so deeply into the memories that he saw you embedded in them. Interesting, that...talent."

Shit. Kalia remained still, focusing on the ship swaying beneath her. "I don't know what you're talking about," she replied instead. "The king and his guards heavily regulate the use of magic. Alaric must be mistaken."

Rahmi ignored her entirely, and that undeterred smile remained wholly plastered on his tanned face. "I require a djinn for a path I've set myself on. There are two options for you now. One..." He trailed off, and his hand slipped from his cutlass, resting uncomfortably close enough on the gunnel that she felt the heat of his pinky finger on the long edge of her foot. "You can come with me, help me with my endeavors. Or, two, I can turn you into the crown. Tell them you're a magic-user and watch from my ship while they execute you on the hill."

Kalia's first thought was to ask what in the name of the gods a *djinn* was, but she tempered back the question. There she was on a pirate ship surrounded by an armed crew led by an *insane* captain. She didn't have the leverage, and if he found out, she wasn't what he thought... Her eyes slid to his belt, where a dagger was tied alongside the cutlass. She ran her tongue over her bottom lip, tasting the brine of the bay, and she was unhappy to note how he tracked the motion with his eyes.

"Your men came into the bordello," Kalia finally said, fixing him with a deadly stare that promised retribution. "They stole from the madam. They *killed* her servants. And that is far worse than anything you could turn me into the crown for." She bent down, kneeling until she was at eye level with him. She couldn't read him through his mask of impenetrable boredom. And, as someone who made a living on reading people, that thought snuck a feeling of uneasiness into her chest. "She'll hunt you, and she'll hunt me. There will never be an end to what she can do. I'm bought and paid for. It's in your best interest to return me immediately."

Rahmi's smile froze, and he almost laughed in the face of it. "You speak under the assumption," he said slowly, "that I haven't counted every one of my sins. I keep them locked away, but I remember them every night." His hand reached upward, clamping around her arm. "I'll be sure to remember this one, too."

Kalia reached down with her free hand and grasped the dagger she still had strapped to her thigh. In a move he hadn't anticipated, she whipped out the blade and plunged it into his forearm. Blood splattered, the warm, sticky liquid leaking onto her hands. His fingers unfurled as he let out a grunt of surprise that turned into a low, mirthless chuckle, twisting her belly into knots.

"Oh, *ruehi*," Rahmi mumbled, as though the word were something he whispered into women's ears at night, but Kalia was no longer listening.

Kalia stepped away from the ropes and turned back to face the shore. She wouldn't stay on this ship, pretending to be this *djinn* in the hands of a man who would use her magic for gods knew what. But she wouldn't return to the madam either. She would disappear, make a new name for herself, get back to Sha'Hadra, and buy an old shop at a fraction of the cost. It didn't matter that she had no money. She would forge a path for herself. She had done it as a child. She would do it again.

There was a pull at her soul, a hooking probe that anchored her in place. Slamming her mind closed, she whirled around to see the captain staring at her, his eyes darkened and murderous. His hand was wrapped around her dagger's hilt. He pulled it from his arm with one smooth tug, the blood running from his wrist and pooling on the deck beneath his boots.

Kalia's body lurched as those hooks ripped away, and a pained dizziness swept through her. Is this what it felt like when she used her magic on others? When she sent those guards into the recesses of their minds? She didn't want to know more. She scampered to the edge of the gunnel and threw herself over the ship's railing, readying for the bay's water to swallow her whole.

Instead, a hand shot forward and caught her arm. Kalia fell against the hull, her body cracking loudly as she swung into the side of the ship. A scream erupted from her, the spikes of it embedding into her throat. The pain was both hot and cold, a burning mixed with the cool sheen of nausea cresting through her. She thought she was going to be sick. She was sure she would pass out again. It was a miracle her shoulder was still in place.

Kalia was hauled upward before she was rolled over the gunnel, and she slipped in the pool of the captain's blood when her feet touched the deck.

"I *said* that you're staying here," Rahmi seethed, spinning her around to face him again.

Kalia had done many fucked up things in her life. The stealing, the fighting, the luring men into the bordello...it was all more ethically and morally questionable than the next. But when she reeled her fist back and connected it with the captain's nose, she knew this *might* have been the biggest mistake she had ever made.

Rahmi's head jerked back as a new throbbing pain lanced through her knuckles, and she could hear his teeth grinding with how tightly he clenched his jaw.

But she was too mad to care, too angry at the captain before her to realize the grave she had dug for herself. They glowered at one another, and Kalia kept her glare trained on the captain's. His eyes, she realized, weren't a single layer of brown but the colors of wet river rocks that shone in the morning sunlight. She could sense the tremble in his hands as they awaited her next move.

"Keep that look of satisfaction off your fucking face," Rahmi finally said, his breath ghosting over her face. "You're still on my ship, and we're sailing away." He seemed to suck any remaining light away from the stars, further reminding Kalia that he was nothing but a controlling void. And she was unwilling to be trapped in his gravity.

To his credit, Rahmi's pinched lips and rigid stance conveyed that he thought the same of her.

Indeed, the city had shrunk since she had been hauled back aboard, and the wind that filled the newly unfurled sails nipped at her bare arms. One of the crew tried to step in, but from the corner of her eye, Kalia saw the rope in his hand. *Absolutely not*. A darkened rage flashed through her gaze, and Rahmi's eyebrow quirked in reply to the sudden shift in her demeanor. He seemed to think it was amusing. Though he hadn't seen the sailor yet, who was likely thinking he was helping the captain subdue the woman beating the shit out of him.

When the man had come close enough that she could feel the heat of his body, Rahmi's eyes finally flicked over to him. But it was too late. Kalia thrust out her elbow, catching the sailor in the middle of his throat.

The man dropped, clutching his hand tightly against the bobbing column of his neck. His cough was harried and choked as he struggled to draw in breath. Alaric bent down to grasp the collar of the man's tunic, pulling him to his feet before shoving him back into the crowd of pirates who had finally dropped the pretense of working.

"That's enough of that," Rahmi said, reaching forward to pin her arms tightly to her side.

Kalia hated the feeling of being trapped, hated that it brought back flashes of memories that pried open her past with the ease of a crowbar to rotting wood. She couldn't get the breaths in fast enough. The thoughts pelted her...drowned her, and made her flail against him. Her wriggling only made him wrap his arms around her. She received a faceful of freshly chopped cedar and dried rosemary, a stunning contradiction to the stained tunics and bloody puddles surrounding her.

Suddenly, Kalia was airborne. Her hips were slung over a broad shoulder, her hair threatening to dip in the bloody mixture of seawater filling the crevices of the wood. She spotted her footprint, and the smear from where she had slid was still painted against the deck.

"Let me down," she growled over her shoulder, grappling with his tunic. She managed to clutch the hilt of his cutlass long enough to draw it from its sheath merely an inch, but the blade was taken from her a heartbeat later.

"You've exhausted my measures of remaining *pleasant*," Rahmi retorted, his tone bordering a hiss.

An arm clenched the backs of her thighs. "Watch where you put your hands!" There was a rumbling chuckle as they moved, and Kalia began to pound her fists against his spine.

"I wouldn't dream of it," Rahmi grunted just as Kalia dug her long, painted nails into the corded muscle of his back. "And you shouldn't either." The tremble of his wicked laugh set every instinct of hers to stand on end.

Whatever piece of him that may have been considered redeemable immediately fell away.

CHAPTER ELEVEN

RAHMI

What had Devlin called djinn? Unpredictable? Fickle? Easy to anger?

Rahmi sure had a few more words he could use to describe the djinn he was currently walking toward the brig of his ship. Callous? Certainly. Temperamental? That was an understatement. Prickly? He had a distinct feeling that he would find out just how *prickly* she could be. But he was sure, based on the depiction Alaric had used upon their return to the ship, that this woman was exactly who they were looking for.

And Rahmi was always sure.

But still, it was all a bit too easy. The thought wormed a doubt-filled path through his mind, one that he struggled to part from. Devlin had made it sound like tracking down a djinn would be the most challenging thing they could do. Liddros agreed. Beginners luck, perhaps? Rahmi didn't believe in that. He fought his entire life to be decisive and control his destiny. Was it truly going to be this simple?

Rahmi flipped the djinn off his shoulder, planting her feet firmly on the soggy floor of the brig. He ignored the pools of water that splashed onto her bloody skin with every rock of the ship, ignored the shudder of anticipation that trembled through her body, and definitely ignored the high slit of her dress that ended just above the middle of her thigh.

"Would you like to paint a picture?" the djinn snapped, pulling him from the stare he had fixed to the bare side of her leg. "I'm sure we could find an artist of some kind for you on this gods-forsaken *raft*."

Rahmi ground his teeth. The number of people he had allowed to mouth off to him in the last three centuries was zero. Alaric had the flogging marks to prove it. And Rahmi wasn't particularly fond of allowing it to continue now, actively fighting against putting her in her place, in fact. But he needed her, and he knew he wasn't going to get anywhere by poking at the steeled exterior she had built around herself.

Capricious, indeed.

The single sconce bolted to the side of the hull swung with every roll of the ship, the flame flickering an orange glow that cast the iron bars of the brig in sharp relief. Despite the low lighting, it still managed to wink against the exposed nails that held his ship together. The echo of the waves against the keel was louder than it had been two decks up, and dribbles of seawater eddied down the wooden interior. Rahmi took note, knowing he would need to fix that leak sooner rather than later.

"Skirts up," Rahmi said to the djinn, gesturing for her to lift the red satin dress. He watched as the woman's gaze slid away from taking in the small cells and settled back on him. Somehow, she managed to look down her nose at him, an incredible feat, considering he was nearing a full head taller. He would need to remove that ability from her stores, too.

"Excuse me?" she asked incredulously just as the man in the cell beside hers said, "I beg your pardon?"

Annoyance raked through him, and Rahmi inhaled through his nose that smelled heavily of moldy bilge water and softly of…was that nutmeg? Cinnamon? Whatever it was, it was warm and reminded him of the home he had grown up in. And it was coming from *her*. That was the very last thing he needed.

"One way or another, *ruehi*," Rahmi replied, ignoring the man in the cell next door. I'm going to check you for weapons. You can make this easy for both of us, or you can make it difficult. It's your choice, but remember that I'm in the position to win."

Her stare smoldered, the green of her eyes shining brightly against that soft, golden glow. Oh, she was pissed…not that Rahmi could blame her. "Do you expect me to have a second blade hidden under my dress? Or perhaps I have a cannonball up my—"

"I didn't expect you to have the first blade," Rahmi interrupted her through gritted teeth, crossing his arms over his chest. He didn't enjoy being interrupted either. "And lest you have forgotten the last five minutes, *you stabbed me with it*."

The woman went quiet, and Rahmi watched as she ran her tongue over her teeth in thought. She was easy on the eyes, at least. He had half-expected a wretched hag, wart-covered and hunched. He moved his gaze over the tangles of her long, dark hair. Took in the forest green, almond-shaped eyes that promised revenge…*gods*, he hoped she was one to go through with it. He would never admit it, but Alaric was right. It had been boring lately. She was curvy beneath the satin dress, and the delicate bangles on her ankles only seemed to enhance the length of her legs.

Once upon a time, he would have done many cruel things to bed a woman like her. He might still try to. He hadn't entirely decided.

There was no doubt in his mind that she would be a wild, untethered ride.

"I can have one of the men come down here instead," Rahmi offered after a second long moment of silence, dipping his head to better catch her eye. "But I can't promise you'll love who I bring—"

"Fine," the woman finally spat, holding her arms out to the side. "Fine. Check me then, but make it quick." Rahmi kneeled in front of her, and he glanced up in time to see her eyes flash again. "But watch your hands, or I'll remove them myself."

The man in the cell behind Kalia watched the interaction with a sharp gaze. He had been brought aboard by Alaric and witnessed the encounter. Rahmi was of the mind to execute him, but Alaric had reminded him of their need for more able men. And the man was that Rahmi couldn't deny it.

Rahmi started at her ankle, checking the bangles for small blades before sliding his hands up the sides of her calves. He cupped his hands around her knees, prodding the underside of the fabric for hidden pockets. He was slow to slip his hands away from her thighs, enjoying the feeling of the tips of his fingers inching up her warm flesh before coming to rest on the holster she used to hide her dagger.

It was higher than he expected. One flick of his finger upward would have him brushing the apex between her legs. By the way her skin pebbled and her eyes darkened as she peered down at him, she seemed to realize it too.

He smirked up at her, deftly unfastening the sheath and letting it fall from beneath her skirts, clattering to the ground. "I'm shocked there wasn't more than one dagger on there."

"There wasn't enough time," the woman replied, lifting her gaze to stare at the swaying lantern. "But I would have if I could." She swallowed, and Rahmi watched her throat bob. "Why are we down here?"

Rahmi couldn't quite conceal his chuckle of amusement. "Because you tried to kill me," he responded, his knees cracking as he stood. "Do I need to check for that cannonball, by chance? Since you offered."

"I didn't," she said, her eyes tracking the movement of his fingers, now grazing the sides of her hips. Her inhale was quiet, as though she tried to bite back the reaction to his touch. He tucked that knowledge into the back of his mind, hoping to forget it for eternity. "And that would be one way to ensure the removal of your hands."

Rahmi paused at her waist, digging his fingers into the boning of her dress. "'I'm curious. Does your cunt have teeth? Or would you use your mouth to bite them off?"

The man in the cell choked in surprise, but the woman merely narrowed her eyes. "Somehow, I think you would enjoy that a little too much." She paused as his hands graced an inner pocket, and Rahmi reached inside to pull out a small jar. "It's a salve. You know, for injuries. I guess you have a use for it after all."

Rahmi glared down at her condescending tone, the pinching soreness of the puncture wound in his forearm beating to the front of his mind. "I'll allow you to hold onto this," he replied, sliding it back into the pocket. "As a gesture of faith between us."

"I have no small amounts of gestures for you, captain," she murmured in response. "Most of them vulgar."

Rahmi snorted as his hands rose to her breasts, and he cupped the sides of them, making the search as quick as possible. Her brows still quirked when his fingers kneaded under the boning, but he dropped his hands to his sides just as she opened her mouth to speak. "What's your name?" he asked, trying to forget their feeling beneath his touch.

The woman remained silent for another minute, long enough that Rahmi was sure she wasn't going to respond. "Kalia," she finally said softly. "Kalia Salam."

A sound of indifference grunted from the back of his throat, but his thoughts spiraled elsewhere. *Interesting*. A name from the interior of the continent...an interior of the continent that once housed an ancient city built by djinn, according to Liddros. Rahmi rarely encountered citizens from the desert plains, but he had now experienced two in weeks. He didn't believe in coincidences.

"Wonderful to make your acquaintance, Kalia Salam," Rahmi said as he turned his back to her and stepped over the cell's threshold, pushing the door closed behind him. It shut with a *clink, and he grabbed the key from the opposite wall before sliding it into the hole and* locking the mechanism with a turn of his wrist. "We'll certainly be in touch."

Kalia hurried forward, her bare feet pattering against the wet floorboards, to wrap her hands around the vertical iron bars. "Are you going to leave me down here?"

The vexed exasperation in her tone surprised Rahmi, and he turned to face her once more. "You tried to kill me," he said slowly. He hadn't realized Kalia was missing half of her brain, though he should have guessed from the vapid cruelness of her personality. "This can't come as a shock to you, *ruehi*."

"Killing you is not off the table," Kalia retorted, reaching a hand through the bars to swipe at his tunic. Rahmi stepped back, and her fingers merely grazed his core. "Let me out."

Rahmi leaned his shoulder against the bulwark where the lantern was bolted. The swaying shadow from it danced back and forth on her figure. "The crew would prefer that you remain here to cool down. We don't need you stabbing more of my men. I'm sure you understand."

A wave of fear crested through Kalia's glare, an emotion Rahmi hadn't reasonably expected from an all-powerful djinn. His smug satisfaction leaked out of him at the harsh bite of it, but her following words contradicted what he knew she was feeling.

"The crew that didn't tell you where they had found me? The crew who were busy sinking their cocks into the women of the brothel while you awaited their return?" Kalia crooned, hooking a foot onto the lower crossbar of the cell door. She lifted her chin, her cutthroat stare boring into him. "Fabulous men, captain. A raise of confidence to the sailors under your charge."

Rahmi tempered the urge to reach through the cell doors and wrap his fist around her exposed neck. To strangle her? He would have tossed her overboard the moment she unsheathed a dagger in his presence if she weren't necessary to the trajectory they had found themselves on. Instead, he let a vying smirk lift the corner of his mouth. "I'm still not against killing you." His words mirrored her own.

A challenging gleam entered her eye, one that he was sure promised a slow and painful death. "Only if you dared."

CHAPTER TWELVE

KALIA

Kalia didn't know how long she sat in the cell. She took turns watching the swaying lantern, listening to the churning waves blast against the keel, and tracking the water that leaked down the side of the bulwark. The man next to her, sickly pale with a smattering of freckles that coated the bridge of his nose and a bruise that purpled his left eye, had attempted to make conversation a few times, but she ignored him.

She remembered him, of course. She remembered his ridiculously chivalrous pursuit to rescue her from the men of the crew. It had only led him here, locked in a musty brig in the bowels of a pirate ship next to her.

But it wasn't long before he got the hint and fell silent. Not long after he was pulled from the brig, Kalia's magic was still too dull to inflict any damage on the men who had forced him from the cell—not that she didn't try.

She vaguely tracked the passing of time by how much of her power had returned. First, she felt the dregs of it in her mind, a flicker of light in the depths of her soul. Next, it hemmed to her heart, filling the voided spaces and strengthening the wall she had built around herself before finally sinking into her bones and tingling the ends of her fingers. That's when she knew she was ready.

The door to the narrow passage squeaked open, and Kalia lifted her head from where she rested it against her knees. She shot to her feet, readying to wield her magic like a sword, piercing whoever thought it a good idea to waltz over the threshold.

However, Kalia's brow furrowed when a woman not much older than herself peered around the door jam, curly blonde locks framing her round face. The woman crept in, grimacing with every noise from the floorboards beneath her feet. Kalia got a good look at her when she was a series of steps into the brig.

Mousy was the best way to describe her. The shawl wrapped tightly around her shoulders, and the cotton skirts tied around her waist were both a size too large. Small scars littered her chin and cheeks, presumably from where she had anxiously picked at her acne, and her rounded shoulders did little to exude any semblance of confidence.

"Can I help you?" Kalia drawled, draping her arms through the iron bars.

The woman jumped, clearly unaware that Kalia had been watching her, and a hand flew to her chest. "I—I...oh, I'm sorry," she stammered, tightening her hand around the napkin she held. "I didn't know—I didn't think—" She hesitantly swept her gaze toward Kalia as though she were afraid Kalia would turn her to stone if she made eye contact. "I brought you some bread."

Kalia held out her hand, and the woman shuffled forward, depositing the lump of bread into her upturned palm before hurrying back. Kalia studied the woman as she unwrapped the napkin, assessing her wide hazel eyes and skittish demeanor. She had half a mind to push her magic into this woman, to take over her thoughts and memories, and force her to bring the set of keys still dangling across the room. But as she called it to the forefront, she paused, instead watching as the woman wound a loose thread around a finger.

Kalia couldn't help the oily slide of pity in her chest.

"What are you still doing here?" Kalia asked against her will, picking a corner from the bread and placing it between her lips. It was stale, and she was sure it was a few days old, but it was something.

"I'm Elodie...I mean, I was just wondering if—" The woman named Elodie paused, seemingly centering herself before speaking again. "I thought you asked my name. I— I was told to bring you some bread."

Kalia's brows rose again as she broke off another piece and popped it into her mouth, chewing slowly. "And you didn't think to ask what a djinn was before tromping down here?" Kalia herself still didn't know what a djinn was. "Aren't you afraid that I'm going to turn you into some slimy aquatic animal and pitch you over the side of the ship?"

Elodie's face blanched, the scars appearing more like specks of blood across her pale face. "I—I—the men thought you might have a soft spot for—you know—" she trailed off, gesturing vaguely down the front of her skirts and stays. The right side of the shawl slipped off her shoulder, and Elodie adjusted it before opening her mouth. Nothing came out.

Kalia's amused expression slid from her face. "The men sent you down here hoping I would have a soft spot for you?" She shook her head. "What a bunch of bastards."

Elodie giggled, the sound bouncing off the wooden walls like tinkling china. "You know," she breathily gushed, taking a tentative step forward, "I— I read in one of the captain's scrolls that djinn don't need to eat." She looked at Kalia expectantly, her bright eyes dropping to the bread in Kalia's hand.

For a moment, Kalia didn't quite know what to say. She shifted on her feet. The crusted blood and dirt on the soles had long begun to itch. She washed away as much of it as she could, but the puddles of leaked seawater had quickly turned to muck. She didn't *think* Elodie was trying to trick her into revealing herself, but she nonetheless leaned on the woman's soft sweetness.

"A common misconception." Kalia made a show of breaking off more of the stale bread, a move that Elodie watched with wide, curious eyes. "Did the captain say whether or not he was going to let me out of here?" Her eyes flicked toward the keys on the wall, and Elodie glanced over her shoulder to see what Kalia was staring at.

"The better question is," a low voice from the shadows of the passage said, the tone coating Kalia like a silk blanket, "are you going to behave if I let you out of there?"

Elodie jumped for the second time as the captain stepped over the threshold, his presence only shrinking the size of the room. The markings on his forearms, the first time Kalia had noticed them, seemed to absorb the golden light from the lantern. Kalia locked her gaze on him, her focus zeroing in on the captain's gentle hand on Elodie's shoulder.

In response, Kalia shot a tendril of her magic forward, piercing the first layer of the captain's mind. He grunted as he shook his head, as though hoping he would dislodge the hooks she had begun to sink into him. She had expected that. Many men she used her power against could sense the first few seconds of an assault, but something far more interesting followed.

A calming peace slid down the bond between them, her soul singing and bowing to his own. She felt the warmth of it, and her magic immediately loosened its lethal grip on him. It was her turn to shake her head, and she glanced up, surprised to see Rahmi crossing the brig and stopping in front of her cell.

"There's a good girl," he said with a smirk, jingling the keys to the door in his left hand.

Kalia sneered up at him. "You disgust me."

Rahmi shoved the key into the lock, turning it until the mechanism clicked open. The door swung forward, and Kalia quickly pushed past the captain in case he changed his mind. He would have to wrestle her back in the cage if he attempted to put her back in.

"That's not the worst thing a woman has ever said to me," Rahmi retorted, reaching over her head to hang the keys back on the hook. "You're to go with Elodie; she'll show you your new lodgings."

"Aren't you afraid I'll jump from your ship again?" Kalia called as he turned to leave the brig. Elodie's gaze darted between the two, uncertainly flashing over her features.

"Be my guest," Rahmi responded with a shit-eating grin, gesturing freely into the dark passageway. "We're three days from shore. It's quite the swim." He pivoted back, grasping her upper arm long enough to yank her toward him. His face was mere inches away, and she was sure she could head-butt him if she reeled back far enough first. "If you do anything to my men, I will tie you by your ankles and drag you behind my ship. Do I make myself clear?"

Kalia ripped her arm away from him, not wanting his touch to foul her already filthy skin any longer. "Crystal."

At the realization that Captain Rahmi-*fucking*-Abada had locked her in the brig just long enough to get her far away from shore, Kalia was fuming. She hated him. She *hated* him. Ideas blew through her mind, primarily of different ways she was going to kill him, but mostly...she wanted to make it hurt. She wanted him to bleed. And to think that he orchestrated her capture.

But, mostly, Kalia was kicking herself. The madam had always told her that she had a knack for trouble and a nose for curiosity, both of which were going to get her into a pile of shit one day. And here she was, in the biggest pile of shit there was.

Kalia was trembling from anger as she followed Elodie up the three flights of stairs, the ship creaking with every roll of the waves. She didn't know when she had gotten used to the stale humidity of the lowest deck, but the sudden burst of fresh air on her face was welcome. The salty breeze was heated in the morning sun, and, in turn, it coaxed the wood of the deck to release a shaved cedar scent. The rays reflected brilliantly off the white caps in the water, and small rainbows danced in the mist created by the ship carving a path through the sea.

It was almost peaceful. Almost.

"Just this way," Elodie prodded, doubling back to Kalia's side when she halted to watch the quarterdeck.

Men flittered every which way, their bronzed faces hidden beneath the brims of their tricorn hats, but Kalia felt their side-long gazes fixed on her. She began to walk again, lifting her chin in defiance as she passed a group of sailors huddled near a bucket, the soap suds overflowing onto their boots. They hadn't seemed to notice. She briefly thought about digging into their minds, but she stopped herself just as quickly.

She had heard of men getting keelhauled and had overheard the sailors in the bordello tell their haunting tales of their involvement with it. She had envisioned the missing skin, the screams of pain...that was, if they came back up alive. It was a torturous, brutal punishment. And, from the gleam in Rahmi's eye, she knew that he wasn't fucking around. Given the right motivation, he would overlook whatever he needed her for, whatever she was on board his ship to do. She wasn't interested in allowing him to have it.

Kalia crossed the deck with Elodie, watching closely how the men jeered in their direction or how they turned away from Elodie long enough for her to walk by. She wasn't particularly popular, Kalia gathered. From how her eyes were set too close together and how her top lip was a thin line compared to her bottom one, Kalia could see why. The woman wasn't a rare beauty, and paired with her seemingly low morale— that wasn't quite something that interested a man.

But she had kind eyes, Kalia noticed, and she was the only one brave enough to venture to the brig to give Kalia a piece of bread. That certainly counted for something.

The two women descended another set of stairs near the stern. Kalia glanced up as she set foot on the top step, spotting Alaric near the helm. He hadn't noticed she was there, and his stare glazed over and far away. She paused long enough, her hand still on the jagged, wooden railing, to send him a vision of him being mauled by a bear. The animal thrashed, tearing an arm away before clamping its large teeth around his neck. Blood spurted, and a second bear appeared, tearing off a leg.

She watched with satisfaction swelling inside of her as Alaric shuddered and shook his head while darting his narrowed eyes around the quarterdeck. She strolled down the stairs before he could catch her preening, gratified smirk.

The stern side of the ship was vastly empty, save for the dozens of hammocks hanging from the ceiling of the berth. Some were already occupied, their attendants snoozing with handkerchiefs draped over their eyes, and some were filled with extra pairs of boots or piles of sun-dried laundry. The faint scent of body odor and sweat was eye-watering, though it had an undertone of citrus and tallow, which told Kalia that someone had *tried* to clean.

Elodie pressed forward, and Kalia didn't fail to notice how her steps became disjointed and hurried, as though she were desperate to leave the confines of the berth. She also didn't fail to see how some men lifted their heads as they passed, not bothering to hide that they were staring. Kalia's skin prickled, and the hair on the back of her neck stood on end. It wasn't the same predatory gaze Rahmi had fitted her with— it was something darker, more sinister. She leveled them with a menacing look that was only reciprocated with raised brows and heavy smirks.

Kalia wasn't a fan of that one bit.

Elodie led her through a hallway, then a second one, before pausing outside a door near the middle of the ship. It was quiet and seemingly forgotten down this passage. Kalia opened her mouth to ask where *exactly* Elodie was taking her when she said, "This is where you'll be staying." She planted a hand on the brass knob, shouldering the door open with extra force.

The room on the other side was small, even compared to the brig. Three framed beds were wedged next to one another, each decked with a worn, thin quilt that had seen better days. A single circular window was the only opening to the outside, and the glass panes rattled in the frame with every wave strike. There were no personal effects within the room, aside from an open trunk that displayed stacks of neatly folded skirts and stays.

"You'll take the one on the left," Elodie said, gesturing toward the bed. "There were three of us, but... anyway, the metal basin was, you'll take the one on the left."

"We aren't staying with the rest of the crew?" Kalia asked, taking a step further into the room. A metal basin was already half-filled with water tucked just behind the door.

"Unless you want to," a second voice retorted wryly from the opposite corner. "And I highly suggest that you don't."

Kalia whirled on her toes, facing the stranger who had hidden herself in the shadows. "Why is that?"

Elodie sighed, sinking onto the edge of the bed on the right side as the second woman leaned forward, planting her elbows on her knees. "Terrible things happen in the dark. Do I need to explain it to you any further?"

"Shirin, that's not the best way to welcome our new roommate to *The Mark of Malice*," Elodie chided, threading the same loose string around her finger. A nervous tick. "We should—"

"It doesn't *need* to be welcoming. It *needs* to be practical. And she *needs* to know," Shirin interjected. She tilted her pointed chin toward the row of beds. "Heard you were coming. I took the liberty of hauling some extra clothes up from storage. They sure won't be as nice as—" She paused to wriggle a calloused finger at Kalia's red dress. "But they'll keep you warm on the open water. The tub is full, too; I thought you wouldn't mind cleaning up."

Kalia slid her gaze from Shirin, landing on the small pile of clothes nestled at the foot of the bed. She let out a huffed laugh, shaking her head. "I don't wear wool."

Shirin cocked her head, studying Kalia with the same guile of an owl watching a field mouse. Kalia momentarily wondered what was with the crew and their preternatural stares, but Shirin shrugged her shoulders and leaned back in her seat. "Suit yourself, but you'll get mighty chilly in *that*."

Kalia took a long moment to assess Shirin. Her black hair was braided and slung over a shoulder, nestled against the tunic she wore in place of the stays a woman outside of the capital would generally wear. Her deep, tawny skin was sun-kissed and smooth, and her brown eyes seemed to glow against her complexion. The frown lines on the sides of her lips were harsh, as were the ones that furrowed her brow, making it seem like she spent most of her time pondering.

"Fine, I'll *change*," Kalia said, sighing through her nose as she slunk out of the straps of her dress. She let the garment fall to her feet before kicking it to the side, turning just enough to step into the tub. She was careful not to let the women peek at her scarred back.

Elodie let out a gasp of surprise that made Kalia chuckle. Nakedness had never bothered Kalia, even before her time at the bordello. Her mother had taught her that natural forms were nothing to be ashamed of.

Her mother.

The unexpected thought squeezed tightly against her chest, and Kalia dipped a toe into the cooled water to distract herself. She shivered, the water already balmy and room temperature, but she sank into the tub nonetheless, thankful for the chance to scrub the blood and seawater from her body.

"So what is your guilt?" Elodie asked, though her voice was muffled from how hard she had pressed her face into her worn quilt. "What are you here for?"

Kalia grabbed the linen from the side of the basin, drenched it in water, and rubbed it on the bar of soap until it lathered. It certainly wasn't the lavender and coconut oil of the bordello, but it would do in a pinch. "My what?" Kalia asked, running the cloth down her arm. The dirt-smeared linen and brown droplets plunked into the bathwater.

"Your guilt!" Elodie repeated brightly, though Shirin shot her a glare of warning that she could not heed with her eyes still covered by the quilt. "Every one of us on the ship feels guilt over something. That's why we're stuck here. Shirin feels guilty over embezzling money from her business partner, a move that sent her friend to her death—"

"Elodie!"

"And I feel guilty for...for..." Elodie groaned, flopping to the side.

"It isn't so easy when it's *your* guilt, is it?" Shirin said, crossing her arms over her chest. "How will you learn to move on if you can't even say it out loud?"

"It's a work in progress, okay?" Elodie replied, rolling onto her back. She loosed a breath, pinning her gaze on the ceiling. "Anyways, Kalia. What are you here for?"

Kalia wrung out the linen and carefully placed it over the side of the basin. The water was already murky, flecks of mud floating on the surface. She trained her face to remain impassive, looking down at her nails instead. "I have no guilt. I was taken from my home and brought here." She offered no further explanation.

Shirin whistled in disbelief as Elodie flopped onto her stomach, blowing a single frizzy lock from her eyes. "Djinn don't have guilt then?"

Kalia stood from the basin, allowing the water to sluice into the tub, before grabbing a piece of dry linen from the seat of a glossy wooden chair. "Sure. If that's the way you want to look at it." She hoped that would be the end of it.

It wasn't.

"And what about—"

"Elodie, she doesn't want to talk anymore," Shirin shot back. "Look at her."

Kalia stepped from the tub as Elodie stilled and dressed in record timing, considering the delicate nature of the skirts and stays. The fabric smelled like old storage crates and felt scratchy against her skin, but she tried to ignore it. "I'm going to find the captain," she announced to neither one in particular. "Hopefully, he'll agree to take me back to shore now that he's had his fun."

Shirin's snort was filled with unkind irony. "I think you're better off asking a ghoul to accompany you to a palace ball."

Kalia tucked that thought into the back of her mind. That was one idea she could use to torture Alaric while she was stuck here.

CHAPTER THIRTEEN

RAHMI

G *ods,* he needed this.

Rahmi glanced down through lust-filled, hooded eyes to see the crown of Cora's head, her dark locks tied back in a knot. She moaned, the sound vibrating his cock.

Cora looked up at him from her kneeled position on the rug, her cheeks hollowed and her lips shining as they pistoned around him. Rahmi grabbed the back of her head, forcing her deeper. It only made her moan louder. *Gods, yes.* Today had been a bitch. He *needed* this.

"What are you doing?" The sharp voice was undoubtedly Alaric's as it echoed through the passage leading to Rahmi's private quarters. "Stop with the bears—" There was a soft chuckle, a mocking one that Rahmi had more than enough of in the last few hours. "You can't go in there. The captain is busy."

The sudden set of voices made Cora jolt, and she began to turn her head to glance at the closed door, but Rahmi intercepted her. Placing two fingers onto her cheek, he guided her mouth back to his cock. She happily obliged, though her gaze remained wary and unsure.

"Eyes on me," he commanded, tipping his head back. "What goes on in my office is none of your concern."

Cora's replying smirk promised filthy things, and she took him even deeper than she had a moment before. This time, it was Rahmi who let out a groan of satisfaction. He imagined sinking into her heat, thrusting into her until she cried out...screamed his name... It had been some time since he took Cora to his bed. He half-wondered if he should pick her up and sling her onto the mattress now.

"You can't—"

Footsteps stormed down the hallway just before the door swung open, the brass knob banging loudly against the opposite side of the wall. Rahmi's head whipped up, his hand remaining on Cora's cheek to keep her in place. She lapped at his cock, her tongue swirling around the tip. She hadn't seemed to notice who entered the room.

Kalia's brow rose in surprise, her eyes darting down to Cora, to Rahmi's exposed cock, and then back up to his face. Where he would have expected any other woman to turn away in embarrassment, Kalia merely leaned against the door framing and crossed her arms over her chest, watching intently. She had changed since leaving the brig, the wool skirts and stays doing her figure no favors. She still managed to wear it like armor.

Cora moaned again.

"Well, well, well," Kalia said, pushing herself off the framing and sauntering forward. "Isn't this a delight?" The gleam in her eye was gleeful, bordering menacing.

Cora pulled herself off Rahmi's cock with a soft *pop*, her eyes widening. Cora narrowed her focus onto Kalia, leveling her with a territorial stare that Rahmi knew Kalia had no interest in staking a claim to. Rahmi cursed under his breath. What he didn't need right now was *this*. He jumped as Cora planted her lips back onto him, sucking with a renewed enthusiasm that was quickly nearing pain.

"Do you need some tips?" Kalia asked as she reached Cora, a hand lifting to stroke the woman's hair. Rahmi watched Cora shiver, her skin unexpectedly pebbling. "I would be happy to oblige." She clicked her tongue against the roof of her mouth, her lips parting as that gleeful gleam turned lethal once more at the sight of his half-hard cock. "Seems you may have lost his interest. May I suggest—"

"Just ignore her, Cora," Rahmi began to say, though he trailed off with a grunt as Cora's teeth scraped over his shaft. "She's just pissed that she's been outwitted, and there's nowhere for her to go now that she's on my ship."

Rahmi tipped his head back once more. He could do this, even with Kalia in the room. He just needed to focus. *Cora. Cora's cunt. Cora's wet heat around his—*

A startling vision panged to the forefront of his mind. He opened his eyes to find himself still in his private cabin, but something was...decidedly wrong. The colors were too bright, the edges of his furniture blurring enough that they appeared fuzzy against the back-drop of the floor-to-ceiling windows that overlooked the wake of his ship. His eyes threatened to roll to the back of his head as another full draw on his cock nearly made him come right then. He glanced down, expecting to find Cora looking up through her thick lashes at him. Instead, he saw—

"A troll?" Rahmi asked, placing his hands on the thorned, green shoulders of the creature and forcing it from his dick. It grinned up at him, toothless and heady. It tried to scramble forward, shuffling noisily through its snout-like nose as Rahmi took several steps back. He shot an annoyed glare at Kalia, who had fixed an innocent expression on her face. "Get out of my head, *ruehi*." She had some fucking nerve. And the largest set of balls he had ever seen.

Kalia canted her head, an icy look passing over her innocent expression. "It would be so easy to kill you in here."

Rahmi stepped forward, nearly trodding on the troll in the process, and raked a hand toward Kalia. All he got was a fistful of salty air. It was so *real.*

"You're going to take me back to shore," Kalia said from across the room with a quiet fury, leaning a casual shoulder against the window. The sun beamed through the glass panes, lighting an ethereal glow around her silhouette. "And you're going to let me return home. You and your crew have had your laugh."

Rahmi dug into the recesses of his memory and ripped it away from her. She let out a pointed gasp as they both fell into a darkness of his own making.

Rahmi opened his eyes, staring toward the ceiling. He was back in reality, everything around him distinctly clearer and crisper. He sat up, shaking the dizziness from his mind. It had been a long time since anyone had gotten the jump on him, and he was going to make sure it didn't happen again. He sat up, glaring toward the woman who had collapsed near the windows, her silky sheet of hair fanned above her head.

"Don't fuck with me," Rahmi growled as he stood, reaching over to his bed to snatch the pair of breeches he had absent-mindedly thrown there. "Go," he spat to Cora.

She didn't need telling twice. At least one person in the room listened to him.

"It's easiest when you're distracted," Kalia said, any trace of that menacing smirk fading from her lips. It was replaced with a tight glare, her jaw ticking with the effort to swallow back whatever it was she wanted to say. She pushed herself up, smoothing out her skirt with an easy brush of her hand. "And I'm sure I'll have another go at you soon." She paused to slide her gaze down to his cock, now limp and hanging precariously between his thighs. "It won't take me long."

The djinn was reckless...an unchecked force for evil that Rahmi hadn't quite expected. He knew better now. There was a wicked, dangerous storm lurking just under her skin. This was a game he could play, a game he could win. He reveled in the challenge.

Rahmi tugged his breeches on, tying the laces into place. His eyes never left hers, brown boring into green. "And what if I refuse?" he asked, changing his demeanor to swagger toward her. She blinked, her brow knitting just enough to tell him that he had successfully caught her off guard and wrestled that control away from her if even just an inch. He was within a breath of her now, and he watched her hair flutter with every puff of air from between his lips. "What if I keep you on this ship of mine? Force you to do my bidding? What then, *djinn*?"

Rahmi had backed her into a corner, and he knew by the cold flash of her eyes and the flare of her nostrils that she was not used to her back being against a wall. She reached between them, her fingers dipping into the folds of her thick skirts. Her hand withdrew, a brass embossed letter opener pointed at him, one that he knew had been snagged from his desk in his office. He was going to have to lock every damn door on this ship if she was going to keep finding things to use as weapons against him.

Kalia pressed the knifelike tip into his sternum, and he felt the prick of it against his flesh. "I don't think you understand your position, *captain*."

Rahmi could feel his stare melt into one of glassy annoyance. He opened his mouth to speak but thought better of it and stopped himself short. His shoulders stiffened with the effort to remain quiet, and he found himself counting to ten if only to keep from wringing her neck. He even calculated how pissed she may get if he tossed her in the brig again. He briefly wondered if it would be worth the trouble.

That is until a growing, overly confident smile replaced the sneer that had taken residence on her face. "That's a good boy," she crooned, a simmering satisfaction clouding the air.

Rahmi decided to remain quiet, instead allowing his actions to speak for themselves. He lurched forward and impaled himself on the letter opener, burying the dull blade to the handle. Brass scraped against bone, and he barely managed to stifle the grimace of pain, but seeing her mouth fall open and hearing her shaky, shallow breathing was victory enough.

"That's the second time you've come at me with a blade," Rahmi said, taking a step closer to her as he reached up to wrench the letter opener from his chest. Kalia stood her ground, though he didn't miss the tremble of her shoulders. "It isn't going to happen again." He let the opener clatter to the ground, the sound dulled against the rug.

A measure of resolve darkened her eyes, and, for a long minute, Rahmi thought the shock had won. In the next breath, Kalia tilted her chin up to better look at him, and her initial surprise had been swept away by determination.

"You're a specter, a curse." She didn't pose it as a question. "Turns out I have heard of you after all. Rumors of your existence have traveled with the sailors for as long as I was at the bordello." She huffed a laugh. "I didn't think they were true."

The casual hint in her tone took him by surprise. Most people were drowning in their fear at the near mention of him. He had hoped that she would as well.

"Are you scared of me now, *ruehi*?" Rahmi asked, taking one final step forward. It was enough to close the gap between them that his chest brushed against hers when he took his next deep breath. "You should be. I've been collecting souls for centuries now. It's only a matter of time before I also claim yours."

"I've met many monsters," Kalia replied, side-stepping him and aiming for the cabin door. "You're going to have to try harder than that." That shit-eating smirk reappeared, and she threw it over her shoulder at him. "And all I'll be able to think about now is the mighty cursed captain with the troll on its knees before him. You might want to get your cock checked the next time we port. You never know what types of diseases are carried these days. I'm sure you would be very unhappy if it fell off."

Rahmi opened his senses, attempting to find any crack in her hard-owned veneer. She had shut himself off to him, and rightfully so. It still didn't edge away the frustration that bit at him. "I ordered you onto my ship for a reason," he shot at her back. She paused, placing a hand on the door frame. "Or has your curiosity disappeared with your need for the last word?"

Kalia tapped a red-painted fingernail against the wood. "Why?"

Dark clouds had begun to gather on the horizon, casting the sun in shadow and smearing the sky in a gray sheen. Footsteps made their way down the narrow hall and stopped nearly halfway to Rahmi's cabin before turning around and creeping away. Muffled shouts echoed from the deck, the faraway hauling of ropes against sails drumming a rhythmic beat into the charged, heavy air. A storm was coming. Rahmi was sure of it.

He crossed the room, navigating around the locked chest at the foot of his bed and the well-used armchair, where an overturned book was perched on the seat. He placed a hand on the door above her head and pushed it closed. It clicked into place, dousing them in silence. "I'm hunting for a gemstone that a djinn can power. You're going to help me find it."

Kalia stilled for a moment before spinning on the balls of her feet, the scent of nutmeg and cinnamon on the phantom breeze she created. "That's presumptuous of you. I have no interest."

"You're going to tell me where to find it."

"You would get further in life if you weren't so demanding." She leaned against the door, hooking one ankle over the other.

"I've gotten this far in life being demanding. There's no reason for me to stop now." It was an effort, a concentrated one, not to throttle her. Rahmi listened to the soft *tsk* of her nail scratching against the wood pattern of the door. "This is non-negotiable, *ruehi*. If you disagree, you will be on this ship for a very long time. I have time to wait. You, on the other hand—" He trailed off and was pleased to see that she was smart enough not to argue immediately. Thank *fucking* Liddros for that.

And as though Kalia could read his mind, her lips twitched upward. She weighed his stare. "How do you think you would fare as a beetle, captain?" she purred. "Do you think your men would listen to you then?"

Rahmi's growl of displeasure was drowned out by the turn of a knob and the squeaking of a door. Kalia had reached behind her back, peeling the door open. She slipped from the room before he had time to reply, and he told himself he had let her go. She might be venom incarnate, but he would find a way to survive her. He remembered what Alaric had said when he arrived with her in tow back to his ship. How she had been trying to help the others, how she had put herself directly in the middle of the conflict.

A wry, involuntary smile split Rahmi's lips. An idea sparked. And he knew what he had to do.

Chapter Fourteen

Kalia

K alia blew out the breath she had been holding as soon as she got far enough from the captain's cabin, finally allowing the fear that had taken root in her belly to grow. It had begun to rain when she was in the cabin; the light droplets adhered to the wool of her skirts and stays. It was ridiculous— absolutely abhorrent— that Rahmi had even entertained the possibility of her helping him. His crew had burnt the bordello to the ground and had probably killed all of those inside who were unable to escape. And he thought *she* would help *him*?

And, gods, she had threatened to turn him into a beetle. Could Djinn even turn people into beetles? She had no fucking clue. That was something she needed to figure out...and fast. Preferably *before* someone realized she was lying.

Scowling at no one in particular, Kalia pushed through a small gathering of the crew, making sure to march straight up the middle. Luckily for them, she could stalk through without an issue, though one of the men made a gesture of prayer toward the gods in her wake. She didn't bother giving him a second glance.

She continued her trek along the ship's side, feeling the wind rush through her hair, flapping her skirts like the black sails from above. Blue extended as far as her eyes could see, blurring with the horizon as the rain lashed in the distance. She...hated it. She wasn't built for the salty, wet air, much preferring the dry heat of Sha'Hadra. Even the fresh scent of oncoming storms didn't quite temper back the body odor and sweat wafting from the crew. But she had learned from a young age that nothing was permanent, and this wouldn't be either. She needed to ride it out and wait until the captain got bored with her and released her back to the continent.

She didn't know if she could wait that long. There had to be coins on the ship. They had to come close to land at some point. The better play would be to prepare a stash for when she could jump off and swim ashore. A plan, that's what she needed.

Kalia placed her forearms on the gunnel, staring into the white-crested waves below. They slapped against the keel, churning beneath them with every slice forward. She couldn't remember much from her childhood, but she did remember that her mother loved the sea. She talked about it often, explaining in detail how the tides rose and fell with the moon, how the starfish and barnacles cling to the rocks, and how fish of all colors and sizes dart along the sunny shore. She had expected to see the coast with her mother, not...

She shook her head and cleared her throat. She didn't need those memories, so she tempered them back, too.

"Ghoul in your graveyard?"

Kalia sighed, not bothering to glance at the man she knew who stood beside her. She hadn't seen him since he had been taken from the brig. "What?"

"It's just— it's a saying my grandmother used to say. You know...ghoul in your graveyard? Bee in your bonnet? Is something bothering you?" the man chuckled, light and airy. "It's silly, I guess, but I always think of her when—"

"Is there something I can help you with?" Kalia interjected. The storm clouds were marching closer, their edged wisps gathering above the masts of *The Mark of Malice*. The men had already begun pulling in the sails.

"I'm the man who—"

"I know who you are." Her words were a stone barrier she erected between them, refusing him the opportunity to come any closer.

There was a short pause, a gust of wind billowing over the quarter-deck before the man laughed again. "Are you always this pleasant, or are my good looks winning you over? It has to be my looks."

Kalia blinked as glaring irritation kindled in her veins. "Just so we're clear—" she started to say, turning to scold him— and wanting to look in the eye while doing so— but stopped short. She hadn't seen the man up close, and not in the daylight, but she hadn't recalled the split lower lip, the second purple bruise underneath his right eye, and the gouge mark on his cheek that looked like it could have been from the pommel of a cutlass. "What happened to you?"

The man smiled, the cut on his lower lip opening enough that Kalia's stomach flipped out of disgust before dragging a hand through his mop of dark curls. "Just the crew joking around. I think it's what one would call a *rite of passage*. But I could be misusing the phrase."

She looked at him further, studying the young, bronzed face she once thought was pale. The smattering of freckles was nearly blending now. His brown eyes exuded joy and lightheartedness despite his injuries. It seemed all he needed was a hot meal or two.

"I think they just beat the piss out of you, no rite of passage involved," Kalia finally said, turning back to face the open sea. The rain droplets were heavier now, plunking against the deck's wood.

He laughed. "It's a possibility, I suppose." He paused, and Kalia felt his stare boring into the side of her head. "Are you going to tell me your name? Mine is Reshef."

She narrowed her eyes. "Do you need to know my name?"

"It's common courtesy," he said with a simple shrug that made him appear unbothered despite her standoffish attitude. "And only polite, considering I *did* try and rescue you from being carted off by a band of bloodthirsty pirates."

Kalia sent him a sidelong look, catching the black stone on the end of a silver chain that hung around his neck. "Stunning rescue, Reshef, considering a band of bloodthirsty pirates *carted me off,* and we *both* ended up here." She let him hear the mercurial bite to her tone. It didn't seem to faze him.

Thunder rumbled, close enough that it shook the gunnel under her hands, and a second gust of wind lifted mist from the cresting waves. There was a snap of rope and a series of shouts as something heavy hit the deck behind them. Kalia glanced over her shoulder, noting the collapsed rigging that had tangled with a set of ropes from the mainsail. There was a second snap and another outcry as Alaric brought down a piece of the broken rope across another man's back.

"That's Karim," Reshef said, answering a question Kalia hadn't deigned to ask. He leaned an elbow against the gunnel, shifting his weight onto one foot to cross one ankle over the other. "He's been struggling since he came aboard the ship. Turns out, the captain took him, too."

Kalia licked her lips, tasting the salt from the breeze on her skin. "How do you know all of this?"

Reshef leaned forward, gesturing for her to come closer as though it were an important secret he wasn't meant to share. When she was within a few inches of his mouth, he whispered, "Because I talk to others like a normal, friendly person." He fell back, resuming his casual stance against the gunnel, and reached up to slide that black stone along the chain. "Did you know this is one of those cursed ships that travel the seas? The captain can only go ashore once every seven years. Can you imagine? I would kill someone over a hot buttered biscuit before then."

Kalia couldn't quite stifle her grin. "Mine would be pastries stuffed with almonds and sesame seeds and coated with honey. It's a sweet cookie from the city I was born in, and—" She trailed off, suddenly realizing she was about to share something personal. She cleared her throat and asked, "What do you know about the curse? I just learned about it, too."

If Reshef noted her shift in conversation, he didn't comment on it. "Enough to know that most of the crew is over one hundred years old and not enough to know why I haven't been asked to join." His gaze became inquisitive. "Do you think I should take that personally?"

"It's probably because you're chatty," Kalia informed him, and he looked at her mildly affronted.

"Boy!" Alaric called over the heads of the men, pointing a thick, accusatory finger at Reshef. "Get back to your position! We have sails to bring in—!" A third gust of wind blew, drowning the rest of his statement and catching a half-furled sail with enough gusto to split the seam.

"I guess it's my time to be *unchatty*," Reshef said, pushing himself from the gunnel. "Thank you for your honesty. Though, as an aside, you could be a bit gentler on the delivery."

Kalia didn't know why she did it. Something about his boyish charm and wide, innocent eyes reminded her of a brother she had long ago. "Wait," she said, reaching out to clasp her hand around his forearm, tugging him back. "Take this." Letting go of his arm, she reached into the pockets of her skirts and fished out the small jar of salve she had been carrying around. "Use this for the cuts on your lip and cheek. *Don't* use it all in one go. You strike me as someone who needs direction." She placed the jar into his palm. "But it'll heal you right up."

Reshef stared at the jar long enough that Kalia wondered if he would say anything. Finally, he glanced up, a wry smile plastered on his face. "Consider this the start of a very long friendship," he said, stuffing the jar into his breeches pocket.

"We aren't going to be friends," Kalia replied, crossing her arms over her chest.

"You're right," Reshef amended with a wink. "We're going to be the *best* of friends."

By the time night had fallen and the crew navigated the ship around the brunt of the storm, Kalia had managed to make her way back to the room she shared with Shirin and Elodie. It took three wrong turns, four dead-ends, and an oddly timed run-in with two men attempting to wrestle the torn sail into storage for repair, but she finally made it just as the night crew went to their stations on the quarterdeck.

Kalia wedged open the door with a shoulder, stumbling over the threshold to see Shirin reach under her mattress and withdraw the hilt of a small blade. Elodie jumped, the soup she was holding spilling over the bowl's rim and dripping onto the front of her dress.

"Oh, it's just you," Shirin said, straightening to a stand. She angled her head as she studied Kalia, raising her brows at the wool skirts and stays she still wore. "Did you find the captain, then?"

"And more," Kalia replied, though she couldn't stop herself from coolly adding, "I met Cora."

Elodie let out a slight, choked sound as the corner of Shirin's lip curled into a smirk. Shirin reached down to pick up Kalia's red dress, freshly laundered and without the stiff, bloody stains. She tossed it onto Kalia's new bed, where it crumpled against the flattened pillow. "It's been quite some time since I've heard those two names in the same sentence," Shirin casually said, picking up another skirt and carefully folding it. "You must have stressed him out more than he's used to these days."

Kalia considered her momentarily before she sank gracefully into the wooden chair next to the basin, now empty and upturned, to drain the rest of the water onto the worn, frayed rug. "I certainly wouldn't recommend his ship as a luxury passage. However, it seems we can have the pick of the litter when it comes to sexual exploitation as long as one can settle for scurvy and bad teeth. A single rating for that."

Shirin paused as if debating saying something else but continued folding the laundry silently.

"I brought you some soup from the galley," Elodie said, holding out the bowl. After spilling it, her flush deepened from a dusky rose to crimson. "How often do djinn eat? Do you need to eat more than once?" Her eyes gleamed with intense curiosity. Kalia reached forward to take the bowl, sniffing it gingerly. "It's just fish stew. Doc, the ship's galley lead, caught them in the sea last night."

The stench was acrid, bordering on sickening, and the overt fishiness nearly made Kalia's eyes water. She almost set the bowl on the end table next to the bed when she glanced up to spot Elodie looking at her with those wide, curiosity-ridden eyes. Something squeezed in her chest from the innocence of it, and she lifted the bowl to her lips to take a small sip instead. It tasted just like it smelled. Kalia made a concerted effort to force it down.

"Mmmm..." Kalia said, managing to swallow her grimace with it.

Elodie opened her mouth to respond, but Shirin cut her off, not bothering to look up from her laundry folding. "It's disgusting. Doc should be a better cook than he is."

"He's only been in the galley for thirty years!" Elodie retorted, much to Shirin's chagrin. "Remember when Isaiah was the galley lead? He had been there for nearly eighty, and his beef still tasted like—"

"Thirty years is long enough to figure out how to make a simple stew," Shirin shot back. "He's made it every single day."

Kalia made a noncommittal noise of agreement. She harkened back to the first time the madam had made her dinner while traveling from Sha'Hadra to the capital. She fumbled over the wood-burning stove and burned two different chicken breasts before finally giving up and handing Kalia six coins to order them food from the tavern's kitchen. It had been the most money she had ever held— at least to that point.

"Not everyone can be as good a chef as you. We should give him the benefit of—the benefit of—" Elodie trailed off with a loud yawn, covering her open mouth with the back of her hand.

Shirin looked at her with a gentle look that could have been from a mother to a child. "Why don't you lay down and get some rest? I'll take the first watch tonight." She bent over, snagging the pile of laundry and dragging it from the middle bed to the one she was standing to the side of.

First watch? Kalia's brow furrowed as the ship creaked, another wave hitting the hull. Elodie smiled gratefully as she pulled back the corner of the middle bed, revealing a stained white sheet. Almost as though she could sense Kalia's question bubbling to the surface, Elodie said, "There are bad people on the ship. It's unsafe for both of us to be asleep at the same time."

The soft sound of the fabric against leather garnered Kalia's attention back to Shirin. An incredulous expression passed over Kalia's face as Shirin pulled out the blade from beneath the pillow completely this time. Kalia finally looked over Shirin and then Elodie's faces. It was the first time she noticed their drawn, dulled gazes, the dark circles beneath their eyes, and the sallow tinge to their skin that only extreme exhaustion could bring.

A shiver of rage ran through Kalia's veins, but not at the thought of being on the ship and surrounded by a group of violent men. *That* she was used to. No, it was at the thought of the two women in front of her feeling so unsafe that they took turns every night keeping watch with a dagger resting in their laps. She forced herself to hold Shirin's sharp stare, her glare daring Kalia to say *anything* about their current way of doing things.

Kalia raised her brows and held out her hand, balancing the untouched bowl of soup in the other. "I'll take the first watch," she said, tilting her head. "Unless you—" She was cut off, interrupted suddenly by the gong of a bell ringing from the quarterdeck above them.

Elodie groaned as Shirin tossed the petticoat she had been folding back onto the pile, turning to take the bowl of soup from Kalia's hands and placing it on the end table. "Captain's summoning us to the deck," she explained as Elodie bent down to retie her boots onto her stocking-covered feet. "Can't be good if he's doing it this late."

As Shirin wrenched the door open, Kalia stood from her seat, following her into the narrow hallway. Elodie shut the door behind them, the sharp snap echoing down the empty hallway. Shirin led the way, finally joining the group of men from the berth as they bottlenecked the bottom of the stairs, their empty hammocks still swinging fruitlessly with the ship's sway. She met Cora's stare from across the room, the woman sending her a sneer that would have rivaled Mintie's.

Kalia merely licked the pad of her thumb before wiping the corner of her mouth with it.

The stairs opened to the deck, and the fierce winds hadn't quite settled from the storm. Kalia reached back to quickly braid her hair to keep it from tangling. She was jolted forward as two men who hadn't been paying attention bumped her back, and she glanced over her shoulder with the coldest stare she could muster, one that sent both men fleeing into the crowd. She swore Shirin snorted in amused appreciation as they crossed the quarterdeck.

The scene before her became clearer the closer she got. Three men stood on a makeshift stage created by a series of crates. Each man stood just high enough to be seen at the back of the crowd. Kalia recognized Reshef as one of the men on display, and he sent her a friendly wave when his scanning gaze landed on her.

She looked at him wide-eyed in disbelief, shaking her head at the casual way he leaned against the mainmast, how his arms dangled carelessly at his sides, and how he mouthed *great salve* before mimicking holding a jar between his thumb and forefinger. From how the two other men trembled, their throats bobbing with forced swallows, Kalia thought Reshef should be far more concerned with what was about to happen.

On the other end of the stage stood Alaric and Rahmi, both watching the gathering crew with a hand planted on the pommel of their cutlasses. Rahmi looked the part of a cursed captain with his fitted long coat, the additional daggers strapped to his waist, and the way his sculpted jaw tensed with every pass of his gaze over the crowd as though he were looking for someone.

The moon shone brightly behind the last clouds blanketing the night sky. The shadows' cast caught him at an ethereal angle, bringing out the wild manner in which he held himself.

He was handsome; she would give him that. If she were honest with herself, she would have admitted that he was one of the most beautiful men she had ever seen. It was too bad that he was about as well-received as Doc's fish stew. It was also too bad that she was going to rob him blind and, hopefully, kill him in the process. She took a moment to send a quick flash of a vision down that bridge, one of her gleefully feeding his dismembered body to a school of sharks.

Rahmi's eyes snapped to connect with hers, a devious smile playing on his lips. Like a predator scrutinizing his prey, it was not reassuring. Kalia briefly wondered what lay up his excessively expensive, gold-trimmed sleeves. She raised a brow. He quirked one in return. She sent him a second vision of an alligator eating his hand, and his smile only deepened. He pulled one of the daggers from his belt, a hand wrapped tightly around the hilt.

As the crowding began to slow, Rahmi broke his eye contact and turned toward his crew. "I've been a fool," he began, his tone methodically controlled. The murmurs came to a screeching halt, silence falling over them. For the moment, the only sounds were the creaking of the ship in the waves and the rustle of the ropes against wood. "I've been a fool because I've sent us on countless journeys, bartering for souls and looting cargo ships."

"Like we've had much to complain about!" A man from the middle of the deck piped up, and the outburst was followed by a smattering of hollow laughs that skittered over the crowd.

Rahmi's smile went glacial, the merit of a man who didn't enjoy being interrupted, and the low chuckles ended immediately. "When we visited Captain Devlin Cato of *The Phantom Night*, he expanded on the makings of a gemstone that could break bonds and shatter curses. He was resolute that such a stone existed. And we've found a djinn to make that very gem work."

Oil slid through Kalia's gut as the men all spun around to survey her, some resorting to standing on their toes to get a better look. Reshef stiffened, his smile sliding into a tight line as though he were on the verge of being sick. She kept silent, fixing a mask of neutrality on her face. Where was the captain going with this? She wasn't too sure she wanted to know.

Rahmi didn't give her an option.

"Our djinn has made it clear in her first few days that she is unwilling to help us with our endeavors," Rahmi went, and those men glared at her with the ferocity of one nearing a pit of venomous snakes. "We're here to convince her otherwise." He crossed the crates, each groaning dangerously under his weight, and held the dagger to the throat of the first man. "We have three men. Three innocent men. You have three chances, Kalia Salam, to change your mind. With every refusal, one of these men will die."

Kalia said nothing as the crew's glares turned wary, shifting from the captain to her and then back again. She crossed her arms over her chest, surveying Rahmi with a look of utmost boredom. He wouldn't do that to his men, wouldn't—

Rahmi said nothing as he wrenched the edge of the blade into the man's throat, ripping it across his neck before withdrawing it with the stomach-twisting crunch of metal against bone. Kalia started as the man scrambled for the gaping cut, the blood streaming and bubbling with every futile move he took. He fell to his knees, losing his balance and tipping off the edge of the crates. He writhed on the deck momentarily but didn't stand up again.

Kalia lifted her gaze back to Rahmi, who stood there watching her with a wide grin playing on his lips despite the blood dripping from the long edge of his dagger and onto the toe of his boot. She watched, still silent, as he moved to the second man, who trembled like he was caught naked in a snowstorm. Rahmi held the blade to the man's throat, cocking his head.

"What do you say?" he asked, digging the point into the man's flesh. "Would you help us?"

The man let out an involuntary whimper, one that tugged at the spot behind Kalia's navel. But still, she remained silent. She wouldn't bend to this *insane* man's whims, wouldn't dare fold to his manipulations.

"No?" Rahmi went on. "I can keep going, *ruehi*. I have men aboard this ship who would happily be given to Samael, God of Death." When she said nothing, he shrugged a single shoulder before wrenching the blade into the man's throat and ripping it out again. Just like the first, the man gave a strangled, gurgled cry before staggering backward and falling from the crates. His body hit the rungs of the anchor drop, a sickening *crack* reverberating over the deck. The crew surrounding her winced, some shifting to distance themselves and Kalia.

Rahmi moved toward Reshef, who was still lounging casually against the mainmast, picking at the cuticles of his nails. He hadn't seemed to have noticed the deaths of the two men despite the blood splattered on his right forearm. Alaric reached him first, grabbing his upper arms and forcing him to straighten. Reshef looked up, surprise flitting over his face, as though he suddenly remembered he was late for an important meeting.

"I just want to point out," Reshef said quickly as Rahmi placed the blade just above the silver chain around his neck, "that I certainly did *not* volunteer to be given to Samael, so if someone wants to meet him in my stead—" Blood gathered where the blade pricked into his flesh.

Something broke in her at the sight of the young man with the blade against his neck, all innocence ebbed from the previously joyous glint in his eyes. Gods, he looked just like her brother at that moment, a brother who had done everything to protect her from the guards who had broken into their home. Given everything...

"Wait," Kalia said, her voice hoarse from the lump in her throat. "Wait."

Rahmi paused, though didn't remove the dagger from Reshef's neck. An artery bulged, frantically pumping beneath the point of the blade. He quirked an expectant brow, his lips curving into a menacing smirk.

"I'll do it," Kalia finally said, sighing through her nose as her heart thundered against her chest. She was going to hate herself for this. She already knew. She would hate every moment of being on this ship, every second she was in the presence of Rahmi-*fucking*-Abada. Still, she continued, "I'll help you find the gemstone. I'll help you use it. Just...just let him go."

Rahmi seemed satisfied, offering her a conspiratorial wink that made her want to reach up and rip his eyes from his sockets. "Gladly." He pushed Reshelf forward, who caught himself before stumbling from the crates. "Alaric set our course for the Eerie Isles. We need to pick up Wright Thackeray." He looked over the heads of the men in front of Kalia, pointing the dagger at her. "If you go back on our deal, *ruehi*, I know just what man to come to first."

CHAPTER FIFTEEN

RAHMI

R ahmi was immensely fucking proud of himself, *immensely fucking proud*. He kicked off his boots, letting them fall in a heap on the worn rug, and tugged off his long coat before tossing it over the back of the armchair. He swore he could almost smell the satisfaction in the air. He outwitted the djinn with nothing more than his dagger, a daring chance, and two men who would never admit to their guilt.

They had been on board *The Mark of Malice* for nearly fifty years, and neither one of them showed any indication that they were working on learning from their mistakes. He did what any good captain would have done.

On the other hand, the third man was one Rahmi had witnessed talking to Kalia. He had chosen the man merely to fuck with her. Rahmi was still debating whether it was worth keeping the man aboard his ship, considering not a shred of guilt marred his soul, but keeping him aboard *for now* was good enough for him. Primarily when the decision resulted in her finally bending to him. The last few days had been harrowing, and he wasn't keen on repeating them.

Rahmi collapsed on the mattress, slipping a hand behind his head to brace against the pillow. If the weather behaved, the sailing to the Eerie Isles would take a few days, but getting his former crew member would be difficult. The Eerie Isles were only the first step in getting to The Labyrinth of Lost Souls, the prison where he knew Wright Thackeray had landed himself after his discharge from *The Mark of Malice* nearly twenty years ago. If Rahmi didn't desperately need him and his irreplaceable skill set...

He had almost fallen asleep, nearly drifted off to the sound of the waves and sails creaking, when his eyes snapped open at the whisper of feet against wood just outside his cabin door. He raised his head off the pillow, peering down the length of his body to stare at the gap between the bottom of the door and the floor. He watched it momentarily and almost readied to collapse back to the pillow when a shadow ghosted across the gap in the frame.

Rahmi's lips curled into a broad smile, excitement thrumming a powerful beat through his veins. He had expected..., but not this quickly. At least when she promised to do something, she followed through with it.

He rolled from the mattress, his feet landing with feline grace against the floor. In no uncertain terms did he want to spook her. And he was nearing absolute certainty that it was her on the other side of the door. He grabbed his belt from where he had placed it on the seat of the old armchair, unsheathing his dagger with a quick tug. Just in time, too, because the brass knob had turned once, slowly and methodically before he heard something being inserted into the lock.

Did the djinn need to pick a lock to break through the door? From what Liddros made it sound like, they were the second most powerful beings on the continent. Wars had been fought to subdue their power. And here she was...using a pin like a pickpocket in Sha'Hadra. Perhaps she didn't want to waste her magic before coming face-to-face with him.

He slunk into the corner of his cabin, hidden from the moon's silver light that finally broke through the end of the storm clouds. It cut a cool path across the room, casting the armchair and the posts of his bed in sharp relief. The lock clicked, and the door cracked open. Rahmi was able to spot a single almond-shaped eye. He pressed himself further against the wall, feeling the ship's swaying at his back.

Kalia placed a hand on the door, slowly opening it wide enough that she could slide her body into the cabin before shutting it with a soft *click* behind her. Rahmi watched as she froze at the door, glancing over her shoulder toward the bed, the blankets in a rumpled heap against the mattress. From her angle, he imagined it could appear that he was merely sprawled across the sheets.

She crossed the sliver of light, and Rahmi was pleased to see she had changed back into that red dress, leaving her feet bare and free of stockings or boots. She was a smart woman. The thick wool was harder to navigate in, and the boots would be loud against the wooden floorboards. She was a master of secrecy, as he could attest.

Rahmi left the confines of the corner, sneaking behind her just as she reached the edge of the mattress. Just as she raised the knife—where had she gotten a knife?— and plunged it into the mass of furs and sheets. It stuck in the bed with a loud *thunk,* and she let out a sharp sigh of relief, mirrored in how her shoulders sagged.

But Rahmi couldn't be killed that easily, even if he were impaled to the bed.

"I think," he said slowly, watching with unfiltered glee as Kalia started and whirled on the balls of her feet, her hand releasing its firm grip on the knife, "that you need to try some other way of killing me. You've already attempted the use of a dagger."

"That was a kitchen knife," Kalia corrected in return, her green eyes glinting with white-hot fury.

He would have to talk with Elodie and Shirin about watching what kinds of utensils they brought back to their makeshift room. She twisted to try and grab the knife, but Rahmi grasped her wrist and a hip, pinning her to the post at the bottom corner of his bed. She let out a huff of air when her shoulders smacked against the column, and that breath warmly caressed his cheek. His hips pressed against her waist, and he could feel her wriggling against places he wasn't interested in having her.

"I would stop moving like that, *ruehi*, unless you've suddenly come to your senses and want in my bed." Her immediate stiffening garnered a chuckle out of him. "You've already stabbed me. Twice, I'm afraid. What's next? Poison? I'm afraid I don't have many pistols aboard my ship, but if you were to come across—" His mocking came to a clipped and grunting end when she trod on his toes, rocking her full weight onto his bare foot before kneeing him in the balls.

Kalia skidded away from him, coming to a halt on the other side of the armchair. Like fuck that rickety, old piece of furniture would keep him from ripping apart this room to get to her. As soon as he could stand straight.

"Why are you in here?" Rahmi asked as he sank onto the edge of the mattress, breathing through the radiating pain that was surely going to make his stomach overturn.

Kalia scoffed, though it seemed his stare pinned her in place. "I made you a promise. You killed two men, you—" She went utterly still as he rose from the bed, stalking toward her. "Don't come any closer to me."

Rahmi stopped, he didn't need to come any closer. Seeing her shrink under his gaze was the finishing touch of the day that he needed. "What's your plan here? Kill me? My crew'll rip you apart before I rise from the depths of Samael." His mouth twisted to the side when she shifted in discomfort. He quickly knocked aside her bond when she tried to bridge their minds. He had already locked himself up, a steel wall between them. "I don't think so, *ruehi*."

"Why do you call me that?" Kalia shot back, taking a sliding step toward the door. It wasn't lost on Rahmi. "*Ruehi?*"

Kalia didn't quite say the word right, not placing enough emphasis on the final inflection, but his nickname on her lips made him stand a bit straighter. He wouldn't admit it; he would rather die with that knowledge than allow her to be privy to it.

Instead, Rahmi sighed and jerked his chin toward the door. "Get out of here, Kalia, before I change my mind."

For once, she didn't need telling twice.

"We lost two men," Alaric said, pacing the floor before the desk. "Two men who worked the sails. And some of the newer ones are afraid you'll chuck them overboard before the end of the week."

Rahmi leaned back in his seat, chuckling as his quartermaster lifted a hand to rub the back of his neck. "And you think that's a bad thing, Alaric? Respect from the crew?"

Alaric stopped his pacing, squaring his shoulders to face Rahmi. "Respect is earned, captain, as you well know. Fear gets us nowhere except an eventual mut—"

"Don't," Rahmi cut him off, shooting him a warning glare that Alaric didn't back down from. "Do not use that word in this cabin."

Alaric leaned forward, placing his knuckles on the edge of the desk. He sent a menacing glare through one blue eye, the patch still tightly secured over the other. "We've been lucky, captain. Lucky with the men you force on this ship. Remember, you will lose this ship the same way you took it."

Rahmi looked away. Alaric liked to remind him of that from time to time. Liked to remind him that he was the captain of a merchant ship long ago and that he once led a mutiny when the old captain of *The Mark of Malice* had captured him. And that Rahmi had won. "What would you have me do, Alaric? Would you have me forget this business Karim put on our doorstep or—"

"All I'm saying," Alaric interjected, standing straight to cross his arms over his chest, "is not to throw away what we have on this ship over the whims of this djinn." He shook his head, gazing at the round window just over Rahmi's shoulder. "There's something funny about her."

Rahmi snorted, picking up the quill he had tossed on the roll of parchment in front of him and running his finger along the edges of the feather. "You mean, besides the fact that she's repeatedly tried to kill me? Or beside the fact that she seems to enjoy torturing you in particular?"

"If she does manage to kill you, we're all in for a load of trouble." Alaric sighed, ignoring Rahmi's quip. "Tell me the truth, captain. What does she mean to all of this?"

His quartermaster was the only person Rahmi would allow to give such demands. They had been together for centuries, had weathered storms, had sacked ships, and had been through an endless amount of shit. Rahmi set down the quill and tapped his finger on the folded map set to the side of the desk. "The gemstone we seek, Karim may have made us aware of the path, but we've been set on it by Liddros." He lifted his eyes and watched Alaric's expression range from confused to horrified in seconds.

"Liddros? *The* Liddros? I thought the two of you weren't on speaking terms."

"We weren't—aren't," Rahmi amended, planting his hands on the desk and pushing himself out of his chair. "I summoned him to inquire about the truth of the legend. Once he discovered the gemstone's survival, he propositioned me for its retrieval—an accord I could not step away from."

Alaric's brows flew high on his head. "And you think you can trust him to keep his promise once you hand it over?" He clicked his tongue against his teeth. "This is far more complicated than I thought."

"More complicated than hauling a man from the capital aboard my ship under the guise of keeping our djinn's capture a secret?" Rahmi smirked. He let out a bark of a laugh at Alaric's gaping, open mouth. Just as Alaric was the only man allowed to challenge him, Alaric was the only man Rahmi allowed himself to joke with.

"That isn't—I didn't—We—," Alaric sputtered, and Rahmi laughed again at the flush that crept up his cheeks. "He was chasing us through the streets of the capital!"

"And it was quite convenient that he just so happened to be your type," Rahmi said, a teasing, shit-eating grin on his face. He picked up the cutlass and the set of daggers from the desk, strapping them quickly to his belt. Relief fluttered through him at the change in conversation, one that he wasn't sure Alaric would allow. More often than not, Alaric didn't let things slide. "I saw the way your hands tightened around him when I threatened to execute him. I—"

A shout emanated from the deck below, one that had Alaric and Rahmi glancing at each other in alarm. They thundered from the cabin a moment later, Rahmi tossing open the door and letting it hit the wall with a loud *bang*. He squinted against the deluge of sunlight reflecting brilliantly off the calm sea. Sweeping his gaze over the quarterdeck, it didn't seem any chaos required reining in.

But one of his crew, Dagwood Thorpe, a middle-aged man with salt-and-pepper hair chopped close to his skull, thumbed in a gesture over his shoulder at the question Rahmi hadn't yet voiced. "The berth," he shouted over the *thwap* of the sails, his hands gripped tightly around the rope as the men to his right and left tied it in place. "A card game." He returned his attention to the rigging, grunting as the rope slipped from his grip and hauled him forward. He caught himself with an expert foot against the mast.

Rahmi's eyebrows snapped together, and he frowned. It was the middle of the day, and while he knew that card games were popular in the late night hours, it was rare that the night crew was still awake. He crossed to the hatch that led to the berth, his boots splashing in the puddles made by the men scrubbing the deck, and clomped down the wooden stairs.

It took another moment for his eyes to adjust from the afternoon brightness to the dim, windowless cavern of the berth. While the lanterns were already lit and swung against their sconces, there wasn't enough light to give the space more than a dull, orange glow fragmented by the dozens of hammocks hanging from the ceiling. While some men still slept, their hats pulled tightly over their eyes and cotton stuffed into their ears, a gathering toward the back of the berth immediately caught Rahmi's attention.

Four men sat around the old round table, its legs long gone and its surface propped up by three crates. When the fifteen men in the crowd shifted just enough to create a gap, Rahmi spotted the familiar red dress and flow of dark hair, delicate forearms braced against the edge of the table. She had pulled on the spare pair of boots Shirin found for her, their heaviness in direct opposition to the lightness of her dress.

"Did your mothers tell you that it's okay to cry?" Kalia said, laying down the cards she had in her hand, a probing, smug smile on her lips. The men seated groaned again as one of them slammed his cards on the table, letting out a shout that was nearly identical to the one Rahmi heard from his office. "Apparently not," she mused, reaching forward to swipe the small pile of pipe tobacco and silver coins to join her growing collection. "Better luck next time."

The man who had yelled, a younger man named Hollis Bane, stood abruptly from his seat and pointed a thick finger in Kalia's direction. "You cheated," he snarled at her, his reddened face contorted with rage. "I *know* that you cheated."

Kalia didn't flinch as she gathered the cards, shuffled them a few times, and began to deal them back to the remaining men. "Alternatively, you're a terrible player with no understanding of when you shouldn't go all in on your hand." She glanced down at her new set of cards. Directly behind her, Elodie bit the nail of her forefinger.

Hollis stormed away from the table, leaving behind all of the coins and pipe tobacco he had lost to Kalia, and breezed past Rahmi to take the steps two at a time. He hadn't even seemed to notice his captain was there. No one had, not yet.

Rahmi watched closely as Kalia's eyes darted down to her cards and back up to each man, her gaze clouding over just enough that he had to bite his lip to keep from chuckling. He knew that look. Had seen it aimed at him a time or two in the last few days. And he had an instinctual feeling that she was hustling his men, a sorceress of secrets indeed. Rahmi recognized Reshef on Elodie's other side. He bent down to whisper something in Kalia's ear, who promptly waved him off and set down her first card.

The next hand proceeded, the stakes increasing with every new card draw. The winnings pile in the middle of the table grew, and it didn't take long for the final three men to eye it hungrily. Rahmi knew what things that kind of currency would buy on his ship— days off, extra stew at dinner, more *fion* when the barrels were close to running dry. And from the way Kalia seemed to skillfully weave in and out of each man's mind, she must have realized that, too.

When she laid her final card, the three men groaned again, and another one fell to her hustle. Kalia reached forward and slid the pile toward her, no longer bothering with the self-righteous smiles, as a second man rose from the table and threw his cards down. Rahmi knew it would take him weeks of gambling to earn back what he had just lost.

Rahmi had been around long enough to know that he could spot a con faster than he could spot the king's prized warship against the horizon. And he had indeed seen enough out of Kalia.

He stepped forward, shouldering through the multitude of men before coming to the seat that had just been occupied. He felt the stares of his crew on him—he had never ventured down here to participate in a card game before—and dropped into the empty chair just as Kalia finished shuffling the cards. If he were right, which there was no doubt in his mind that he was, this should be quick.

"Deal me in, *ruehi*," Rahmi purred, leaning forward to place his elbows on the table.

"Are you sure that's wise, captain?" Kalia retorted, though she still included him when she began to deal the cards. "We all need something to bargain with." Her green eyes slid to his lap, and she regarded it with the utmost disdain. "I'm not sure you have much to offer."

Rahmi concealed his agitation with a smirk as mutterings and chuckles broke out within his surrounding crew. "Cock jokes, both charming and ladylike. Come on with it, then, unless you're afraid. If I win, you have to work in the galley for the rest of the time you are aboard my ship."

"And if I win?"

Rahmi's smirk deepened, and he watched as her eyes shifted to the single dimple on the left side of his mouth. "If you win, I'll take you to shore right now."

Kalia's hands faltered as she dealt the last of the cards, and he felt a worm of pleasure threatening to overtake him as her gaze darted upward to connect with his. "You're lying."

"I'm not," Rahmi replied, picking up his cards and looking them over. As if on cue, he felt her power begin to needle into his mind, and he slammed the steel door shut, severing the bridge between them. He swallowed his chortle at the apprehensive look on her face. "You should know, I'm not sure I ever want this to end. Especially if it means not having those little moments like last night."

The crowd jeered as Kalia huffed a breath, though he didn't miss the squirm of discomfort as she looked down at her cards, then lifted her eyes to look at the back of his as if she could see right through them if she tried hard enough. She shifted her sight to Searle, the man to her immediate left, and Rahmi watched as her stare went a tad hazy before clearing again. She set down her first card, keeping the rest tucked tightly to her chest.

"I've never felt so wanted. I think the first thing I do will be to use my winnings and hire a crew of my own," Kalia said sweetly as Thorne, the man to her right, set down his first card. "I haven't forgotten my promise."

"To kill me?" Rahmi asked in confirmation, setting down his card. Searles thumbed through his stack before laying one down, and Rahmi reached forward to take the hand. "I hope you haven't forgotten already. It's been the most exciting thing to happen to me in decades."

"I just need to get back to my roots," Kalia responded, laying a card on the table. "Stabbing isn't usually my thing."

Rahmi flicked up his gaze, locking eyes with her over the tops of the cards. "What is your *thing* then? What should I expect from you?"

She didn't respond, letting her stare intensify as she laid down her hand.

Kalia had won the second set. Searles won the third. Rahmi won the next three, much to Kalia's chagrin. Rahmi felt her assaults on his mind, still steel-trapped against her attempts. And she was becoming desperate.

A thin sheen of sweat glistened against Kalia's hairline as her eyes slid from Rahmi to Thorne to Searle and back again. Searle was the first to lose, his hand of cards deposited in the middle near the ever-growing pile of coins and pipe tobacco. Rahmi had even flicked in a few silvers to appease the grumbling men at his back—men who didn't believe the captain should be down in the berth gambling with the crew.

But Rahmi had a point to prove, and as he laid down his final card, sending a saccharine smile to Kalia, he made it.

Rahmi reached forward and pulled the pile of winnings toward his end of the table, most of it from Kalia's now dwindled stash, divvying it up between the men who had already lost it. "I expect Elodie to show you to the galley starting this evening. I like my stew on the saltier side so that you know." If looks could kill, Rahmi would have been dead on the floor. He reached into the remaining pile, grabbed a coin, and flipped it into the air before tossing it to Kalia. She caught it in between her palms.

"Oh, and *ruehi*?" Rahmi tacked on just as Kalia rose from her seat. "If I hear you using your magic to hustle my men again, I'll lock you in the brig until you forget what the sun feels like on your face."

Kalia rolled her eyes, and it took significant effort for Rahmi not to react. "You're coming up with an awful number of rules," she merely drawled in response, slipping that mask of indifference back onto her face.

"Only for you, it seems."

CHAPTER SIXTEEN

KALIA

The nightmares had returned.

Kalia didn't know if it was the stress of her newfound life or involuntarily leaving her old one behind, but they had returned. Her dreams were filled with shouting female voices, the angry, muffled sobs of a small boy, the sharp *zing* of swords leaving their sheaths, and a loud cry before the world turned bloody and dark. Soon after, Kalia began walking her path alone, without a family and the safety of a home.

She woke with a start that night, breath sawing her throat as she sat up in bed, a hand clutching tightly to her chest. It took a moment for her mind to realize where she was and another for her to blink the foggy vision away. When she finally did, she noticed Elodie seated in the chair at the door and Shirin staring at her from bed.

Kalia swallowed and pressed her palms into the corners of her eyes before lifting her hands to her brow, wiping the clammy sweat away from her hairline. Her heart still hammered, quivering her already queasy stomach. Blowing a breath, she reached over and lifted a shaking hand toward the porcelain pitcher to pour herself a glass of water.

It was empty.

Swearing under her breath, Kalia tossed the quilt to the side and swung her legs over the edge of the mattress. She needed some air, some water, *something* to get her through the roaring headache and the endless stream of nerves that blasted through her veins, coursing through her like a pulsating, ice-covered monster.

"Are we going to ignore that you were just thrashing around like a fish out of water?" Shirin asked, her brown eyes still settled heavily on Kalia's face. "Or are you going to tell us what that was about?"

Kalia picked up the pitcher from the end table, letting it dangle at her side. She bounced it against her thigh in tune with the ship's swaying in the waves. Above them, the overnight men scuttled over the quarterdeck, their muffled shouts still sounding through the floorboards. She swallowed the thrumming tension and fixed a cool mask on her face.

"There's nothing to tell," Kalia replied, crossing her arms over her chest, the pitcher still hanging by the tips of her fingers. "I was just dreaming about Doc's fish stew. It came to life."

Her first night working in the galley and seeing Doc's cooking process solidified Kalia's resolve never to eat anything from the head chef, even if that meant starving. The one good thing she could glean from the galley was the crates of apples and root vegetables she could use to make an escape stash. She may have snuck a few on her way out and hid them with the single coin Rahmi tossed her after the card game.

Fucking bastard.

Shirin's sardonic snort of laughter was unladylike enough that Kalia instantly flashed back to it. Still, Elodie's the madam laying her whip across her back when she had done something similar, but Elodie's innocent, doe-eyed gaze only widened.

"You were moaning. It sounded sad," Elodie piped up, grimacing slightly as she shifted in her seat. "You were saying *momma* or *mommy*. It was hard to tell at first, but—"

Kalia felt her nostrils flare as she took in a deep, noisy breath. She curled her hand around the pitcher's handle hard enough that a piece of the chipped porcelain dug into the creases of her fingers. "I said there is nothing to tell," she replied coldly. Elodie shrunk away from the bite in Kalia's tone.

"There is no reason to get upset with us," Shirin snapped back, swinging her legs over the edge of the bed. "We're just trying to talk to you. We've found it's helpful to get things off of your chest if you—"

"Is this the part where you say *all you need is love*? Or y*ou can do anything as long as you have friends by your side*? How about *keep pushing yourself, no matter how tough it gets*?" Kalia interjected, turning to square her shoulders toward Shirin, who had stood with her feet planted wide, color rising into her cheeks. "Because I think I'll skip that, thank you very much. I don't accept empty platitudes, especially from people I don't know."

Elodie huffed a quiet, wounded sigh that bordered on pity, but Shirin's direct stare and set jaw lacked any discernable warmth. Kalia returned it with ease.

"She's the one that's got to be stuck here, El," Shirin finally went on after a long moment, waving a dismissive hand toward Kalia as she broke the eye contact. "It isn't any of our business if she would prefer to be sacrificed to Liddros instead of healing her guilt. You and I will have moved on, and she will be here still lamenting about the world being unfair, and *if only she had one more person to scream at, it would all be better*."

Kalia glowered, opening her mouth to send a storm of insults toward Shirin, but Elodie stood from the seat to step in between the two women with a difficulty that caught Kalia's gaze.

"It's okay, Shirin," Elodie managed to say, her face contorting into a grimace of pain she could no longer hide. She leaned over to desperately grab onto the foot of the nearest bed, her hand sinking into the mattress as she struggled to remain upright. "Do you remember when I came on this ship? I didn't speak for—" She let out a hiss as a hand flew to her lower back, and she nearly collapsed back into the seat. Shirin wound a gentle arm around Elodie's waist, attempting to guide her toward the chair.

"You should sit," Shirin said, her brows furrowing with concern as she looked over Elodie. "It's been a distressing day; you don't need to—"

"Are you hurt?" Kalia asked, though her tone was markedly sharper than she meant it. Shirin bristled as Kalia curved a path around the three beds, coming to a halt in front of Elodie. "What happened?"

Elodie sucked in another breath, one that whistled between her clenched teeth, as she straightened her hunched shoulders. "It's nothing, truly," she began, but Shirin cut her off.

"It isn't nothing. That *monster* and no one came to your aid..."

"Shirin, I'm *fine*—"

"You are not *fine,* Elodie. You can barely stand up straight."

"It won't take too long to—" Elodie didn't finish her sentence, interrupted by her cry of pain. Her knees buckled, forcing Shirin to tighten her grip around Elodie's waist.

"What is wrong with you?" Shirin snarled at Kalia, who was already removing the finger she had prodded into Elodie's lower back, but Kalia wasn't listening. Balancing the water pitcher on the foot of the bed, she was busy tugging on the laces of Elodie's stays, loosening the garment enough to peek through the sheer fabric of her shift. "What are you— oh, Elodie..."

Shirin peered over Elodie's shoulder, her horrified stare locked on the purpling bruise that swelled Elodie's lower back and left flank. Elodie dropped her chin, and Kalia knew she had begun to cry from the thickness of her voice when she said, "I didn't want you to know. It was...I was coming back from the galley and—"

This time, it was Shirin yanking at Elodie's garments. The loosened stays tumbled to the ground, followed by the stained skirts, and Elodie shivered as Shirin pulled up the hem of the shift, her skin pebbling against the stale air of the lower deck. It wasn't the flash of pale, bare skin that drew Kalia's attention, but the defined boot print stamped in a painful shade of blue across Elodie's body.

The three were silent, save for the small sobs that had begun to shake Elodie's shoulders. Kalia didn't necessarily *like* the woman. She was young and naïve. She was nosy and unsophisticated. But Kalia knew what kind of man had done this to her, what variety of men had *allowed* this to go on. The roaring in her ears was no longer from the crashing of the waves against the hull, and the tenseness in her jaw had nothing to do with the argument she was readying to have with Shirin. Pure hatred coiled in her belly, gripping the edges of her and preparing to spring free.

"Why didn't you tell me it was this bad?" Shirin asked, her fingers brushing over the tender pattern. Even with the feather-light touch, Elodie winced.

"Who was it?" Kalia's question was a whisper, so deadly quiet that Shirin lifted her gaze twice from the wound.

Elodie sniffled, glancing over her shoulder to look at Kalia and Shirin. She blinked slowly at whatever she read in Kalia's eyes. "I—I..." Elodie started before trailing off. She inhaled a shaking breath, her chest rising slowly as she filled her lungs. "It doesn't matter. He had his fun. He'll leave me alone now." Her eyes brimmed with tears, and each one glistened in the dim glow of the candlelight as they dripped onto her heated cheeks.

"I didn't ask if he had his fun. I didn't even ask if you think he'll leave you alone. I asked who it was."

Shirin's swallow was audible as she fixed her stare on the dark shadow that had eclipsed Kalia's face. A series of heartbeats passed as the two stared at one another before, finally, Shirin curtly nodded her head once. She slid her gaze back to Elodie.

"We should go to the captain, El," Shirin began, but Elodie violently shook her head, grimacing again when the movement twisted her back.

"Y-you know th-that will j-just make it w-worse," Elodie said through tears. "Ralston, he..." She trailed off, her body stiffening as she looked at Kalia.

Kalia tipped her head, quirking an interested brow. "Who is Ralston?"

Elodie turned on the toes of her boots, ripping the hem of her shift from Shirin's hands. She clamped her fingers around Kalia's forearm, her cheeks paling considerably. "Oh, gods, he's—he's no one, Kalia. Don't think about it. He's dangerous, he—"

Kalia swapped a look of indifference with Shirin, who seemed on the verge of storming from the small room herself but only shook her head. "One way or the other, I'm going to find out who that is. You can tell me now, or I can figure it out myself." *One way or the other, Ralston was going to pay.*

Shirin's eyes grew darker as she narrowed them on Kalia. "Why?"

Kalia leveled her calm gaze on Shirin, taking in the tangled braid still matted from sleep and the frown lines that etched the sides of her mouth. "Because even you two helpless pairs of wet stockings should feel safe."

The corner of Shirin's lips curled into a half-smile as though she appreciated the quip, but Elodie wasn't nearly so convinced.

"What are you going to do?" Elodie whispered shrilly. Her trembling chin and overly bright eyes only made her look smaller, and Kalia felt her spirit squeeze at the sight of it—that damn empathy.

Kalia used two fingers to scoop up the porcelain pitcher again, letting it dangle precariously in the air by the handle. "I just want to have a chat," she said.

The berth was louder than usual, thanks to the calm sea keeping the quarterdeck crew at a minimum. One of the men had left the hatch above the staircase ajar, allowing the breeze to waft in. It cut through the otherwise stifling room with the precision of a sharp knife and cleared the stale stench of the lower deck in the process. Kalia stepped out of the shadowed hallway and into the long room, Shirin and Elodie tight against her heels.

A group of men gathered near the far wall, their low chuckles heard through the conglomeration of swaying hammocks and discarded piles of dirty laundry. In the opposite corner, a woman was on her knees before another pirate, his head titled back to rest on the ship's framing. A guttural groan worked its way up his throat as he came. One of the men faked a theatrically loud moan, another round of raucous laughter filling the berth.

The woman pulled away from his cock with a soft *pop*, wiping the corners of her lips as she stood. A silver coin was dropped into her outstretched hand— payment for a job well done. She turned back toward the men, beckoning the next one forward with the curl of her finger.

Working at the brothel had numbed Kalia to the sight of women exchanging their services for coins, but the thought of them doing it on the pirate ship...

"It's their choice," Shirin muttered over Kalia's shoulder, seemingly reading the unasked question that clouded her mind. "They were allowed to house with us. Some had, for a while anyways."

Kalia recognized Cora, the woman she had come across in Rahmi's private cabin a few days before, as she emerged on the staircase, her dark hair tousled and tangled. A smirk appeared on her lips when she locked her gaze with Kalia, and Kalia had to refrain from rolling her eyes. Cora sauntered past, her grandstanding gait reminding Kalia of the peacocks she saw strutting through the palace gardens when she had made a trip with the madam as a teenager.

She briefly wondered how often Cora had landed on her back in the captain's quarters to feel she had the right to flounce around the ship like that. With a zip of irritation Kalia couldn't entirely control, she shoved a kernel of her power toward Cora, just enough for a flash of a vision to spark down the bridge. One of Cora being pleasured by the rotten tentacle of a dead squid. Kalia made sure to add in the sour, fishy scent just for extra measure.

Cora stumbled, tripping over a set of boots she hadn't seen. Kalia didn't bother watching to see if Cora recovered, instead turning back toward Shirin to ask, "Which one is Ralston?"

From the corner of her eye, Kalia saw Elodie begin to wring her hands, her pale face shining in the slivered light that managed to slide through the hatch above the staircase. "This is a terrible idea..." she began, but just as quickly clamped her lips shut at the look Kalia shot at her.

"He's there," Shirin answered as she leaned against the wall, jabbing her chin toward the far corner where the men had gathered. "In the dark tunic, blonde hair. Has a stare that makes you want to put on every article of clothing you own."

"With the smug smile and is looking over this way?"

"That's the one," Shirin replied. She casually picked at her nails as her gaze flicked back to Kalia and the pitcher she still held in her hand. "You said you just wanted to *talk*, right?"

"Mmmhmm," Kalia countered, further stepping into the berth. The men lifted their hungry gazes at her sudden appearance, their eyes roving the thigh-high slit in the satin red dress. "That's one way to put it."

"Kalia," Shirin said sharply as Elodie let out a shrill squeak from the back of her throat, but Kalia took another hurried step forward to avoid their scrabbling fingers. "*Kalia.*" One hand clawed into her shoulder, but she easily slipped from it.

It was effortless to ignore them as she pressed further into the berth, her stare locked Ralston. His oily smirk reminded her of Cranford Reed, and she remembered watching Mintie crawl down the grand staircase, blood smearing on the marble behind her. Never again, Kalia had told herself. *Never again.* These preening assholes would never learn, not if she didn't teach them.

Ralston's gaze flickered away from her only once, looking around in sudden disbelief that the newest woman on the ship would have her eyes set on him. Kalia tugged on a honey-sweet smile as she approached him, one she had learned from watching Nadine work, and Ralston reached out a hand to set in the crook of her neck.

Kalia tempered back the shudder of disgust that threatened to cannon up her spine. He must have taken her reaction as one of shy nerves because he let out a huffed, uneven laugh.

"You're a right sight to behold," Ralston started, tilting his head down to look her in the eye. "I'm sure nothing good can come from you." Low bouts of laughter echoed around them, chuckles from the men who had turned their attention away from the two women still on their knees across the berth. Ralson's hand slid from her neck, his calluses pricking at the skin of her shoulder. "What do you say we go somewhere a little more private? I'm sure you don't want to be heard the first time you scream a man's name."

"Not that there's much privacy, girl," another man said. "We'll hear you wherever you are. I can promise you that."

The men around them laughed again as the tips of Ralston's fingers glided along the edge of Kalia's hand before lacing it with his own. He began to pull her toward the hallway, where Shirin and Elodie still stood in waiting, but Kalia firmly planted her feet.

"Just one thing," Kalia countered, biting her lower lip as she took a small step back from him, keeping her hand tightly wound within his.

Ralston's eyes flashed, anger replacing blind lust at her defiance, but he leaned a shoulder against the nearest wooden framing pole to showcase his casual appearance. "And what's that, lovely?"

Kalia didn't waste another moment before swinging the porcelain water pitcher upward, slamming it against the underside of his jaw. Ralston let out a shout as the pitcher cracked against him a second time, this one catching him in the nose. He fell to his knees. Blood splattered and teeth scattered to the floor, plinking on the wooden planks like grotesque water droplets.

The men let out shouts of protest, jeers, and sneers echoing through the berth as they reached to draw their cutlasses. But Kalia smashed the pitcher to the ground, allowing the porcelain to shatter, before crouching beside Ralston. She picked up the nearest piece and shoved the sharp edge into the column of Ralston's throat, forcing the flow of blood to bisect the porcelain and run down her hand. In another breath, she stopped the men in their tracks with a flash of her power, freezing them in place with a vision of her own making.

"I saw what you did to Elodie," Kalia said calmly, brushing a strand of hair from his sweat-covered forehead. He reeled his head back, knocking it painfully against the wooden pole behind him. "I saw that bruise you and your boot left on her back." She shoved the porcelain piece in further, and Ralston winced. "You touch her again, and I'll be back. And I'll do worse than this."

Kalia stood, wiping her hand on the front of his tunic and dropping the porcelain piece to the ground. It clattered next to him, and he lifted his murderous stare long enough to bore a promise of retribution into her own. Kalia withdrew her power, and the men stumbled as they lurched forward, one tripping across a worn rug and landing with an *oof* on his stomach.

But Kalia had already stepped over Ralston and wiped the blood from her hand onto the back of his tunic. She swept past Reshef, who was peeking over the edge of his hammock, a sly grin curling the corners of his lips. She ignored him, too.

"You have immense amounts of power," a male voice called from the staircase, and Kalia glanced over her shoulder to see Rahmi had been watching from his perch on the bottom step, Alaric nestled behind him. Presumably, they had heard the shouts of the men from above. "I'm surprised you didn't use more of your magic, djinn."

Kalia bristled at the amusement dancing in his eyes as she squared her shoulders to face him. "Do you find this funny, *captain*?" she bit back through gritted teeth. "Do you find it funny when your men attack the women on your ship? Or are you so oblivious to the go-ings-on with your crew that you didn't realize what was happening?" She jabbed an accusatory finger toward him and felt a swoop of anger that the same glittering joy had slid from his face. "Some things require a response that the other person understands, and your *crew* under-stands violence."

She pivoted on the toes of her boots, storming past Elodie and Shirin back toward the small room they shared.

The following morning, Kalia emerged from the lower decks to find the wind whipping through the sails and the sea spraying a cool mist onto her cheeks. She shivered from the cold as her gaze planted on the gathering of pirates at the base of the far mast and lifted her eyes to where they were looking.

Ralston hung from the crow's nest, his bloodied and bloated body covered in lesions that could only have been made by the barnacles on the underside of a ship.

"Is that better for you, *ruehi*?" a voice murmured in her ear, like a caress against her soul. "Keelhauling is a fair punishment on my ship."

Kalia didn't say anything as she turned away from the dead man and the captain and walked toward the hatch leading to the galley.

CHAPTER SEVENTEEN

RAHMI

"Every light should be extinguished," Rahmi ordered as he descended the steps from the stern to the quarterdeck at record pace, Alaric tightly behind him. "Every torch, every lantern, every dimly lit candle. No light should come from *The Mark of Malice* the moment we pass through the mist."

Rahmi had expertly navigated them away from the continent's coast and kept a fair distance from Kalia in the process. He hadn't even approached her in the five days since he had tossed Ralston overboard before stringing his nearly-dead corpse from the crow's nest. It was there that he died, and it was there that Rahmi kept him for three days as a reminder to the rest of the crew.

He would be lying if he said he hadn't felt shame in allowing his crew to run the lower decks. He wanted to be a just captain, allowing his crew to choose how they spent the remainder of their time healing from guilt. More than anything, he wanted them to make the *right* choice.

But Rahmi had known how uncomfortable Shirin and Elodie felt in the berth and knew enough that he had assigned the two of them—and Cora—a spare storage closet. But Cora had split off from them nearly a decade later, and adding three more women to the ship in recent years made Rahmi believe there were enough willing participants to satisfy the men in his crew.

He didn't like to admit when he was wrong, but he knew he was wrong now. And he needed to make that apology up to Elodie, though he knew words alone would not be sufficient.

"How are you planning to sail us through, captain?" Alaric asked, his single eye widening as he clomped down the stairs after Rahmi. "The clouds covering the stars tonight are—"

"Then we go through the old-fashioned way," Rahmi interjected with a grin. He reached up to snuff out the nearest lantern with a quick pinch of his fingers. "And we use my memory of the path through the wreckage."

"And hope that is enough to get us through," Alaric grumbled.

Rahmi slid his gaze to his quartermaster, who had already pinned a longing stare on the newest crew member, Reshef. He was busy assisting Thomas in securing the sail's rope to the mainmast, his lean muscles rippling through his tunic. Rahmi cleared his throat once, then again with no response before finally knocking Alaric in the ribs with a quick elbow tap.

Alaric started, turning a sheepish look to the deck. "The Eerie Isles are not a place we want to get stuck," he went on after a moment of recovery. "Are you sure there hasn't been another ship to go down since last we've been here?"

Rahmi didn't answer for a long minute, instead turning his attention toward the wall of seemingly impenetrable mist that loomed before them.

The Eerie Isles, though named as an archipelago, was a graveyard for ships set behind a dense wall of fog. Once within the barrier, Rahmi knew he could barely see the bow of the ship from his place at the stern, but he had enough experience sailing through the waters that he wasn't worried about the sunken ships held aloft by the reefs. He hadn't thought twice about the broken masts bobbing in the sea or the rigging waiting for the next ship to tangle in.

No, what set his teeth grinding and his nerves on edge were the creatures that lived within it.

"Extinguish the lights, Alaric," Rahmi finally commanded, retrieving the small piece of wood and the carving knife from his coat pocket. "My ship pierces the veil."

Alaric didn't argue, though Rahmi knew what he was thinking from how his brow flashed to his hairline and his one eye dropped to look at the wood. Rahmi only whittled timber when he was nervous and needed to keep his hands busy. It didn't happen often, but now...

Rahmi leveled him with a look of warning as he pocketed the wood and knife and crossed the deck to the next lantern, pinching the wick just in time for the front of *The Mark of Malice* to disappear within the fog. A shudder of anxiety rippled through the men as the mist hit their faces. It was a sensation that Rahmi never quite got used to himself, the clawing and the biting. The staring, the assessing. It was as though the fog were alive, that every molecule of water was sentient and turned toward him—a monster waiting in the shadows for any flicker of light to set it free.

And Rahmi knew precisely what that monster looked like.

He took a breath, then another, as the ship glided through the veil. Turning on the heels of his boots, Rahmi clambered up the stairs, reaching for the wheel's spokes to steady their entry. There was a broken mast a few meters to their left, and an overturned keel to their right. He needed to thread the ship just enough that— yes, that would do it. Turning the ship was damn near impossible, even at their crawling speed, but keeping them on course was going to be necessary.

Rahmi spun the wheel to his right just as Alaric shouted an order from the bottom of the stairs. There was another ship they would need to avoid about a hundred meters along, but that would give him enough time to navigate past it. *The Mark of Malice* shuddered as the rudder scrapped along the side of something he hadn't anticipated, and Rahmi gripped the wheel tighter to keep it in place.

"Alaric, check the keel!" Rahmi shouted to the quartermaster, who had thrown out a hand to steady himself on the railing of the stairs. "From the feeling, it could be one of the storage rooms." He let go of the wheel, allowing it to center, before removing the wood and carving knife. He began to whittle, swallowing back the nerves that sat like a rock in his stomach.

"Aye, captain," Alaric replied, curtly nodding his head. He took off at a brisk pace, nearly avoiding colliding with someone as he went deeper into the dense fog.

There was a growl and a male shriek of panic before another figure emerged from the gray, a saccharine smirk on her lips. Another set of wool skirts had replaced the familiar red dress, though Kalia had pinned the hem to expose her legs. Rahmi let out another breath, but this one had nothing to do with creatures in the sea.

Rahmi watched as she sidled up to the gunnel, resting her forearms on the wood's edge. "You shouldn't provoke him like that," he called over to her, delighting when she jumped in surprise. "He's my second on this ship. He could have you thrown into the brig before you give him another of your visions."

Kalia straightened, strolling to the bottom of the steps. She rested one foot on the step above and paused, assessing him with a gaze that pierced him just as deeply as the surrounding fog. "I don't think he would dare," she responded, tracing the wood pattern of the railing with a finger. "Something tells me he's scared."

Rahmi couldn't argue that.

"And anyways," she went on, taking another step upward, "I felt the ship shake and came to see what that was all about. I should have known you two seaweed brains had something to do with it. But this fog is..." She glanced around, her eyes skimming along the mist.

Rahmi scraped the carving knife against the corner of the block, and a ribbon of wood fluttered to the deck. "Hiding things that, I promise, you want no part of."

Kalia finished climbing the stairs and edged to the gunnel near the wheel, peering over the ship's side. "Is that why all of the lanterns have been extinguished?" she asked, crossing her arms as she stared into the abyss of the water below. For the things that lurk in the watery grave?" Her words had a spin of sarcasm on them, but Rahmi had seen those things firsthand, and he had no interest in seeing them again.

He let another ribbon of wood fall to the deck. "I don't want to take any chances." He looked up, momentarily taken aback to see that her green eyes were now locked on him. "I've made that mistake before."

"Like the mistake you made with Ralston?"

"Yes." Rahmi's blunt answer made Kalia blink, but he went on before she could respond. "But not in the way you think." Another curled ribbon fell to his feet. "I should have stepped in long ago when the women asked for a separate room. You were right to challenge me on it. And I was right to punish Ralston the way that I did."

Where Rahmi had expected a smug, shit-eating, *I-told-you-so* grin to appear, Kalia only turned away. She rhythmically rapped her knuckles against the gunnel, brow furrowed in thought. "I've been expecting you to toss me overboard. String me up on the mast next to him," she said in a surprisingly light tone.

"Is that why you've been avoiding me?" Rahmi asked after a barked laugh. He hadn't expected to have a decent and friendly conversation with the djinn, but he would take what she would give.

"I haven't been *avoiding* you," Kalia retorted, her shoulders stiffening as though she had been caught sneaking a bag of treats before dinner. "I've just been aware of where you are at all times and have made an effort to be elsewhere."

"Call it what you want then." Rahmi reached over to grasp the wheel again, steadying it to the left. Shouts echoed from the quarterdeck, the sole indication that they weren't the only ones on board the ship. A gust blew from the east, swirling the fog in a dance of briny, water-logged scents. "I still need you. There will be no tossing you over...at least, for now."

Kalia rolled her eyes at the wink he sent her, but her gaze quickly snapped to the waves below. "I just— I just saw—" Her cheeks paled, the rosy coloring from the wind bright against the sudden paling shift under her skin.

Rahmi allowed the wheel to center again before walking over to the gunnel. He knew what she saw and didn't need to glance into the waves below to confirm it, but he did anyway. There was a flash of graying skin, water sluicing from the limb as it surfaced, and a sickening *thwack* as the body slammed into the keel of the ship.

Keeping a steady hand on the carving knife, Rahmi sliced off another ribbon of wood from the block, allowing it to drift down, down, down until it settled on the rolling waves below. They watched it silently for a series of heartbeats before a single hand, rotten and clawed, emerged from the depths. The creature captured it with one swipe, dragging it into the sea.

Kalia continued to gape at the scene that had unfolded before them, her wide eyes still fixed on the waves.

"Nasnas," Rahmi murmured, answering a question she hadn't asked. "They were once human, prisoners in the realm we're sailing toward. The ones who died while held captive there turn into—" He trailed off to gesture below. "They usually stick to themselves, preferring to stay beneath the surface. But they're attracted to light."

"Hence the lanterns." Kalia's skin had turned clammy, a sheen appearing on her brow that Rahmi knew wasn't a layer of mist from the fog. She inhaled deeply, nostrils flaring. "And was this a shortcut to the prison, or do you have a horror kink that we should know about?"

Rahmi chuckled again, resting a hand on the gunnel beside Kalia's forearm. "It's the *only* way to the prison." He could feel her heat on the long edge of his pinky, and when he glanced down, he was made aware that his hand had prickled her flesh. Silence stole the space between them, and a long minute later, Kalia finally cleared her throat.

"What are you making?" she asked, moving her arm away to wave a dismissive hand toward the timber.

A rush of cool replaced her warmth, and Rahmi ignored the sinking feeling in his chest as he lifted the half-carved block into the air. "A carving of my cock for you to go fuck yourself with."

Kalia laughed as she reached over to pluck the wood from his hand, planting her elbow on the gunnel to keep it between them. She scrutinized it with narrowed eyes, but Rahmi still saw her nervous swallow when another nasnas surfaced below them. "It truly is that small. I didn't get a good enough look, but—"

It was Rahmi's turn to pluck the carving from her hand. It was the beginning of a horse's head, one that he had carved from memory before. One that was stark in his mind when he reflected on his childhood. The horse that had hauled his family's things around as they moved from dune to dune on the outskirts of Sha'Hadra.

"Do you want to see it again?" he countered instead, sliding a side-long gaze toward her. "Wouldn't want you to feel like you were missing out."

Kalia shook her head, the ghost of a smile still on her lips. She opened her mouth to retort, and Rahmi had begun to lean in to better hear her over the shouts of the men on the deck, but a particular chorus of yells caught his attention.

"No! *No, no, no!*"

Rahmi's gut hardened into lead, and bile burned the back of his throat as he launched himself down the stairs of the stern deck, landing with a heavy *thump* against the wooden planks. A flicker of light, the tiniest flame from a struck match, illuminated the deepest recesses of the fog. It was barely seen, barely glowed against the thick gray that surrounded them, but it was enough.

"Blow it out!" Alaric cried out from an unseen position. Rahmi heard his thundering footsteps, too. "*Blow it out!*"

It was too late.

Rahmi tore his cutlass from the sheath at his hip as Searles emerged from the fog, his dagger drawn and held tightly in his fist.

"How fucked are we, captain?"

Rahmi ran a hand over the top of his head, his fingertips catching in the wind-swept tangles that escaped his bun. From his periphery, there was movement on the side of the ship, and he briefly closed his eyes long enough to let a sigh escape his nose. Opening them, he turned his head to look toward the gunnel, where a wet, gray hand had planted on the flat surface of the wood.

"Fucked, Searles. If I do say so myself."

But it wasn't himself that Rahmi thought of as the hand pushed itself further onto the ship, where it became a wrist, elbow, and shoulder. No, it was where he had left Kalia in his desperation to snuff out the flame. And as Rahmi turned to look toward the staircase, unseen against the thick wall of fog, the nasnas lurched into a ferocious attack.

CHAPTER EIGHTEEN

KALIA

The Mark of Malice had gone quiet, hauntingly so. For the first time since Kalia was brought aboard the ship, she could have heard a coin drop against the deck. The flicker of light, the one Rahmi had sprinted toward, had gone out, but a chilling fear still trickled into the crevices of her chest. It froze her in place long enough that she didn't know when her fingers had begun to tremble.

The fog had become a prison, pressing on her from all directions. It caressed the exposed areas of her throat as though whispering promises of what it was readying to unleash. But she was alone on the stern deck, alone as the wheel creaked an unearthly song that only heightened the stillness around her. A stillness that was steadily broken by the whisper of wet flesh against wood slopping behind her.

With a cold, oily dread, Kalia slowly turned toward the ship's side, where rotting fingers had curled around the gunnel. The creature hauling itself aboard wasn't anything she could have imagined, even in her wildest nightmares. She got a better look at it as it slopped onto the deck, spilling into a pile of seawater that washed over the toes of her boots.

The nasnas was half a man, but not in the way of sirens or satyrs like she had heard in the bedtime stories from her childhood. No, the creature was *literally* half a man. Shaped as though someone had cleaved him from the crown of his head to the meeting of his thighs and then had lost the other piece of him long ago. The nasnas pushed itself to stand, and it was terrifyingly agile, having only one leg and one arm. It swayed with the ship's rocking, which scraped against the unknown obstacles to the left now that Rahmi was away from the wheel.

Kalia took a step back, her mouth drying despite the sea breeze and fog, as the nasnas locked its single eye onto her, cocking its head to the right. The half brain and guts sloshed inside the exposed cavity, nothing but unseen magic keeping everything from tumbling onto the deck.

She quickly realized she had no weapon as the shouts of men and the preternatural roars of the creatures rose from the mist beyond her. She took another step back as the nasnas hopped toward her, its arm stretched in front of it, a hungry glint etched onto the half-face. She did the one thing she could think of doing and prayed to the gods that it would work.

Building that tendrilled bridge Kalia had come accustomed to connecting, she pushed into the mind of the nasnas, hoping she could convince the creature to hobble over the side of the ship. Or confuse it enough with her placement on the stern deck that it fell over the edge anyway. She closed her eyes, tearing through the layers of consciousness to find something she could latch onto.

But Kalia fell into an impenetrable darkness. From somewhere above the surface she had slipped under, someone was screaming. Pins and needles pierced her flesh as though she had been plunged into a frozen lake. It was pain, unimaginable pain, and it was never-ending torture. There was nothing; the creature was an abyss of mindlessness she couldn't escape. She lost the bridge in the depths, scrambling and clawing as she was dragged deeper.

She was thrown back onto the stern deck, snapping back into her own body like a band. She was flat on her back, skirts and stays soaked from the pool of salt water the creature had dragged upward.

"Wh—what?" Kalia managed to gasp, the words sawing against the soreness in her throat. *Shit.* It was she who had screamed. She glanced around, frantic to lay eyes on the creature, to keep it from coming any closer to her, but her stare landed on Rahmi instead.

His chest heaved as he dropped his cutlass to his side. The ship rocked, a sickening screech coming from the keel below. Bile rose to the back of her mouth when movement drew her gaze away from the captain, and she twisted to vomit as the head of the nasnas rolled toward the staircase, thumping down each step.

"Don't let them touch you," Rahmi growled as he grabbed the wheel, desperately turning it to the right. "We're weighing anchor until we can get them off the ship. In the meantime—" He paused to wrap a hand around her bicep and haul her to her feet before taking a dagger from his hip and pressing it into her palm. "The only way to kill them is to remove their heads."

Kalia glanced down at the dagger, the leather hilt smooth against the skin of her palm. "*This* won't take the head off of *that*."

"No, but it'll buy you time to get away. Nasnas know nothing except for what is directly in front of them." The ship lurched, and Kalia stumbled as a heavy splash echoed through the fog. "The flame is out. We shouldn't worry about attracting more of them, but we have to get the ones off the ship."

Skirting around the gray, rotten body of the nasnas Rahmi had beheaded, Kalia followed him down the stairs and into the chaos of the quarterdeck. Shrieks and screams split the night, slicing through the mist and bounding off the shipwrecks just out of sight. She looked down at the dagger once more before lifting her eyes toward Rahmi, startled when she saw that his brown ones were boring into her own.

"I gave that to you out of faith that you won't bury it in my back," he hissed, taking a step forward. "Can I trust that you'll give me that much decency?"

Kalia lifted her chin, tempering back the fear and anger his darkened glare provoked. "Fair is fair, I suppose." He had saved her, after all. It was the least she could do.

"Good." Rahmi wrapped the crook of his arm around her neck, dragging her into him as he slashed the cutlass through the air. Her cheek pressed against his tunic, and she could feel the thrum of his heartbeat on her temple. He smelled like used gunpowder and briny sweat, a faint hint of spiced cinnamon underneath it all. Behind her, something heavy fell to the deck with a *thud*. "If your plan is still to kill me, dare to do it while I'm facing you." His voice ghosted against the shell of her ear.

She pushed away from him, a sneer curling her upper lip, "I haven't forgotten." A gunshot fired, the sharp ring rattling her eardrums.

Whipping around as Rahmi reached for her again, Kalia watched with horror as the closest nasnas swiped a mottled hand in her direction, the hefty claws missing her by a hair's width. It let out a strangled roar, hobbling toward them on one unsteady leg. Another blade cut through the smoke and fog, the metal glinting against the moonlight that slivered through a break in the clouds.

The blade sliced clean through the neck of the nasnas, sending the head rolling toward the deck. Kalia glanced up to send a grateful look toward the person who had leaped in, but the man's eyes were wide and shocked. The body of the nasnas had fallen back onto him, the corpse colliding with his chest. Kalia stepped forward, unsure how to help, but Rahmi pulled her back. All she could do was watch as the man's face contorted into a silent scream. Dust trailed from his fingers, wrist, and forearm before his entire body disappeared in a hazy cloud. Only his clothes remained, crumpled into a pile on the ashy sand.

"Don't let them touch you," Rahmi repeated, his voice low and gruff.

Kalia's gaze darted around, and it registered for the first time that the remaining men fighting on the deck were layered in the white dust, piles of clothes haphazardly strewn about the deck.

"Kalia!"

She didn't have time to respond. In the span of a heartbeat, two hands shoved her back, and she was sent stumbling across the deck. Hands scrambling to catch anything that would keep her from falling, she twisted as her boots caught in the ropes coiled against the bulwark. But the push had been too hard, and she stumbled too fast.

Someone screamed her name again as she tumbled over the gunnel, pitching headfirst into the fog surrounding the ship.

Time ticked as Kalia fell. It could have been a hundred minutes; it could have been a hundred seconds. It wasn't until she breached the icy waves below that she knew the mindlessness of the nasnas did feel like drowning.

She was being stabbed, she could have sworn it, and the coldness of it sank into her chest. The sudden rush of freezing water made her brain momentarily stall. Her woolen skirts, made to keep her warm in the harsh sea winds, only dragged her further into the depths. Cracking her eyes open and ignoring the burning from the salt that followed, she couldn't even see how far the surface was.

If Kalia was even facing the surface.

There was no indication of which way was up or down. She thrashed, kicking her legs to gain momentum over the current, but the coiled rope had fallen with her. It wrapped around her ankles and calves, tangling in her sodden skirts. Panic flashed through her, and her racing heart did nothing to lessen the burn that built in her chest.

She needed to breathe. *Oh gods*, her lungs were on fire. There was a final gasp playing at the back of her throat, one that she knew would be her doom if she couldn't...if she didn't... She might not have the choice. Her mind was numb, her chest was screaming out, and there was no way to stop the heaving gulp that would only flood her lungs with seawater.

Something heavy plunged into the water behind her, and an arm wrapped around her waist. Kalia's mind went fuzzy, the corners of her thoughts beginning to blacken and wither. She was being pulled to her left, but it was too slow, and it would be too late.

They stopped, and Kalia lay suspended in the sea. Her skirts were torn off, quickly followed by her stays, and the rope around her feet was tugged at. It must have been too knotted and tangled because the person abandoned it a moment later. She moved easier through the water without the heavy wool layers weighing her down, but it still wasn't fast enough.

Kalia sucked in a breath, one that filled her mouth and chest with sea foam and water, just as her head broke through the surface. She coughed and gagged as the air— *had anything been so precious to her before?* — graced her cheeks. The briny water burned her throat as she vomited, but that arm around her waist remained steady and unyielding.

The waves washed over her, plastering her hair further to her head, and Kalia didn't know where her tears ended and the sea began. She finally turned her head toward the heavy breathing that echoed into her ear, the weight of her body making her feel muddled.

"I've got you, *ruehi*," Rahmi said, tightening the grip around her as they bobbed in the sea. He jerked his head, a poor attempt to clear the water-logged locks of hair from his brow, but only showered Kalia with droplets that stuck in her eyelashes. "I've got you."

Her teeth clacked together, and her entire body shuddered, but Rahmi's grasp on her never faltered. He lifted a hand, swiping the locks that clung to her lips and temples. Did he always have a dimple on his right cheek when he frowned? She knew about the left one. She hadn't noticed the right one before. Nor had she spotted the freckle that had taken up residence just on the outside of his nostril until that moment.

A rope fell from above, hitting the waves with a loud *splat*. "Captain! Grab ahold! We'll pull you up!" The voice came from impossibly far away, and when Kalia squinted, she could barely make out the gunnel of the ship through the thick, rolling fog.

"You— you came after me," Kalia started, the cold threatening to strangle whatever she had left in her chest. From the worrying look Rahmi tore over her face, she wondered if her lips had already tinged a dangerous color of blue.

Rahmi loosened one hand from her waist to grab the rope, pulling it over to Kalia. He deftly tied it around her, looping it behind the back of her thighs so the knot he created would act as a cradle. His brown eyes sank into hers, and Kalia felt like she was again falling into the sea depths. "Yes." It was a complete sentence, and he didn't elaborate further.

CHAPTER NINETEEN

RAHMI

"I s finding Wright Thackeray that important to you?" Alaric asked, leaning his shoulder against the windows that lined the ship's stern. The heat of his body created a fog against the glass, though it didn't make much of a difference when the clouds of mist still surrounded the ship. It had thinned in the last day, though it was still difficult to see past their wake.

Rahmi sighed, lifting his head from the map he had laid out on his desk. "Thackeray has something of mine, or at least he knows where it is. I need it back if we're going to make any sense of this." He waved a vague hand over the old, water-stained parchment.

"And you think it's worth getting into the prison rather than finding another way around it?" Alaric's single blue eye leveled Rahmi with a stare. He shifted on his feet, crossing his arms over his chest just as *The Mark of Malice* dropped the anchor. The shuddering splash echoed through the gorge they had sailed through, reverberating over the shipwrecks just out of sight. "We lost thirteen sailors to the nasnas. We can't afford to lose anymore."

"If we get this stone, we won't have to worry about losing anymore," Rahmi countered, placing his knuckles on the desk's surface to bracket the map. He scoured his eyes over it for the hundredth time that day. "I'm not concerned about getting into the prison. I'm concerned about getting out." His hand itched to reach toward the block of wood, the horse head taking more of a shape in the last few days.

Alaric was quiet for a moment, running a contemplative finger over his lower lip. "And say you do get out. What then? Do we remove Karim from the brig and allow him the freedom to roam the ship after he almost killed Doc in the galley?"

The map thief had become a thorn in Rahmi's side, but it was true. In his desperation to leave *The Mark of Malice,* there had been an incident involving a wooden mixing spoon, three fillets of fish, and a crate of potatoes. And after last night, Rahmi certainly wasn't going to be looking at potatoes the same way again. In the melee, Rahmi was also sure Kalia had slipped an apple or two into the top of her dress.

"Karim's usefulness is running its course, but I still need him to guide us to the correct cave once we are in the vicinity of the archipelago," Rahmi went on with a sigh. He scrubbed a hand down his face, feeling the stubble scratch against his calloused hands. "We'll only have a limited amount of time for the islands to appear, and if he is to be believed, there are hundreds of them."

Alaric looked away, jittering his foot against the floor. "And you'll be taking the djinn?"

Rahmi scraped his hand into his hair at the mention of Kalia, but he promptly ignored it. She had pushed him away when her boots hit the quarterdeck and hadn't bothered looking back to acknowledge further that he had jumped off his ship after her. He had muttered the word *atira* in her direction, most easily translated to *bitch* in his native tongue. From how her eyes narrowed at him over her shoulder, he was sure she caught the gist.

"Yes, I'll be taking the djinn. Her abilities should come in handy if we run into any trouble."

"You're awfully trusting, considering you expect her to help you infiltrate the prison, locate Wright Thackeray, and get both of you back to the ship." Alaric scoffed, shaking his head. "She's tried to kill you every chance she gets. What makes you think she'll bend to you this time?"

Rahmi smirked as he straightened. He casually picked up a brass compass and tossed it into the air, catching it in his other hand. He had seen the lengths she would go to protect others. That side of her would be an effortless target. "She's not as prickly as she likes to believe," he replied, setting the compass down with a *thunk* on the desk. "She does have some soft spots that will be easily manipulated. There's one on this very ship."

Alaric's blank stare flashed momentarily before roaming around the cabin. Rahmi tracked it with interest, watching as the quartermaster's gaze glided across the pile of parchment stacked on the side of the desk, the collection of broken quills that Rahmi had tossed in frustration into the corner of the cabin, the half-drunk bottle of *fion* precariously balanced on the armchair seat, and the single corked glass bottle of dried herbs that his mother had given him for luck when he left to join the king's navy. A crease notched between his brows as Alaric finally lifted his eyes toward Rahmi once more.

"Reshef is a valuable crew member, captain." Alaric's voice had taken on a coldness that Rahmi hadn't expected, his cheeks brightening to a red beneath his pale skin. "It would be unwise to—"

"Reshef is a means to an end, someone you brought here, and has somehow managed to worm his way into the heart of our djinn,"

Rahmi interrupted. Alaric's eyes darkened in silent response. Rahmi sucked in a sharp breath, stepping around the edge of the desk to face Alaric head-on. "We've had many years together, and you've been an excellent quartermaster to me. But if you question me in front of the crew, your authority on this ship will no longer be recognized."

Alaric's steel exterior melted into something that Rahmi couldn't identify. "What will you do with him then?"

Rahmi studied Alaric for a long minute before skirting back around the desk. "Bring Kalia to me. She and I need to discuss a few things before tomorrow comes." He sank into the cushioned seat behind him and promptly leaped back up again. Smacking a hand to the stinging burn in his left buttcheek, he twisted around to spot a series of quills protruding from the fabric of the seat. "Bring her to me *now*, Alaric." His words gritted through clenched teeth.

Alaric paused near the armchair, glancing down at the bottle of *fion* for a final time. "There's something you aren't telling us about this gemstone, captain. And as your second, I would appreciate the courtesy of your knowledge." He didn't say another word as he swept from the cabin, shutting the door with a soft *snick* behind him.

"You summoned me?" A bored voice droned from the doorway and the warmth of a spiced scent wafted in on the evening breeze.

Rahmi lifted his gaze, his eyes landing on Kalia's silhouette framed by the remnants of a golden sunset that snuck through the foggy mist. Remaining silent, he tugged a drawer in his desk open and withdrew the sea urchin from inside, gently placing it in front of him. She didn't bother to appear abashed or shameful—confirmation in his eyes.

It was the venom from the urchin that still stung the lump in his ass, even hours later, and Rahmi was having a difficult time sitting down. He willed himself to remain still, a feat he had once prided himself on but now was getting the best of him.

Kalia sauntered forward, a hint of a smug smile pressed between her lips. She stalled in front of the desk, reaching down to pinch one of the spikes between her thumb and forefinger to lift the urchin into the air. "I've been looking for this, and I thought it would make a nice pet. Thank you for finding it." Her bright eyes were positively feral with delight as they washed over him. "Where was it hiding?"

Rahmi rested an elbow on the desk, scratching the stubble on the side of his jaw. "Where did you find a sea urchin?"

Kalia shrugged, carefully setting it on a pile of parchment, where one of the spikes pierced the top document. He swallowed a grunt of irritation. "All sorts of things get pulled up with Doc's fishing nets."

He met her innocent stare with an incredulous one of his own. He would need to have an immediate chat with Doc about what he was allowing Kalia to leave the galley with. A conversation he was beginning to have weekly. "I think it's best if we removed it from the ship."

"You're probably right. It is venomous, after all," Kalia replied, her gaze roving over him as though she were waiting for him to keel over and fucking die.

Rahmi's return smile was tight. "Still won't be enough to kill me."

She looked concerningly unperturbed as she took a few steps back from him to sit on the chair's armrest behind her. "Shame."

Predator and prey, cat and mouse—that's what they were to one another. Dancing around the inevitable, both of them leaning into this merciless game that, one way or another, would more than likely end in bloodshed. It had for Rahmi already. He had the scars to prove it. And he knew that she did, too.

"And after I saved your life." Rahmi clicked his tongue against the roof of his mouth. "When I cut through the laces of your stays to free you, I felt the welts on your back. Didn't think anything of it, not until I was tying you into the rope. Those were deep, weren't they?"

A calm mask descended over Kalia's features, but from the tap of her fingers against the back of the chair and the slight tightening of her shoulders, Rahmi knew he had won. She may be an expert in the physicality of their little game, but he was the one who could play her mind. He swatted away her attempt to claw into his head, feeling her talons rake against the first layer of his consciousness.

"We've talked about that, *ruehi*," he said, sinking back into his chair to cross his arms over his chest.

"Alaric seemed upset when he came to find me. Lover's quarrel?" Kalia didn't miss a beat and showed no notion that he had successfully thwarted her. She began to pick at her nails. "What did you send him to find me for?" *Aside from the sea urchin* was the unsaid piece at the end of her question.

The indifference she showed was impressive, even for her.

"Tomorrow, we'll go into the Labyrinth of Lost Souls together," Rahmi said, watching her closely for her reaction. He didn't have to wait long.

Kalia's brow rose to her hairline, and her gaze sparkled with fresh amusement. "Oh?"

"Oh," Rahmi confirmed. He swept his eyes over the red dress she had changed back into before narrowing his focus on the way she was staring at the sea urchin still between them. Staring as though she would like nothing more than to fling it back into his face. "The prison is protected by magic. You're a djinn. You will give us the best chance of making it out alive."

Surprisingly, Kalia's smile turned brittle at the edges, just long enough for Rahmi to notice. A moment later, the overly confident, smug smirk hitched back onto her mouth. "And if I choose not to help you?"

"You'll help," Rahmi noted with a tone of assurance. "Because Reshef is coming with us. I'm certain you won't leave your friend there."

Kalia's smirk slid from her face, and the glare she set in its place was biting. "Reshef isn't a friend."

"Your repeated defense of him isn't helping your cause."

She tapped her nails, the red polish chipped and nearly gone entirely, on the back of the armchair, one ankle crossed over the other. She was seemingly deep in thought, wrestling with herself on how to respond. Finally, she let out a long sigh as she ran a hand over the length of her braid. "What are you expecting to find in there?"

Rahmi shrugged his shoulder and tried to temper the look of pure glee that came with winning his second argument of the day. He didn't want to antagonize her further—not yet, anyway. Something about her always made him want to try.

"I don't know," he answered honestly. The corners of her lips downturned, tugging her mouth into a frown that highlighted the fierce gleam in her eyes. "People go into The Labyrinth of Lost Souls. They don't come back out."

"And what do you expect me to help with?" Kalia retorted. Her fingers curled around the back of the chair, the nails digging into the faded fabric. "If we don't know what we're getting into, how do you expect me to prepare?"

"How you prepare is up to you," Rahmi said. He appreciated her beauty in that moment, appreciated how the light illuminated the green in her eyes, how her thigh peeked from the slit of that red dress. He shifted in his seat, and a new wave of pain crested from the venom still embedded in his ass. That appreciation shifted back to vigorous dislike with his next breath. "But we're leaving at the break of dawn."

"This is a terrible idea," Kalia stated as she slipped from the armrest, planting her boots on the floor. "You're going to get us all killed."

"That's a chance I'm willing to take." Rahmi cocked his head. "And it should be one you're willing to take, too. It's the only way you'll see the capital again."

CHAPTER TWENTY

KALIA

The whole thing was a terrible fucking idea. Considering that Kalia had once poisoned one of the wealthiest dukes on the continent, she had firsthand experience with what may be viewed as a terrible idea. She was itching to get off the ship, itching to return to the continent, itching to get away from Rahmi-*fucking*-Abada and his band of guilt-ridden pirates.

And she was getting desperate. Even the stash of tobacco leaves and coins she had plundered from the crew in the dead of night, now hidden in a slit in the mattress, wasn't enough to save her.

As she tossed and turned in bed that night, loud enough that Shirin let out a groan of frustration and stuffed the flat pillow over her head, Kalia considered marching to Rahmi's cabin to come clean. She would tell him she was a Voyant and say that she had no power outside of her gods-given ability to manipulate the mind.

Then she would get on her knees and beg— or whatever else he may have in mind— to convince him to let her off the ship, preferably not in the middle of the Aeglecian Sea.

But when Kalia imagined how that scenario would play out, she also imagined how his jaw would clench, and his brow would knit together. Rahmi was not a man who allowed disobedience lightly, and she had already pushed her luck a few times. She knew she was fortunate she hadn't been keelhauled and strung from the crow's nest alongside Ralston.

And that was if Rahmi didn't return her to the capital, only to sell her to the king. A shudder ran up her spine. She had heard of Clairs being sold to the palace and how the crown enslaved men and women with gifts of mind magic to do his bidding, to warm his bed.

Kalia distinctly remembered hearing one from Pete about a young girl with the ability to shift the emotions of others. She had lived a handful of blocks from the bordello and used to skip on the cobblestones, careful not to step on the cracks between the stones. Pete had always said he would remember her bouncing, blonde curls for the rest of his days.

Pete had woken one morning to the news that she had been stolen from her family in the middle of the night. The only clue to her whereabouts was a single eagle feather on the kitchen table. The king's calling card. She had never been seen again.

Kalia never shared her true story with Pete, but he had brought up flashbacks of world-ending screams, begging that turned to sobs, blood splashing on the clay-tiled floor that had just been scrubbed the day before. That was always a detail that she remembered. And she had nightmares for days after Pete's bleary-eyed confession.

She reflected on the sea urchin and the mask of irritation Rahmi had struggled to pull over his features. Would it be possible to *annoy* him into letting her off the ship? She considered it for a moment. She may end up in the brig, but it would be better than death. Or to be used as the king's plaything.

Kalia let out a long sigh, flipping over once again to stare at the ceiling of their small room, the bed creaking loudly underneath her. Thanks to the lock Rahmi had installed on the door, Elodie was asleep, but Kalia's mind was too busy coming up with every possibility for tomorrow.

She had no idea what to expect and couldn't even begin to prepare. Rahmi didn't seem to have any idea either.

Kalia sighed again, but Shirin gave a sleep-filled grunt this time and whipped her pillow at Kalia.

Dawn hadn't entirely broken when Kalia stepped onto the quarter-deck, the sudden shift from stifled, stale air to the fresh breeze startling. The impenetrable wall of fog still surrounded them, and the haze that slid over the unknown landscape curled eerily against the gentle waves that lapped at *The Mark of Malice*.

The mist only seemed to magnify the salty scent of algae that must have been coating the nearby shipwrecks, and the cold, dewy sensation against her skin sent her shivering.

The only indication that it wasn't quite morning came from the breaks in the clouds, where Kalia could spot the spackling of stars against the navy sky. Streaks of golden orange had begun to paint the mist's underside, dimming the moon's silver light. The stars started to blink their exit, bowing to the glimmering warmth of the sun that certainly wouldn't be felt on the ship.

"All right, Kalia?"

The voice was an unexpected break against the quiet, creaking from the masts, and it forced her attention away from the beads of water that collected on the gunnel. Reshef approached her, his boyish, brown eyes dancing with joy as he bit into the apple he was carrying. She crossed her arms over her chest, watching the black stone necklace sway in the hollow of his collarbone.

"You're cheery," Kalia replied, catching the second apple Reshef tossed her. She wiped the waxy exterior against her dress before sinking her teeth into the fruit. It was sweet, if not a little bruised, but it would do the trick. It was better than the leftover fish stew Doc had forced on everyone. And Kalia was not convinced that eating fish from this part of the sea was exceptionally healthy, considering what else lurked beneath.

Reshef leaned an elbow against the gunnel as he took another crunching bite. "I heard you and I are going on an adventure today."

A pair of men trundled onto the deck as if on cue, wiping away the sleep crusted at their eyes' corners. They headed directly toward a set of rowboats tethered against the ship's side, yanking at the ropes holding them in place. One of them fell to the sea with a splash, lost to the depths of the fog.

Kalia turned back to Reshef, who had regarded her with a giddy, irrepressible smile. "That's one way to put it. I'm surprised you aren't being dragged on this *adventure* kicking and screaming."

Reshef shrugged. "No point. I was told I was tagging along—"

"Used as collateral."

"And I thought, what better way to spend a morning and early afternoon than with my best friend?" He waggled his eyebrows at her, his smile only growing.

Kalia wrinkled her nose as she took another bite of her apple. "You truly believe that, don't you? That we're friends."

"*Best* friends," Reshef amended. He tossed the apple core over the side of the ship, where it bobbed in the waves briefly before being swept below by a gray, mottled hand. Kalia's stomach turned. "And if anything cemented it for me, it was your brutal beatdown of Ralston in defense of Elodie. You know, some of the men still found his teeth in their hammocks days after his execution." He ran a hand through his dark hair. "I remember thinking— *I would like to have a best friend like that*. Thank the gods I already do."

Kalia shook her head. "I don't have friends. People are only there to betray you in the end."

Reshef didn't miss a beat. "Mmm, deep. But, alas, you aren't an island. You don't need to be alone." And, as if he sensed Kalia's rising discomfort, he let his gaze drop to the half-eaten fruit still in her hand. "I bet you my serving of Shirin's bread tonight at dinner that you can't hit Brett Ike in the back with that apple you stopped eating."

Like a cat stretching after a long nap, curiosity awakened in the recesses of Kalia's mind. "Which one is Brett Ike?"

"The one bent over. Pimples that demand to be extracted, but with an odor bad enough, I wouldn't bother without three layers of fabric and six freshly cut mint leaves covering my nose."

Kalia paused, canting her chin toward the sky. "What makes it smell so bad, I wonder?"

Reshef pursed his lips, squinting at the man still bent over a set of oars, struggling to undo a tightly bound set of knots. "Doc's fish stew, wouldn't you say?" He reached up, zipping the black stone along the chain of his necklace. "Now, will you try, or will you back down? Shirin's bread is on the line."

Kalia set her feet and hitched her arm back, pinning her attention on Brett Ike's backside. Just as she readied to launch the apple into the air, a calloused hand wrapped around her wrist, and another removed the apple from her palm. She tipped her head back, unsurprised to see Rahmi's glowering face within a breath's distance away from hers.

"It's too early for you to terrorize my crew, *ruehi*," Rahmi murmured, tossing the apple over the ship's side. "Even if that one caught Reshef and Alaric in the storage bays of my ship two nights ago." He quickly withdrew his hand from her wrist, taking the heat of his palm with him. Disappointment cannoned through Kalia, though she tucked that feeling into the depths of her soul, hoping it would never surface again.

Kalia scowled at Reshef, but the man merely shrugged. "He ruined my *climax*."

"Ugh, gods, don't say *climax* like that while you're looking me in the eye."

Reshef smirked as he stepped forward, threading his fingers in Kalia's loose locks. He lightly tugged her head back, forcing the exposure of her throat. "Oh, *Kalia*," he moaned gently, a laugh taking over the tone of his voice. "*Climax*."

Kalia swatted him away, though she couldn't quite bite back the grin that stole over her lips.

Reshef removed his hand from her hair, casually leaning against the gunnel once more. If anyone were looking on, he would probably appear unconcerned that he was about to be held hostage in a prison in which no one has ever emerged. "I sense that you're a sensual creature, Kalia. When was the last time you were touched?"

"*That* is none of your business—"

"When was the last time you were touched in a way that made you *aching* for more?"

Rahmi shifted behind her, and Kalia felt his tunic brush against her bare shoulder. Her heart ratcheted at its lightness, and pleasure curled in her core. She stepped forward, putting a measured gap between them as though that could temper the tension in the pit of her belly. Reshef winked as though he knew.

Rahmi cleared his throat just as Brett Ike approached them, though Kalia noticed he didn't quite look Reshef in the eye.

"You gave him quite a fright, did you?" she muttered as Brett handed Rahmi the oars and ropes.

Reshef snorted. "I do this thing with my fingers where I put my middle one—"

"We're ready," Rahmi announced, cutting off Reshef. "Let's head to the boat."

Just as Kalia made to step forward, Rahmi grasped her upper arm. She twisted, coming face-to-face once more with him. The grip against her was possessive and intense, though she may have also imagined it. Reshef was right. It had been some time since she was thoroughly fucked. She suppressed a shudder and the sudden need to arch her back to slyly drag her nipples across his chest.

Gods, this was not the time or the place. Fuck Reshef for putting the thought in her head. And fuck Rahmi for putting her in a position where she wanted one last romp in the sheets before her inevitable demise. Kalia looked at Rahmi again.

The captain would do. He was good-looking enough. She mentally chastised herself. *Good-looking enough* was a lie she couldn't even tell herself. He was one of the most beautiful men she had ever seen. It was too bad that her attraction washed away in a cold bath whenever he opened his mouth.

Rahmi's exploring gaze flashed, and she could have sworn he pulled her closer in a claiming gesture. Kalia's skin was sensitive, her flesh tightening to her bones as his eyes darted to her mouth. His breath rushed out, fluttering the locks that framed her cheeks.

"You get us in," Rahmi said, that exploratory gaze hardening into a steel wall. "You get us out. Or Reshef is executed on the spot. Do I make myself clear?"

Kalia glared up at him, yanking her arm from his grasp. "Yes, *captain*."

Rahmi smirked, taking another step closer and bridging the small gap between them. He lifted a hand, brushing his fingertips against the underside of her jaw as though he couldn't help himself. Her skin turned molten where his fingers had been, a call from her body to his. "You should call me that more often, *ruehi*. I like how your mouth looks when you say it."

Kalia kept her eye trained on the vast, endless fog that stretched out in front of her, ignoring the sickening squelch of nasnas against the underside of the boat as they passed by. Every so often, a rotting, gray hand would tear from the surface of the water, lazily bobbing above the waves before disappearing again. She suppressed a shudder when she caught it from the corner of her eye but never turned to face it.

The rowboat, steered by both Rahmi and Reshef, slid to a crunching stop on the shore of a cove. The surf crashed against the black sand, hissing as it gently retreated into the fog. Kalia stood from her perch on the wooden slab spanning the width of the rowboat and stepped onto the beach. A second wave surged forward, spilling cool water over the toes of her boots and soaking the hem of her dress.

Glancing around, Kalia took in the smooth rock walls that stood tall against the gorge, peeks of spindly trees that grew from the cracks in the stone barely noticeable through the heavy mist. Her boots sunk into the sand as she lurched forward, licking the salt water spray from her lips. A tang of minerals and wet rock was in the air, each coated with a briny layer of mildew and algae.

Rahmi hopped from the boat, landing next to her with a sharp splash in the third wave that rolled against the shore. He bent down to grasp the front of the boat and drag it out of the water. Reshef followed, tossing the oars into the shell with a heavy clatter.

Reshef lifted his gaze, and Kalia looked over her shoulder to see him peering at the high arches of rock, his eyes trailing down to follow the water streams running down the walls. As Rahmi shouldered past him, a sea bird squawking as it flew low over the cove, Reshef quirked a sardonic brow.

"Rumor has it that you can only go ashore every seven years, captain." Reshef's tone was light, though marred by curiosity. He took several steps forward, his boots sinking into the silt. "Does this mean you're using it on us?"

Kalia couldn't help the grin that curled the corner of her lips, appreciating the twinkle of mischief in the wake of his wink.

"No," Rahmi grunted, placing a hand on the pommel of his cutlass as he walked forward, squinting against the sea spray that ricocheted from the rock wall. "Places around the continent have always been infused with the old magic of the gods. Can't you feel it?"

Kalia paused, noticing the crackle of energy against her skin and the taste of ether on her tongue. It was like a brewing storm that swept over the capital's bay or the lightning Pete always joked about bottling for his potions. It felt ancient and penetrating like the fog, watching them closely from a thinly veiled place just out of sight.

"With locations like these, it's a wonder you stay on your ship so much," Reshef mumbled, though he clamped his mouth shut with

Rahmi's scowl. His silence didn't last long. "It's the perfect vacation destination. Soft sand, the blazing sun, not a cloud in the sky—"

Kalia laughed as Rahmi approached the rock wall, his scowl deepening when he assessed it. Clearing her throat, she pressed forward, boots sliding against the sand, and stopped beside him. "I thought the king outlawed magic."

Rahmi's narrowed gaze fell to hers before lifting to plant on the wall once more. "The king is very particular about the kind of magic he outlaws. Have you never realized that he doesn't seem to age?"

Before Kalia could answer, Rahmi withdrew the dagger at his hip and wrapped his palm around the blade. A sound of disbelief rose from her throat as he split his flesh with a quick swipe of the dagger. Rahmi lifted his hand, blood dripping down the creases in his palm, and smeared it across the rock wall.

For a long moment, nothing happened. Kalia turned to send a string of sharply worded curses toward Rahmi, but the ground suddenly began to rumble beneath her feet. Sand bounced and jumped, displacing along the shore. The tremoring deepened, and she threw out a hand to steady herself, accidentally clenching onto Rahmi's forearm. His muscles tightened beneath her touch. Without warning, everything stilled.

Crumbles of rock dislodged from the arch above, falling to the sand around them. Twisted, brown roots dangled from the cracks in the stone, their swaying beginning to slow as a calm spread around them.

But the tranquility of the cove after the trembles felt unnatural, and the hair on the back of Kalia's neck rose in answer to an unasked question. Next to her, Reshef had paled. His throat bobbed with his hard swallow, and his hand lifted to his throat, touching the black stone that rested in the notch of his collarbone.

A hazy shimmer, vastly different from the fog around them, drew Kalia's attention away from Reshef. Her eyes widened as the shimmer grew lighter, webbing from where Rahmi had smeared his blood until the stone itself melted away.

Rahmi sheathed his dagger and took a tentative step toward the new doorway. "This should be familiar to you, *ruehi*. Old magic always requires a sacrifice," he said before passing over the threshold and into the darkness.

CHAPTER TWENTY-ONE

KALIA

I f Kalia felt like she was being watched on the shore, it was nothing compared to how she felt now. The narrow passage pressed in on her from all angles, and the bumpy stone walls seemed to reach toward them. Her very soul was being dissected. The passage was glacial and unforgiving, as though the walls knew she was an intruder and wasn't supposed to be there.

"Where are the guards?" Kalia whispered, though the echo of her voice still barreled into the darkness.

Reshef was tight against her back, and she could feel the shift of his tunic with every step he took. Rahmi paused as they reached the shadows, and his hand lifted to tug a wooden torch from the wall above him. With a series of scraps from the flint stone he removed from his pocket against the rock, a spark lit the end of the torch. Another moment later, a blazing flame crackled merrily along the end.

The heat from the fire washed over Kalia, chasing away the abyss and forcing it into the cave. She blinked against the light, squinting as her eyes adjusted to the shift. She could have sworn a low, angry *hiss* sounded from the walls.

"This prison doesn't require guards," Rahmi said, returning the flint stone to his pocket. "Magic is its source of containment."

They pressed in deeper, kicking aside chewed bones and trudging through the puddles from the rainwater dripping down the walls. The light from the doorway, as hazy and veiled as it was, diminished with each step before disappearing entirely as they rounded a bend. Then, it was only the light from Rahmi's torch that remained.

The cave was silent, unnaturally so. There was only a rushing quiet where Kalia expected to hear the flap of a bat's wing or the scuttle of a beetle against the rock flooring. She couldn't help but notice how the phantom sound was still loud enough to be jarring, that the *whoosh* of her heartbeat in her ears was relentless and never-ending. She focused on that and that alone as they moved forward, rounding a second bend and then a third.

Nerves settled in the pit of Kalia's belly, and she wondered what Rahmi's plan was for her. How could she fake the powers of a djinn to get them out? Or would she merely end up a pile of discarded bones scattered along the passageway by the unseen rodents?

Or worse.

Rahmi stopped in his tracks, swinging the lit torch to his left. Kalia nearly ran into his back, and Reshef did run into hers, but she was able to scramble in time to prevent any contact with Rahmi. Still, she didn't expect to see the man huddled in the carved alcove of the passage. His body curled into a fetal position on the stone floor.

Stomach threatening to leap into her throat, Kalia took a startled step back before regaining the courage to walk toward him slowly. No bars separated the nook from the passage, and it seemed the man had ample opportunities to escape his small section of the prison, though he had never dared to try. She passed over the threshold, sinking onto her knees to place a gentle hand on his shoulder.

The man twitched under her touch, and a haunted expression passed over his pallid, ashen face. His eyes had long grown milky in the dark, though he didn't squint under the bath of golden light from the torch. The odor in the small cell was acrid enough that Kalia was forced to place the back of her hand over her nose, and that scent seemed to permeate every stained article of clothing he wore.

"He's not the one we're looking for," Rahmi grunted, taking several steps away from the cell.

Kalia angrily stood, her hands balled into fists at her side. "Does that mean we should leave him here?" She gestured toward the man on the floor, and she barely swallowed her grimace when the torch illuminated the pus-filled sores that covered the skin over his joints. His mouth had begun to move, low whispers falling onto the stone floor beneath him.

"We've come for one man and one man only," Rahmi said, shouldering past Reshef to grab Kalia's upper arm. "I'm not going to risk my life to save another."

"So these men aren't worth saving?" Kalia asked, yanking her arm from his grasp. Rahmi spun on the balls of his feet and stalked down the passage. She followed him, her anger a storm cloud on the sea's horizon. "These are still *lives,* innocent—"

"These men are far from innocent, *ruehi,*" Rahmi cut in, rounding on her. The torch high above her head placed the angles of his square jaw in stark relief. He closed the space between them and placed a finger under her chin to force her to look up at him. "These are men the king feared to put to death. Sorcerers, necromancers, mind-magic users."

Kalia straightened, though the impenetrable anger was still fastened to her face. "What does the king have to fear from a dead man?"

Rahmi curled his finger along the underside of her jawline. The smirk that pulled on the corners of his lips was knowing. "Dead men can still speak. What is magic if not energy gifted to us by those who are gone from this world?" Kalia narrowed her eyes, but Rahmi was already turning away from her. "Come, we don't have much time."

Reshef rested a heavy hand on her lower back as she glanced over her shoulder to take one final look at the man in the alcove. His milky eyes were still fixed on the threshold, unseeing and unfeeling. "You can't save them all," he murmured in her ear. Guilt settled like a weight on her heart.

Rahmi looked back once, assessing her with an unreadable stare before returning his attention to the passage.

They passed six more alcoves, each man more battered and frail than the last. One of the prisoners seemed to have recently died; his mouth slackened, and his empty eye sockets brittle at the edges. The Labyrinth of Lost Souls already claimed what it wanted from him, and that knowledge haunted every step Kalia took.

The longer she was in the prison, the more sickly she felt. The cold humidity of the underground placed a layer on her skin that she couldn't differentiate from her sheen of sweat. Every few minutes, a moan would reverberate from somewhere in the prison, the sound filled with tragic hopelessness and pain. It would claw itself against the underside of her skin, ripping out pieces of her with every passing breath.

"What did the man we're looking for do to end up here?" Reshef asked, finally breaking the silence. He bent down to avoid a stalactite that hung low from the ceiling.

Kalia slid her gaze to another person in an alcove, this one a woman with matted hair and brown, rotting teeth. She could almost imagine herself there. *Mind-magic users*, Rahmi had said. Would this be the final years of her life if the crown caught her?

"Wright Thackeray has always been a bit of a swindler," Rahmi said, dipping the torch toward the alcove to his right before moving on. "It got him on my ship in the first place. He did alright for himself for the first decade when he was released from his curse. He slipped back into old habits three years ago. It got him locked up here."

"Not a necromancer or a sorcerer, then?" Reshef replied, side-stepping another pool of water.

Rahmi snorted. "Not even close." He swept the torch to the next cell before stepping away. He paused and doubled back, sinking to a squat as he lowered the flame toward the threshold of the carved alcove. "You stupid cunt," he muttered, rising to a stand. He stepped forward and toed the edge of his boot against the man's shoulder. "I warned you about this."

Kalia peered around the captain's arm, her eyes drifting down to the man on the floor. He was in better shape than the others, though not by much. Rats had bitten holes in his clothing, which was still stained with various brown splotches that made Kalia want to breathe through her mouth. His long salt-and-pepper hair was tied in a loose ponytail near the nape of his neck, though it had long been matted and untouched. A bucket was perched in the corner, one of the only alcoves to have that, and a moldy loaf of bread sat next to his outstretched hand.

Like the other prisoners, the man made no impression that he knew three people were standing before him.

"Meet Wright Thackeray," Rahmi said. "Kalia, you're up." He motioned to her with two fingers, jutting his chin toward the old crew member sprawled against the stone.

"And do what?" Kalia asked, her voice shakier than she meant it to be. She tried to hide her wringing hands in the creases of her dress, but she knew that he had seen her nervousness from Reshef's eyes dropping to her thighs. For some reason, that thought didn't sting as much as before.

Reshef took a step forward. "Why don't we try just waking him? Is there a reason we need Kalia's magic to free him?"

Rahmi's lifted a sardonic brow. "Go ahead." He pressed his lips into a tight, unyielding line as his hand came to rest on the pommel of his cutlass.

Kalia and Reshef exchanged glances before she lightly pushed him forward. A low cough hid his scoff, but he crossed the threshold of the alcove nonetheless. He first planted a hand on Wright's thin shoulder, shaking it gently. Reshef reached down to dig his knuckles into Wright's sternum when the man didn't wake.

Wright let out a rattling snore but continued his slumber.

Reshef cleared his throat as he stood, studying Wright with a pinched expression. He finally bent down to grasp Wright's wrist, beginning to tug him toward the threshold of the alcove.

"I wouldn't do that," Rahmi cautioned as he leaned his shoulder against the nearest wall. "They won't like it."

"Who are *they*?" Kalia began, but there wasn't a need for an answer. A Crackling and ominous power rose around her. It pressed at her from all angles, piercing and cruel. This was a clear threat, unlike the intense scrutinizing of their arrival at the prison.

Rahmi crossed his arms over his chest. "I spent many years ferrying prisoners to this cave. I watched them go through the doorway and never come back out. There is a magic at play here that you don't understand. So maybe, instead of questioning me, Kalia can come forward to release Wright from his captivity, and we can leave—if we'll be allowed to leave."

Kalia felt the sweat break out on her palms as she took a tentative step forward, avoiding Rahmi's merciless scowl. She knelt beside Wright, grimacing when her knee made contact with a sharp stone just inside the alcove.

"What do you sense?" Rahmi pressed, shoving himself off the wall to stand directly behind her.

"I— nothing. There's nothing." Kalia closed her eyes, racking her brain to try and figure out what the *fuck* she was supposed to do. She felt Reshef and Rahmi's gazes boring into the back of her skull.

"Are you going to—" Rahmi started, but Reshef shushed him just as quickly. Kalia could almost picture the arrogant look of disbelief that was certainly clouding Rahmi's face.

Kalia formed a tentative bridge with Wright, ignoring the sinking feeling that she would regret what she was about to do next. Peeling back the layers of his mind, she accessed the memory with one final tear at his subconscious and tumbled to the deck of a ship.

She pushed herself up, quickly glancing around. It was undeniably the deck of a ship, that much she could see through the lashing winds and pelting hail. Even in the memory, it pierced through her dress, leaving small welts in its wake. Men scurried around the ship, and, at closer inspection, she realized with a start that they were faceless.

Except for one.

"Crew to starboard!" A man yelled from the mainmast, the drenched and slick rope clutched tightly in his hands. He struggled to tether it down, the storm washing wave after rolling wave onto the deck. "Tether it down! *Tether it—*" But he was cut off with a gasping shout of surprise as a third wave knocked his feet from under him, sending him clattering across the deck.

Kalia hurried over to where he struggled to right himself, clutching the gunnel to keep her balance, but she was too late. A fourth wave caught him in the side, and he went careening over the side of the ship. Kalia gaped at the space of the deck as the faceless men slowly made their way back to their original stations, not bothering to give a second glance at where the man had been swept over.

But Wright reappeared a moment later next to the mainmast, gasping and coughing a lungful of water. He gulped and shakily pulled himself up, using the large hooks on the mast as counterweights. He hadn't even noticed Kalia yet as he leaned a shoulder against the wood.

"It was your fault," a small, childlike voice echoed over the roaring sea, drawing Kalia's attention to the top of the stern deck.

The girl stood stark against the heavy black clouds, her white nightdress whipping around her ankles. A small handmade doll was tucked into the crook of her arm, and her eyes were rimmed red with tears. Kalia darted her gaze back to Wright, who had begun to quiver against the mast.

"Please," he begged, kneeling against the deck and clasping his hands together. "Please. It was an accident, I didn't mean to—"

"I died in this storm," the girl started again. "I—" She began to gurgle, water slipping from between her lips as she tried to draw breath.

Kalia took off toward the girl, her arms pumping and her feet pounding against the deck, fighting against the wind, rain, and rolling sea. She reached the bottom of the staircase as the girl's face turned blue, a starfish appearing just at her hairline. In the next breath, her eyes sunk into her hollowed sockets, and her skin pulled tight against her bones. A crab skittered from her open mouth, and Kalia froze with one foot on the bottom staircase.

The girl crumpled to the deck, her doll falling from her arms and sliding with the river of rainwater toward the helm.

Wright's anguished yell was strangled and dulled against the rising storm, though it morphed into one of shocking pain as a rope above him snapped. Kalia watched in horror as a chunk of the mast broke off and fell down, down, down. In a split second, short enough that she was unable to scream for him to move, the shard of wood pierced the man in the back of his neck. He immediately went limp, his head hanging grotesquely toward his chest as blood dribbled from the sharp end of the wood that penetrated the column of his throat.

Kalia swallowed hard, looking back toward the girl at the top of the stairs. She was gone. Furrowing her brow, Kalia swung her gaze back toward Wright, who had also disappeared in a shimmer of darkness. She blinked twice, at a loss for words or thoughts, just as Wright gasped to life again, this time at the helm behind her.

Taking the stairs two at a time, Kalia launched herself to the landing of the stern deck just as Wright clutched the wheel's spokes, throwing his weight against the helm.

"*Wright!*" Kalia yelled against the roaring wind. Lightning flashed above them, forking a path through the clouds. "*Wright Thackeray!*"

His eyes widened as they settled on her, as the ship dipped into the valley between two waves. "What fresh plague of Liddros has come to haunt me this time?" he yelled. He reached to his side, struggling to unsheathe his blade while attempting to control the wheel.

"What?" Kalia retorted, flinching as the boom of thunder hit overhead. "I'm not— I'm not from—"

Wright seemed to make his decision, stumbling away from the helm to aim the tip of his cutlass at her. His hand was steady despite the roiling storm that continued its march across the sky. There was no horizon in the distance, just rainfall so pronounced that it streaked the clouds. His chest heaved with every breath, eyes wild as he waited. *For her to attack*, Kalia realized. *For her to kill him.*

"I'm here on behalf of Rahmi Abada," Kalia rushed out, dodging the blade's edge as he swiped it toward her in a devastating blow. "He's in the prison. We need you to wake up."

Wright sliced the cutlass up once more, catching a pleat in Kalia's dress. It tore clean through, nicking her thigh. She hissed as she felt the warmth of her blood trickle to the surface of her skin.

"Captain wouldn't *dare* come to the Labyrinth. Not for me," he retorted, his eyes shining bright as another flash of lightning illuminated the faceless men on the deck. Kalia felt a jerk of surprise behind her navel when she realized the men had all turned to face them. "He's not stupid enough to—"

"He found a way to the *Luminaria*," Kalia rushed out as Wright whipped the blade through the air, sending her a rush of brine on a phantom wind. "He needs your help to get it."

Wright scowled, and the wrinkles in his aged face tightened. "The *Luminaria* is a children's story told to those who climb out of their beds too much. It doesn't exist. And I won't have you killing me, not now. *Not again.*"

"It does exist." Kalia hurried out of the way once more, the tip of the blade embedding in the wood of the wheel as Wright lunged for her. "I'm not here to kill you. I need you to wake up."

Wright hesitated, his stare darting back and forth between her eyes. Water dripped from his nose, catching in the white of his beard. He looked at her, taking in the earnestness in her expression. The rain still pelted against the deck, pooling in the cracks of the wood. He swallowed, and, from her periphery, Kalia spotted the crowd of faceless men slowly making their way toward the stern.

"How do we wake you up?" Kalia hurriedly went on as one of the faceless men began to climb the steps. As he drew closer, she saw that a thin layer of flesh covered the sockets of his eyes, nose, and mouth. "How do we—?"

But Wright was already rushing toward her, his hand outstretched. It gripped her arm, tugging him behind her as he slashed the cutlass toward the nearest faceless man. "You need to go deeper," he said, yelling at her over his shoulder. "If you got in, I know what you are. *Deeper.*"

His instructions may have been vague to anyone else, but Kalia knew exactly what he meant. She placed a hand on the back of his balding head and threw out the tendrils of her power, forming a bridge to his soul that she tried so hard to avoid in others. It connected them, cell to cell, dust to dust before she could see the ball of energy that resided within the depths of his mind.

It glowed brightly against the darkened recesses of his consciousness, but Kalia noticed something else immediately. Like a dead vine, a blackened spiral had crept along the outer shell. It squeezed as Wright shook around her, the corners of his mind beginning to fade into nothing.

Kalia approached the vine, wrapping a hand around the deadened spiral. She pulled as hard as she could, and the tendrilled magic suffocating Wright's ball of energy resisted. Black webbed from the vine, plunging into his soul. She pulled harder, fighting with every ounce of her power to force the vine to relinquish its grip on Wright. Above her, a dull scream of agonizing pain sounded, muffled as though she were underwater.

There was throbbing anger, shrieking fear, and sinking grief so bottomless that Kalia didn't know if it came from her or him. But the stress of the vine had finally given way, snapping like the rope on the deck. The spiral shriveled away, curling in on itself as it died.

Then Kalia was thrown from Wright's mind, and she landed back into her own body with an *oomph* against the stone of the alcove. Power rose around them as Wright gasped to life, his sunken eyes popping open. Blood trickled from each of Kalia's nostrils as she looked up to Reshef and Rahmi, both of whom were staring down at her with wide, terror-filled eyes.

She only managed one word through the ether that coated her tongue, through the magic that she had unleashed on them when she freed Wright from his imprisonment. "Run."

CHAPTER TWENTY-TWO

KALIA

The path back to the entrance was drenched in pitch black as that power snuffed out the flame at the end of Rahmi's torch. Cinders remained, just bright enough for Kalia to spot Rahmi pulling Wright to his feet and draping an arm around his neck. Rahmi hitched the man higher onto his shoulder, and Wright stumbled as he crossed the threshold of the alcove. His legs gave out, and Kalia heard Rahmi curse.

"Get Kalia!" Rahmi barked to Reshef, who lunged forward to yank Kalia from the floor. She felt a heavy hand clutch her wrist, felt the black stone against her cheek as she was pulled into Reshef's chest, and felt the pressing magic of the prison skate against her bare skin. She could have sworn her mind-magic dimmed for the moment the black stone touched her skin but returned in full force when it was gone.

The passage trembled beneath their feet as they surged toward the first bend. Kalia planted a helpful hand on the stone wall to her left to feel the curve of the alcoves pass by her palm. Cries and shouts sounded from the prisoners as the crumbling rock fell from the ceiling, pledging to trap them inside.

Kalia was pulled through the second bend, and despite the steel wall she had encased her heart in, she knew the pain in the back of her throat and creeping nausea had little to do with how much power she had exuded. She thought back to the woman with the matted hair and rotting teeth and thought back to the man with the milky eyes. If the prison collapsed, if the cave ceased to exist in its anger for their escape, Kalia knew they wouldn't survive.

"We have to help them," she shouted, and Reshef's hand squeezed her shoulder. "We can't leave them here. *Rahmi*—"

"We don't have a choice, *ruehi*," Rahmi said over his shoulder, his voice no more than a grunt against the nearly dead weight of Wright Thackeray. "It's us or it's them."

Kalia wouldn't take that bullshit for an answer. Despite his protests, she stumbled away from Reshef, landing with a sickening thump against the stone floor. Crawling on her hands and knees, she scraped her palms on the crumbled rocks as she made her way toward the nearest alcove. Another groan and a shuffle of bodies sounded behind her before a set of muscled, strong arms wrapped tightly around her waist.

"We don't have time for this," a voice growled in her ear, the tone familiar in its unyielding nature.

"Let me down," Kalia shot back as the trembling became more violent. She was hoisted into the air, her breath leaving her lungs as her chest thumped heavily against the sharp edge of a shoulder. "*We have to help them*!" She had to help them. She couldn't leave them behind to die.

The spiced scent of ship wax and brine filled her nostrils as Rahmi began to run. "We can't help anyone if we're dead," he retorted.

The tunnel passage opened with a yawn at the fogged entrance, though it had already begun to close. Kalia pounded on Rahmi's back, dust and debris from the falling stone catching in her hair. The wide entrance was half the size, and that shimmering became more opaque with every breath. Reshef limped toward the black sand beach with Wright now unconscious in his grip.

The cave tremored more violently than before as they tumbled onto the shore ahead of Rahmi and Kalia, Reshef dumping Wright onto the sand with little regard for his condition.

"Come on!" Reshef shouted. He sprinted forward, re-entering the cave just as the entrance shrank again.

Sweat dripped from his brow, but the entrance held steady just long enough for them to stumble through. Kalia shrieked as they, too, tumbled onto the shore. Reshef jumped through the doorway, now small enough for a man to dive through, before the rock wall snapped shut, entombing those left behind.

Kalia sat up, rubbing the excess sand from her hair as she stared at the wall. Beside her, Reshef had already stood and was quickly pinning the black stone necklace back into place.

"Are they dead?" she asked quietly as Rahmi brushed off the front of his tunic and headed toward Wright, who had awoken long enough to slump against the side of the rowboat. She sucked in a deep breath, focusing on the fresh scent of algae and salt, the last of the stale air leaving her nose. "Did we just kill them all?" Her heart cracked; the first notch in the wall she had erected around herself.

"I don't know," Rahmi replied, bending to heave Wright into the bottom of the rowboat. "I'm sure we'll find out one way or the other when the crown does their next check of the prison."

Kalia pushed herself up, shouldering past Reshef, who looked more pale and shaken in the dim light that seeped through the fog. "And when will that be?" she demanded, halting in front of him with her hands firmly on her hips. "Tomorrow? Next week?"

Rahmi shrugged, tossing one of the oars from the boat toward Reshef, who caught it with an unsteady hand. "Whenever the king thinks about it again, I suppose." He held out his hand, offering her assistance in clambering inside. His eyes darkened as she planted her feet further into the sand. "We're done here. We got who we needed, and now we're returning to my ship—do not even think about using your magic on me."

Kalia withdrew her power from the impenetrable wall of his mind, sending a seething glare in his direction. "Give me your dagger, then. I'm going back in."

Rahmi threw down the oar in frustration before rounding on Kalia. She didn't step back but lifted her chin in defiance. A shudder of irritation flashed through Rahmi's eyes. "And do what?" Rahmi asked, crossing his arms as he stared down at her. "Get them out one by one while hoping whatever guards the prison will be sympathetic to your cause?"

The wind picked up, sending the sand skittering across the toes of Kalia's boots. Her eyes narrowed onto his, green against brown. "I did what you asked," she retorted through gritted teeth. "You got in, you got out. What I do now is none of your business."

Rahmi's low, humorless chuckle broke through the sound of the waves lapping at the shore behind him. "You're going to wait on this beach until the Royal Navy comes along and beg for mercy?" He took another step forward, closing the gap between them. "Get in the boat, *ruehi*. We aren't finished yet."

Kalia smirked, shifting her weight to one leg, cocking her hip to the side. "Or what?"

"Out," Rahmi ordered Alaric and Thomas as they entered the captain's office to see both men bent over the map spread over the desk. They straightened at his sudden appearance, and Alaric opened his mouth to speak, but Rahmi beat him to the reply. "Wright is in the sick berth. He's been through quite the ordeal and needs some time."

Alaric shut his mouth as he darted his gaze to Kalia, who leered back at him. She had been in an incredibly foul mood since their return trip began. Thomas, to his credit, was already halfway out the door.

"Bring *The Mark of Malice* around the bay, then guide us through the fog. When we're through, we'll get clearance to chart the skies," Rahmi continued.

Alaric curtly nodded in response, and the door shut behind him with a sharp *snick*.

"Are you going to untie my hands now?" Kalia finally asked, lifting her restrained wrists in front of her. "I'm back on the ship."

She knew where his foul mood extended from. Rahmi wrangled her like a newborn calf with the spare bit of rope at the bottom of the rowboat, then tossed her in to sit beside Wright. Despite his tired appearance and ashen complexion, Reshef still managed to bite his bottom lip to keep from laughing every time he dared to glance toward Kalia as he rowed.

Rahmi leaned against the edge of his desk, which creaked in protest against his weight. "I think I'll wait a bit," he replied smugly. He removed the dagger from his belt, stabbing the tip of the blade into the wood next to his hip with a rough downward stroke of his hand.

"Give us time to get out of the bay, just in case you need to jump from my ship while the island is still in view."

Kalia grated her teeth together. The ship shuddered and shouts from the crew working to raise the anchors came from the other side of the closed door. The fog beyond the port hole on the opposite end of the cabin began to swirl as the sails unfurled. She never took her glare from Rahmi.

"And why would I jump from your ship?" Kalia bit out, stepping forward to close the space between them. "Couldn't have anything to do with the people you left behind to rot in that—"

Rahmi's smirk tightened at the corners. "There is no possible way to help them all. There was no room on the rowboat. There is no room in the sick berth. There are not enough supplies on my ship—"

"Just say that you had no interest in helping them," Kalia spat, cutting him off with a scoff that she didn't bother trying to hide despite his clenched jaw and tight fists. "Just say that you would have rather let them all die, just like you do with the people on this ship."

Her words had him rising to a stand, and he reached out to grasp the knot of the rope he had tied around her wrists, jerking her toward him. "Don't speak on things you don't understand," he replied, so close that his breath was like a caress on the heat of her cheek. The tension between them was palpable, so thick that it made the fog outside look like a partially cloudy day over the gorge.

There was a tightness to the corners of her eyes, but she only tilted her chin higher to keep their eye contact. "You're selfish and cruel—"

Rahmi's gaze darkened into feral anger for a split second, but he seemed to temper it back. "I don't think you know how cruel I can be." He lifted a finger to drag along the underside of her jaw, the touch feather-light. "I've been patient with you more than my quartermaster would like to see." He yanked her forward even further, their bodies grazing one another. And, still, she didn't back down.

"No, I've been patient with *you*, captain." Kalia's nostrils flared as she inhaled sharply at the arrogant quirk of his brow. "You strut around the ship, killing those who defy you, all the while ordering—"

Rahmi's eyes flicked to her lips long enough for her to register it before he closed the inches between them and pressed his lips to hers. The kiss was hard and fast and hungry, punishing and demanding. Kalia reeled her head back, her brow furrowed.

"You talk too much," Rahmi murmured, though he never released the curl of his hand around the knot that still tethered her wrists together. He never stepped back to create the gap that had once been the tense barrier between them and never lifted his gaze from her lips.

Heat bloomed in Kalia's core, the sensation familiar and thrilling, even though it was *him*. She could feel her fury punching through her veins and the inferno in her eyes as she glared up at him. An inferno that he welcomed, that he buried within his blaze. Instead of stepping back, as she knew she should have, she lifted onto her toes to scrap her tongue against his bottom lip.

Kalia clamped down on his flesh with her teeth when he opened for her, tasting the blood that pebbled against her tongue. She wanted to hurt him; she wanted to make him regret ever forcing her to step foot on the ship, but most of all, she wanted the release she had a feeling he could give her, even if she would hate herself for it tomorrow.

Rahmi's other hand shot into her hair as he groaned into her mouth, their tongues a sudden tangle of heat and promise and rage. He whirled on her, roughly pushing her against the nearest wall hard enough to force the air from her lungs, but he swallowed her exhale with the kiss he never broke. Kalia struggled against the rope. She wanted to claw at him, tear at his flesh with her nails, leave marks that only she knew about. She curled her fingers into the waistband of his breeches, the only thing she could reach, and felt the stiffness of his abdominal muscles against her knuckles.

"Tell me to stop," Rahmi said through the blur of their mouths, tongues, and teeth, still dancing in a wildfire that Kalia couldn't stop even if she wanted to. It wasn't a plead that slipped from him. No, it was a *command*.

The anger that he would dare demand an order claimed her, sinking her into immeasurable rage. "No," she seethed out, digging her nails into the bulk of his hip.

"Tell me now," Rahmi growled, but his mouth had already broken from hers and had already licked a path up the column of her throat. His hand untangled from her locks. He didn't bother being gentle with that either, as he pinned his hips against hers, pulling up on the skirt of her dress.

The satin fabric, usually so soft, painted another trail of fire along her thigh as it lifted, and Kalia felt his fingers needy and insistent against her skin. He slanted a knee in between her thighs, releasing his hold on the rope long enough to haul her into his arms. Kalia wrapped her legs around his waist, catching his lips with hers once more. He spun them again, this time planting her on the desk's surface, swiping the pile of parchment onto the floor with one casual swing of his arm.

Kalia's back straightened, her legs parting to allow Rahmi to slide between them. She gasped into his mouth as his hand left her ass, sliding between her thighs to land in the crease of her hip. Another flame blazed in her core as he swiped a thumb against her sex, and she let out an involuntary moan when he pinched her clit. His smirk was punishing as he lowered his mouth to nip at her collarbone, at the skin of her neck, at the shell of her ear.

Her hands were caught between them, pinned between his thigh and her knee, and unable to grasp anything other than the fabric of his breeches.

"I knew you would be wet for me," Rahmi murmured, sliding the tip of his thumb into her entrance, teasing her briefly before moving away again.

Kalia moaned again as his thumb pressed against her clit for the second time, and she resisted the urge to tip back her head in pleasure. She didn't want him to know— only wanted to feel that intense hatred, tried to pretend it wasn't him. "You're only a means to an end for me," she finally said, her tone low and husky. She didn't like the way it sounded when it came out, but from the way he set another bruising kiss against her mouth, he did. "And when this is over, it never happened."

"Don't worry, *ruehi*," Rahmi whispered against the shell of her ear, thrusting a finger into her heat without warning. This time, Kalia did tip back her head, groaning to the ceiling as he curled it against her front wall, keeping that pressure of his thumb against her clit. "You're just another mistake in the long line of the ones I've already made."

Rahmi slowly withdrew his finger before adding a second one, sliding back in to curl against her again. Kalia's thighs spread impossibly wide, her body trembling from the tension as he expertly teased and licked and nipped, all the while thrusting his fingers deeper inside of her. His other hand slid to her throat, wrapping to tighten around her neck.

Kalia arched her back into his touch, inadvertently opening that bridge between them. Rahmi, to her surprise, had dropped the wall of protection he usually touted. His fingers move faster, her orgasm blooming in her core. *Gods*, it had been so long since someone else had made her feel this good. And he was responsive to her body, curling his fingers or rubbing her clit or planting open-mouthed kisses on the top of her shoulder in a way that only made her moan louder.

"I bet I could make you come by the filthy things I send down that bond," Rahmi said, and Kalia was flooded with a shot of desire and pleasure so intense that she could feel herself grow wetter with every thrust of his hand. Her hips rolled against him, and she was desperate to touch him, to wrap her hand around his cock, to feel the friction of her palm against his bare skin.

"Make me then." The words were out before she knew she spoke them, and she whimpered as Rahmi applied more pressure to that bundle of nerves between her thighs. "Because I don't think you can."

Kalia lifted her gaze to Rahmi, who was watching with rapt attention to the view of where his fingers disappeared, sinking inside Kalia's tight sex. It only fueled her further, only burst open that wildfire building inside of her. Kalia rolled her hips faster, fucking herself on Rahmi's fingers as her cries spilled into the inches between them. He met her mewls with groans of his own, moving his thumb harder as though determined to, indeed, make Kalia come as hard as he could. His hips thrust against her own, though he was imagining it was his cock taking her instead.

An explosion like a cannon blast flared from Kalia's core, bursting through her. She panted, crying out in loud and unrestrained moans, as her body flared to life with Rahmi stroking her through it. He wrenched a second one from her with the quick pinch of his thumb and forefinger, barely on the heels of her first. Gods, *gods*, why did he have to be so *fucking* good at this? She had half been hoping he would be terrible; then she would have another reason to hate him further.

Rahmi withdrew from her when she finally stopped tipping over the edge, the muscles in her thighs finally ceasing to tremble. Kalia's release shone against the back of his palm as he tugged on her restraints, letting the rope fall loose to the floor. Her heartbeat regulated to a semblance of normal, and time began to tick again, her brain and body connecting once more after her return to the continent. Kalia surged off the table, readying to grab the waistband of his breeches and tug them over his hard length, but he stopped her with a simple hand to her chest.

Rahmi smirked, lifting his other hand to his lips and sucking her release from her fingers. His eyes fluttered closed as he groaned, as though nothing had ever tasted so sweet. Kalia's eyes went wide. It may have been one of the more erotic things she had ever experienced.

"I think I'll take the high ground here, *ruehi*," he said, bathing her in a gloat she couldn't escape. "Knowing you can, and will, come for me...I think I'm going to enjoy this very much."

CHAPTER
TWENTY-THREE

KALIA

"What's the capital city like?" Elodie asked, her wide, innocent eyes trained heavily onto Kalia.

Kalia's hand slowed as she glanced up from the chopped potato. "What do you mean?"

They were gathered around a small wooden table in the corner of the galley, including Reshef and Shirin. The sunlight from the porthole poured onto the floor. It was the first afternoon *The Mark of Malice* had seen any semblance of it in nearly a week, many thanks to the roiling fog now in their wake, and most of the crew were on the deck basking in the warmth.

A large iron pot in the middle of the room was centered directly above an overlay of blackened bricks that held a low flame, the contents simmering inside. The steam from the stew wasn't something Kalia would have described as *pleasant*, but it was fresh enough. A crate of potatoes was nestled between Kalia and Elodie, the lid removed and resting against the nearest wall. Curled skins, loose fish scales, celery leaves, and a flour spread littered the small table.

If Doc were there, he would kill them for the mess, but he had snuck out the moment the sun peered around the edge of the fog.

"I've never been there," Elodie said, pausing to blow a lock of blonde hair from her eyes as she expertly filleted a fish and yanked the bones away from the flesh. "I grew up in Pine Hollow. It's a small port town, nothing like the big city." She sighed, tossing the set of bones into the nearest bucket. "I've always wanted to go."

Shirin pushed the heels of her hands into the dough she was kneading and didn't bother looking up from the flour-covered surface she was working on. "You've had the opportunity. You don't want to leave the ship when the captain ports."

Elodie handed the fish fillet to Reshef, who pinched it between his forefinger and thumb before unceremoniously dumping it into the large iron pot behind him. "Well," she said, a preening bristle entering her tone, "I never had reason to go ashore—"

"You were scared to go ashore," Shirin interjected, folding the dough in on itself and kneading it again. "Reason has nothing to do with it."

Kalia frowned and, from the corner of her eye, saw Reshef pick up the wooden stirring spoon as though it were a sword, dunk it into the stew, and give it a rattling stir. "Why are you scared to go ashore?"

"I'm *not* scared—"

"Could have fooled me," Shirin muttered under her breath. She cupped her hands, spinning the dough around to give it shape before carefully setting it on the counter behind her, where four more loaves were rising.

Elodie slapped the next fish onto the table harder than she meant to and glared at Shirin. "I'm more comfortable in places that are known to me. Then I don't have to..." She trailed off, shaking her head. "Never mind. It doesn't matter."

"Elodie, what kind of men are you interested in?" Reshef asked, blasting through Elodie's discomfort in the only way he could. Kalia noticed Reshef's way of turning attention away from unpleasantness with shocking questions, a trait she was surprised to find endearing.

Elodie sent him a grateful look before sighing. "Oh, Reshef. My type is someone who is far more attractive than me and is very mean about it."

Shirin snorted, and Kalia let out an involuntary clap of laughter as Reshef opened his mouth to retort but was interrupted by footsteps bounding down the narrow hallway.

The door flew open, and a cool breeze cut through the oppressive heat like a knife. Elodie clamped her lips shut as one of the crew, a mangy-looking man with greasy hair and a missing left hand, stalked in. He glanced around, presumably looking for Doc. When he didn't see the galley's head cook, he stuck his remaining hand into a crate of apples, pulled one out, and exited the room.

When Kalia returned her gaze to the half-chopped potato in front of her, she noticed a bottle of *fion* had been uncorked and set in the center of the table. She smirked at Reshef, whose eyes had a sudden mischievous glint, and reached forward to grab the bottle.

She lifted the rim to her lips, taking a swig that tasted too dry and savory for her liking. She preferred the sweeter drinks the madam imported from Sha'Hadra, but this would do in a pinch. She handed the bottle to Shirin, who took it with an appreciative quirk of her brow to Reshef.

"The capital city is dirty and smells like rotting fish," Kalia finally answered Elodie, who declined the bottle and immediately passed it over to Reshef. "Much like this ship. You aren't missing much."

Clambering shouts came from the deck above them. The sun shone blindingly bright against the sea, the gentle waves lapping against the keel. Changing her mind, Elodie leaned over and plucked the bottle from Reshef's hands, taking a large gulp.

"I don't believe that," Elodie replied, dropping the bottle back into Reshef's hands before picking up her knife again. "You think the king will allow his palace to smell like rotting fish?"

"The king himself smells like rotting fish," a voice from the door responded, startling everyone in the room.

Reshef, who had leaned his chair to the back two legs, nearly toppled over while Elodie let out a shriek, tossing the knife over her shoulder. It embedded in the doorframe near Rahmi's face. Kalia watched him with growing apprehension as he sauntered into the room, picked up the bottle of *fion* from where Reshef had set it mere moments before, and took a gulp that made his throat bob.

Kalia looked away, remembering how the corners of his eyes had tightened and his mouth downturned just like that when his fingers were inside her. *Gods*, he knew what she felt like. She didn't lift her gaze to meet his, though she felt his stare boring into the back of her head.

"I didn't realize I had permitted another bottle to be brought up from storage," Rahmi finally said. The tips of Elodie's ears flushed a shade of red. "The crew won't be happy that one of their numbers is pilfering the stock."

Reshef had already resumed tipping his seat back, his shoulders loose and lowered as he casually stirred the pot of stew once more. "Consider it a survivor's tax."

A chair scraped behind her, pulled toward the small table before a heavy body dropped into the seat. From the corner of her eye, Kalia saw Rahmi lean forward to grab a knife from the table and swipe a small pile of dried herbs toward him. Her brows rose as he began to chop them into thin slices before sprinkling them into the simmering pot.

"Doc isn't going to be happy with you," Kalia warned, though her tone remained nonchalant. "He doesn't take kindly to his recipe changing."

Rahmi snorted. "Doc is from the coast. You and I both know the best spices come from Sha'Hadra."

Kalia looked over at him, holding his gaze long enough to draw her back into his office, her legs splayed open on his desk. She glanced away, but his eyes lingered on her for a heartbeat longer than they should have.

"Besides," Rahmi went on, turning away to sprinkle another handful into the pot, "we've eaten fish stew every day for nearly thirty years. We can't make it worse than it already is."

Elodie's tinkling giggle filled the galley as she retrieved her knife from the doorframe and wiped it against her skirt. "You've been in the capital, sir. How is it?"

While Kalia was sure Elodie could coax the dead to talk, she remained stunned and silent when the captain responded to her.

"You should look around for yourself the next time we port." Rahmi resumed slicing another small pile of dried herbs. "Maybe Kalia will show you around, considering her intimate knowledge of the city and its clientele."

Kalia returned a glance of irritation, that stunned silence melting into a puddle at her feet. "My knowledge is quite limited," she corrected him, though her tone had taken on a hard, challenging bite. "I had little more to do with the city than you do."

Rahmi's smile was saccharine, his head tilting in her direction. "Oh? You mean to say that you didn't work for one of the most popular bordellos on the continent?"

Kalia didn't like how Elodie perked up or Reshef's eyes sliding between her and the captain. She didn't like how Shirin's hands had paused, no longer kneading the new ball of dough in front of her. And she definitely didn't like Rahmi's wide grin, one that he didn't bother to hide. Slowly, Kalia resumed chopping the potatoes, though her fingers trembled as they wrapped around the knife's hilt.

"There were rumors," Elodie piped up, another wet squelch from the fillet sounding as she pulled the bones out. Her inability to read the growing tension in a room had never been more prominent than in that moment. "I heard some men talking about it while scrubbing the deck one day. They said that you would—"

"Whatever you heard," Kalia said through gritted teeth, her trembling fingers now shaking uncontrollably, "it was likely incorrect." They had no idea how she ended up there, had no idea what she had gone through, and she had scars on her back to prove it. Instead of voicing that, she reached into the crate of potatoes and slammed it on the table before her.

Reshef opened his mouth to speak, paused as though he thought better of it, and clamped his lips shut again. Shirin even looked abashed, and her stare remained fixed on the dough.

"I'm sure you had to make your coin somehow," Rahmi pressed on. Kalia didn't know where he was going with this...or why. "Don't be remorseful for what you had to do in the dark."

"What the fuck is *that* supposed to mean?" Kalia's anger inside her came to a boil that she knew she couldn't control.

Rahmi casually tossed the final handful of herbs into the pot, wiping his hands together to dust off the residual flakes. "There are plenty of distasteful careers in the capital. Toss a few coins in your face; you were probably on your back for hours each night. *Bought and paid for by the madam*, I believe you told me. You did what you needed to do; there was no shame in it."

Even Elodie turned her eyes from the conversation, though Kalia knew she was still dying to ask questions. And Elodie didn't need the answers to them. She didn't need to know how Kalia's mother and brother had died at the hands of the palace guards, how her brother had tried to protect Kalia until his very last breath, how it all happened thanks to a family friend who had turned them in.

No, none of them were privy to that information.

"Captain—" Elodie started slowly, but the oxygen had already been sucked from the room, the space so quiet that Kalia heard the ringing of rage in her ears.

The knife in Kalia's hand slipped from the potato, slicing across her hand that held it in place. Metal clattered against wood, blood steadily dribbling onto her lap as she stood from the table. The stool scraped against the floor as she kicked it back with her boot.

"Kalia!" Elodie exclaimed, moving to grab the nearest stained rag from the counter, but Kalia was already making her way toward the door.

The cut wasn't particularly deep, but it throbbed enough that she counted each beat. She didn't look back as she opened the galley door, the cool air an immediate relief against her flushed cheeks. And she said nothing as she entered the hallway, not daring to analyze how that shield placed so strategically in front of her heart had finally been pierced.

Kalia didn't bother to go to the sick berth, instead wrapping her hand in a handkerchief she stole from Shirin's trunk to temper the bleeding. She slipped from the room, using her teeth to tighten the knot as she made her way deeper into the ship. She had no interest in going back to the galley or in waiting in the small room for Elodie and Shirin to reappear.

She delved two decks down, deep enough that she couldn't hear the crew's booming laughter echoing over the quarterdeck. The air was stale and humid, the smell a mix of mildew and ship wax, but it was quiet. And that's what she wanted— solitude.

There was no reason for Rahmi to have brought up her time at the bordello, even if it were in jest. Even with the scars from the frequent lashings and the cache of terrible memories that morphed into nightmares, Kalia certainly hadn't wanted harm to befall any of the women. And he had been the one to send them all to their deaths if they hadn't gotten away from the blaze in time.

Tangled in her web of thoughts, she hadn't realized someone was following in the shadows. A hand wrapped tightly around her forearm, yanking her over a threshold to her left. She sent out her mind magic like a whip, threading the bridge with the now-familiar mind on the opposite end.

"Wright Thackeray," Kalia said, pulling back her defenses despite the dagger to her neck. "Isn't this a surprise?"

He looked better than he did a few days before. His hair was washed and combed, the dirt from the prison alcove meticulously scrubbed from his skin. He had put on a new change of clothes that weren't filled with rat-chewed holes and putrid stains, and some of his exposed wounds were on their way to healing. But he was still gaunt, his flesh spread too thin over the bones of his face, and he had been out of the sun for so long that he was still a shade of pale Kalia had never seen before.

And, considering Wright was having a hard time keeping the dagger above chest level, Kalia knew that he probably wouldn't have the strength to cut her throat. At least, not yet.

"Who are you?" he demanded, half his wild gaze glowing a dull gold from the lone lantern in the hallway. She briefly wondered if he always looked that crazed or if it was thanks to the years spent in solitude at the prison.

Kalia pushed away the dagger with relative ease. "What are you on about?"

Wright began to pace, his back facing the doorway. Kalia carefully noted his gait pattern, watching for an opportunity to slip by without him stabbing her in the back. "Captain said there was a djinn aboard," he whispered quickly, lifting his hand to tug at the ends of his hair. He didn't make eye contact with her, giving her the impression that he said it primarily to himself.

"I am the djinn," Kalia replied anyway, though she stepped away from him when he rounded on her, dagger drawn forward once more.

"No...no," Wright went on. He lifted the blade's tip to his temple, tapping it against the side of his head. "I saw you. I saw you in here. Don't lie to me." His knuckles whitened with the grip he had on the hilt.

The lantern in the hallway swayed again, this time casting him in a shadow that darkened one side of his already feral stare. Kalia narrowed her eyes at him, an uncomfortable quiver prickling in the pit of her stomach. He was just paranoid. He had been in prison for too long and had endured too much.

"I *am* the djinn," Kalia repeated, this time slower and with more emphasis, but Wright cut her off.

"You are *not* a djinn." His words clattered through the nearly empty storage bay, ricocheting off the three empty wooden crates and the old folded sail stuffed in the corner. "I've seen a djinn. I'll remember it for the rest of my gods-forsaken life. You are decidedly not that, but I do know what you are—"

This was something Kalia wanted to hear. This man had spent years being tortured inside of his mind. He was half-starved and unable to make prolonged eye contact. This man who...

"You're a Voyant."

Kalia stiffened, the walls of the room threatening to suffocate her. For a long minute, she couldn't breathe. It was a word that only Pete whispered during her weekly visits, a word that only he had been able to put weight behind. Yet here it was, hanging in the space between her and Wright. She took a step forward, and he raised the blade to point at her again.

"Djinn may be powerful, but Clairs are deadly, and a true djinn doesn't have the same magic you displayed in the prison." With every passing breath, Wright's hand had begun to tremble, gravity pulling it toward the floor. "They don't flaunt their power, don't use it for anything, don't want to be found. But Clairs: Voyants, Sentients, the lot of you...you can't help yourselves."

The humorless grin that tugged onto Kalia's lips was lethal, making Wright's already pale face drain even further. "Then you know that I could kill you." She again bridged that gap with her mind, curling a magic tendril against his absurdly thin layers. He wasn't guarded and most likely couldn't hold a steady shield against her again.

Wright's back straightened, and the blade finally fell to his side. "You won't. I've been observing you these last few days. I've watched you with those two women and that man. You haven't hurt them, and you won't hurt me."

"You seem certain."

"I know what you want," he said, though his voice had become strangled and high-pitched. "I've watched other things, too. I've watched you slip dried food into your skirts when you think people aren't looking. I've seen you steal coins, tobacco, jewels, anything you can find that others won't miss. You're planning an escape."

She assessed Wright with the scrutiny of a hawk finding a rabbit, and he squirmed beneath the intensity of it. Finally, she said, "You haven't told the captain yet. Why?"

Wright shrugged, though the movement was clunky and unnatural. "I'm waiting for the right opportunity. And, unless one comes up, I think we can come to an arrangement, you and I. I can get you off this ship and make it possible for you to escape into the night with no way to find you. Or I can tell the captain and see what he says about the whole thing."

With the right motivation, everyone will betray you. Kalia hadn't known Wright for over a few days, yet the stinging words were already coming true. She thought back to the trust she had been attempting to begin with Reshef, and something in her chest hardened into place. She sat in silence for a moment, contemplating Wright, before she let out a huff of a chuckle. One way or the other, she always knew that her and Rahmi's *partnership* would end badly. She just needed to be the one to end it first.

"What do you need me for?"

Wright swallowed, though his free hand lifted to rub the back of his neck. "The *Luminaria* must be destroyed. The sea, this realm, it all requires balance. Allowing the captain what he wants, what he truly wants, is an abomination to nature." He flicked his gaze up to Kalia, if only for the briefest of seconds. "When we lead him there, we must find a way to ensure he can't use it."

The man standing before her was once one of Rahmi's most trusted crew members, one that he specifically sought out...and this man was willing to trade in everything. Was he willing to risk his life to betray the man who saved him? *Why*? Kalia asked him just that, disbelief and distrust at war within her.

"I've had time to reflect, as you can imagine, while I was at the whim of the gods. Nothing should have that much power. Not you, not me, not them, and not the captain. He's been searching for hundreds of years, searching for something that I thought was an impossibility." Clarity shined through his gaze for the first time in their conversation when the lantern's return glow illuminated his face. "The gods may have abandoned us but are no less forgiving. That stone will kill us all if it gets in the wrong hands."

Kalia's stare bored into his, and he dropped his eyes to the tips of his boots. "I don't think you'll tell the captain anything, not that he would believe something that came from your muddled head." She sent another tendril of her power his way, caressing the thin layers of his mind with a phantom touch. "Getting off this ship isn't a problem for me, Wright. I have my plan. I have my currency. My question is: will you be the one to stand in my way knowing what I can do to you?"

A shudder spasmed every muscle in his body, but he still managed to croak out, "You need to listen to me, Voyant. If the king gets ahold of that gemstone, we're all dead. You included. You can run as far from this ship as your stolen coins will carry you. You can try to hide. But there won't be a place where he won't be able to find you."

Kalia ripped her magic from his mind, sending him toppling to the ground. She gracefully stepped over him as she crossed the threshold, only glancing back at him once as she did.

CHAPTER TWENTY-FOUR

RAHMI

W right studied the map with narrowed eyes, his stare flitting from one corner to the other. He certainly wasn't the man Rahmi had released from his ship all of those years ago, his thoughts more panicked and disorganized. It was evident in the way he kept shifting back and forth on his feet, as though determined to pace in any way he could.

"I don't know, captain," Wright finally said, rubbing the palm of his hand down his pant leg. "This seems well past my prime."

Alaric leaned in, his gaze darting around the parchment. "All we need is a direction. We don't even need a pointed location—"

Rahmi scowled, tipping his head back to look at the cabin's ceiling. His inability to read the map itched a part of his brain that he couldn't scratch, and his needed reliance on Wright was a blend of vexing irritation that he couldn't shake. Relying on others wasn't something he wanted to be practiced in, yet here he was...the djinn in one corner and Wright Thackeray in the other.

"Where is the NightWatcher, Wright?" Rahmi asked through his teeth, a painting of forced restraint. His impatience was finally getting the best of him. "I gave it to you when I let you off this ship. I rescued you from the Labyrinth. I want it back."

Wright straightened as he ran a hand through the length of his salt-and-pepper hair, another new feature in the ten years since Rahmi had last seen him. "Now, captain..."

Rahmi drew in a sharp breath and released it before he spoke. "I'm not asking for a story. I want the NightWatcher. You and I know it's the only thing to help you read that map."

Alaric seemed to be holding his breath, his attention away from the desk for the first time in nearly twenty minutes. The ship creaked in the silence, the cool evening breeze that drifted through the open porthole briny, salty, and sweet. The scent of the sea, having the water surrounding him, was usually all he needed to calm down.

But not now. Not when Wright was stalling, and Rahmi's attempts to hurry him along had been failing for *two fucking days*.

"Where is the NightWatcher?"

Wright's mouth fell open. "I stumbled on hard times a few years back..."

"I want the NightWatcher. Now."

"Times were real tough, captain. I—I was living in an animal pen near Amberwick. You've seen that town, it's nothing but mud and cow shit..."

"The NightWatcher," Rahmi snapped, withdrawing his cutlass from the sheath and slamming it down on the desk, rattling the surface so hard that a brass instrument clattered to the floor. He tried not to remember how the pile of parchment had done just that when he had hoisted Kalia onto the edge of the desk only a week before. "What did you do with it?"

"I sold it," Wright squeaked out. Alaric cursed quietly as his one eye squeezed shut. "I sold it. I needed coin."

Rahmi's fingers curled against the blade, feeling the cold metal prick against the callouses. He should have listened to his gut back then. He should have known that he would need the NightWatcher, and Wright-*fucking*-Thackeray would have done away with it somehow. But no...Wright had been a trusted member of his crew for one hundred years. It had been a *gift,* something he had squandered the moment he couldn't keep his cock in his breeches. Was it *fion*? Gambling? Brothels? If Rahmi knew Wright, he would have guessed it was a combination of the three.

"Tell me," Rahmi seethed. His jaw already began to ache with the strain of his clenching.

"A-about six years ago," Wright replied, and Rahmi didn't miss the tremble to his voice. He also didn't miss the details Wright spared as he clamped his lips shut again.

Rahmi's brows rose, an expectant look passing over his face. Though Wright was no longer a true member of his crew, Rahmi wouldn't hesitate to treat him any differently. And from the gulp that worked Wright's throat, he seemed to realize that, too.

"The brig may loosen his tongue," Alaric said, crossing his arms over his chest. "Karim is still down there, they could be cellmates."

Wright's eyes widened. "No!" he exclaimed, approaching the desk to stand before Rahmi. "No, do not lock me up, captain!"

Rahmi glanced at Alaric in disgust before his quartermaster grabbed the front of Wright's tunic and tossed him into the old armchair. The chair slid as Wright collapsed into it with a loud *oof*, the legs scraping against the wooden floor.

"What say you then, Thackeray?" Alaric went on, resting his forearm on the headrest directly above Wright. "Are you going to tell us the truth or go to the brig? Captain is giving you a choice; don't waste it."

Wright's gaze flicked around the room before finally landing on the open porthole, where the stars had begun to glitter against the navy sky. The night was clear, not even a wisp of clouds in the sky, and the streaks of orange signifying dusk had already given way to the depths of the horizon. He sighed, dropping his chin to his chest and shaking his head.

"The si'lat. It's with the si'lat."

Rahmi stilled, and Alaric swore louder this time, pushing himself from the headrest and placing his hands on the top of his head. Rahmi's pulse thundered in his tight chest, and he had to turn all of his attention toward not overturning his desk out of rage, something he hadn't done since he was a young sailor aboard his first ship. It would be fitting now.

"Alaric, tell the crew to set course for the west."

Alaric regarded him for a moment. "The si'lat might not even *have* the NightWatcher any longer," he started, but Rahmi was already shaking his head.

"An instrument used by a cursed captain and traded to them by a *former* crew member?" From the corner of his eye, Rahmi saw Wright wince at the emphasis of the word *former*. Rahmi waved a dismissive hand toward Wright. "Get out of my sight. Now. Before I change my mind about killing you and drown you in a bucket of your piss."

Wright scampered from the room and didn't look back.

"Do you know where to find them?" Alaric asked as soon as the tail of Wright's coat whipped around the doorframe. "The si'lat are notoriously difficult to deal with."

"We have a past, and I'll have to use a part of my day on land to do it—" Rahmi began, though he was cut off by the whine of a door hinge and a sudden shriek, followed by a clang of wood on wood and raucous laughter. He sighed, closing his eyes. "Bring me Kalia." He paused as the shrieking grew louder and more panicked. "And bring me whatever just happened to Wright. I'm sure the djinn had something to do with it."

Alaric's responding nod was curt as he pivoted on the balls of his feet, marching from the room to give the orders.

"Dragging a woman from her bed. It's uncouth," Kalia said as she entered the cabin, stopping a few feet short of the desk Rahmi sat at. With a gloved hand, Rahmi lifted the dead Man O'War siphonophore from the bucket at his feet, tossing it toward Kalia. It wetly slapped against the wood as it slid, its venomous tentacles coming to a halt near the toes of her boots. Her eyes lifted, roving over him with unconcerned interest. "You don't look injured."

"And you're no woman," Rahmi retorted in exhaustion, ripping off the glove and dropping it onto his desk. "You're a plague."

Kalia smiled and looked about to say thank you but thought better of it. It was one of her best ideas since boarding his ship; he was in no mood. "Has Wright been particularly *helpful*?"

She was goading him. He knew it by the smugness that dripped from that smile, a smugness that nearly bordered on scorn. But he needed her, so he swallowed back the derisive comment dancing on the tip of his tongue.

"We'll be at the lair of the si'lat in three days," Rahmi said instead, lifting from his seat behind his desk and winding around the corner of it. He leaned against the edge, amusement kindling in his chest when Kalia's cheeks warmed, presumably at where he had perched himself. Two could play at that game, as he well knew with her.

Kalia cleared her throat, shifting from one foot to another, but didn't look away. "And?"

Rahmi pointedly ignored the quip and went on. "Si'lat are shapeshifters. We'll need to be on our guard when we get to the lair."

At his words, Kalia's brows rose. "*We*? What do you mean by *we*?"

"Do you require a definition of the word, or can I assume that question was rhetorical?"

Kalia narrowed her eyes on him, but he refused to break under her stare. She was deeply perceptive; he would give her that, but Rahmi was the one to give the orders. It would be her who followed.

"Wright sold something of mine to the si'lat," Rahmi said in her silence, picking up an eagle feather quill balanced on the edge of the desk. He looked at it, turning it over, before setting it back down. "I need it back."

"And you need me to come with you, why exactly?"

He still wasn't entirely used to her questioning. And he certainly didn't understand why she was determined to make everything monumentally more difficult. "You were so helpful in the prison, I figured you would want to make yourself useful again."

Kalia snorted, the sound one of the more unladylike things he had heard, and turned to walk back out of the cabin. "You figured wrong."

Rahmi pushed off the desk just as she reached the door, and he held a firm hand to shut it back against the frame. It clicked into the lock with a soft *snick,* and Kalia whirled around to face him, a heavy glare set on her face. He bracketed his hands on each side of her head, trying to get past the smell of her hair and the fullness of her lips. The same scent sunk into every corner of his office for the day following their *encounter*. The same lips that he so badly wanted...no, *needed*...wrapped around his cock.

He was pleased to see a gentle flush spreading at the base of her throat. He suddenly wanted to kiss it, to see if the skin had grown as warm as it looked. It awoke something in him, something that had slumbered until that moment.

"You're coming. I'm not asking."

Rahmi could see her slamming the wall shut behind her eyes, any openness she once held now well hidden behind it. That gentle flush shifted into a rage-filled crimson, and those full lips, once parted, now pressed into a tight line.

"What are you looking for?" Kalia snapped back, placing both hands on Rahmi's chest and shoving him. He didn't budge. "I thought you had what you needed."

Rahmi grabbed her hands and pinned them to her side, his fingers encircling her wrists. He found he liked the feeling of her skin beneath his, and that wasn't something he was r to reflect on. "What I need is no business of yours. You're going to come with me and retrieve it, or—"

"Trust should be shared," Kalia interjected, but Rahmi snorted in response.

"You're going to lecture me on trust?" he asked, and his forced laugh made his smile harden. "I put my trust into those who have earned it, and I can't seem to turn my back on you without you trying to stab me in it." She went quiet, a seething quiet that Rahmi knew meant she was attempting to read him. He sighed. "Wright and I need a special instrument to read the map, one that he sold to the si'lat years ago. I need it back."

Kalia swallowed, her eyes searching his. "What does the *Luminaria* have to do with the king?"

The question was odd, and Rahmi found himself studying her in return. He let go of her wrists, taking a small step back. The cool night air flooded the sudden space between them, pricking at the heat he had come to know. "What makes you think that it is?"

To her credit, Kalia didn't turn away. She held his gaze, crossing her arms over her chest as though battling the open-sea wind. "What happens to the souls on this ship when they are given to Liddros?" When Rahmi didn't answer immediately, she let out a scoff. "If you truly want *my* trust, your honesty would be appreciated."

It wasn't a request. Rahmi heard that loud and clear. Information itself was dangerous, but any information regarding the king was lethal. Rahmi had a sinking suspicion that she would find out one way or the other...or eventually grow tired of his demands.

"What do you know of the king?" he finally asked, and from her furrowed brow, the question seemed to take her by surprise.

"What do you mean?"

Rahmi took a deep breath before replying, the taste of salt on his tongue. "It's a simple question. What do you know of the king?"

Kalia ran a hand through her locks, carefully picking at a tangle in her hair that snagged on her finger. She licked her lips, drawing Rahmi's attention downward. "I know that he's cruel, that he rips apart families without a second thought. I know that he rules the continent with an iron fist. I know he doesn't leave the palace unless it's to watch an execution."

"And what do you know of his age?"

The notch in her brow deepened as she frowned. "His age?"

"Yes, his age. How *old* do you think the king is?"

Kalia opened her mouth to reply before closing it again. When she finally did respond, there was a bite of impatience that marred her tone. "I don't understand what that has to do with—"

"How old do you think the king is?" Rahmi repeated slower, not allowing her to get another word in. Behind him, the sun had set completely, casting them in darkness. He wound around the desk, striking a match and lighting the half-used candle in the copper holder on his desk. The scent of honeycomb wax and burning wick curled around the room, replacing the fresh smell of the sea. "You can guess."

"Fifty," Kalia said with a scowl, placing her hands on her hips. "But I don't know what—"

"He's nearing one thousand." Rahmi blew out the match, and the thin band of smoke danced toward the ceiling.

Kalia blinked, and her grimace nearly looked pained. "One thousand?" she shook her head. "I asked you to be truthful with me."

"From what I understand," Rahmi started, ignoring her again as he lit a second candle with the help of the first. "Liddros was in a bad way with his brothers. He requested to be hidden and used a mortal to mask his powers behind a tethered bond. The king agreed to allow Liddros to use the continent on one condition—Liddros would allow the king to access his magic, enough to make him immortal. But the king deceived him."

"Liddros is just a god of the sea, though," Kalia said. "How is that possible?" Her gaze dropped to the floor, tracing along the worn rug like she would find the answer buried in the fibers. There was a flash behind her eyes, a shift of something thunking into place. "What is he?"

Rahmi hesitated before shaking his head. "I don't know. Liddros's accessible power ran dry about one hundred years into their deal, and he wanted his bond to be broken with the king. The king refused. Liddros was forced to create a set of cursed captains who could harness what little of his power remained—ones who could scour the continent looking for souls that the king could use to stay immortal."

Kalia's eyes looked over his exposed forearms, where the black ink of his curse was written into his skin. He was forced to hand over the souls of his crew, the ones he could no longer save. The ones fed to a greedy king were never allowed to move on. He fought Liddros on it once he realized what he had done and what he was now forced to do.

"And your curse?" Kalia asked tentatively, lifting her gaze to connect with his. Her lingering stare

"I broke the laws of nature when I became this captain and took on the role of Liddros's watchman. I've been punished accordingly." Rahmi scrubbed a hand over the underside of his jaw, feeling the pricks of his unshaven beard against his palm. "I sailed in battles in the king's name and killed many of my brothers in the process. Now, I use my hands to supply those very souls to a king who has locked himself behind the luxury of a palace."

Shame flittered through him, an emotion he wasn't ready to contend with. It pierced through his chest, drawing him back to the last time he felt his way. The only reason he allowed the crew of his ship to reckon with their guilt was the war he once had with his own. But that guilt wormed through his memories, recalling faces and smiles he hoped he would never have to see again. Not even in his mind.

"What happens when you have the *Luminaria*?" Kalia asked quietly.

Rahmi pushed his feelings aside, shrugging his shoulders with a nonchalant raise that he hoped conveyed a casual indifference. "I give it to Liddros and pray that he remembers who helped him. I wanted to sail the seas for an eternity, not take the souls of the men and women who want the same." He cleared his throat, glancing toward the shadows that quivered against the far wall.

Kalia sighed, dropping her head back to look at the ceiling, her lengthy hair draped against her back. "I'm going to regret helping you, aren't I?"

Rahmi chuckled low. "Get me to the *Luminaria*, *ruehi*, and it will be something that I will never forget."

She lifted her head at his words, the intense green of her eyes forging a path straight to his soul. "I'm just praying I'll get back to shore, and you'll forget I ever existed." Kalia twisted the ends of her hair around a finger.

Something about her words sent a shot of discomfort through his gut. "You and I both know that isn't possible."

"I told you once it was over, it never happened." It was the first time Kalia had spoken of their encounter, and Rahmi felt his cock twitch at the unexpected reminder.

His eyes darkened, and he watched Kalia's throat bob with her forced swallow. "On the contrary, a night hasn't gone by where I don't think about how you tasted."

Kalia shifted on her feet, an unfamiliar expression passing over her features. She hesitated, rocking to her toes before pivoting on her feet and gliding from the room. For the first time in a very long time, the certainty and confidence that Rahmi operated on were beginning to waver.

CHAPTER TWENTY-FIVE

KALIA

"That's it?" Kalia asked, squinting against the barrage of wind that whipped around the edge of the rocky cliff. The sun peeked through the clouds, just enough that the rays reflected brilliantly off the waves that snuck into the sheltered bay. A sugar-sand beach stretched along the coast of the isle, and the tall seagrass planted on the shore bowed to the breeze. "That doesn't seem like a *lair* to me." It seemed like somewhere she would sit with a bottle of *fion* if anyone asked her.

Rahmi slid a second dagger into the sheath tied to his belt, the sound of leather against metal soft amongst the flapping sails above them. "No, *that's* it."

Kalia glanced to the left, where Rahmi had gestured with the point of the third dagger still in his hand. "No. No, no, no." She shook her head, taking her hands off the gunnel of the ship to cross her arms over her chest. "There is *no way* that I'm going anywhere near that."

A split was open down the rocky cliff where the rolling waves pounded the wall. From her position on the ship, it looked barely large enough for her to fit through. Sea water entered through the fissure with a boom that sounded like thunder, the wave cresting to fill the space inside before retreating in a hiss of white foam.

"We aren't going *near* it. We're going *in* it," Rahmi amended, turning toward Alaric to take the compass from the quartermaster's outstretched palm and popping it into the pouch tied around his neck.

He had to know that wasn't better. She turned to gape at him, only to find an amused grin quirking his mouth. She scoffed, shaking her head. "You're lying." Gods, she hoped he was lying. He had to be lying.

"I'm not lying," Rahmi replied with a laugh. "We're going to have to swim there—"

"Pardon me?"

"There isn't a place for us to tether a boat, and the si'lat will just steal it even if there was."

Kalia glanced back toward the cliff. A wave slammed against the rock, spraying seawater upward in a rainbow-threaded mist. The second boom thundered through the small bay like a cannon blast. They were both going to die. She could feel it in her bones.

"Don't look so worried, *ruehi*," Rahmi said. He reached up to grasp the rigging, hauling himself onto the gunnel. He turned on expertly placed feet, clear assurance in his movements despite the ship rolling in the waves beneath him. "I'll be with you the whole time," he said.

That didn't make her feel better either, considering she had tried to end his life on multiple occasions. He seemed to have sensed the apprehension in her hesitation because he extended a hand down in compromise. She stared at it for a brief moment before flicking her gaze up to meet his.

The last thing Kalia wanted was for him to show her up in front of the crew. Her pride certainly wouldn't allow for that. She pushed back her anxiety, the feeling like razorblades in her blood, and took his hand. Rahmi easily pulled her onto the gunnel next to him, and she gulped when she glanced over the side.

The wind hadn't calmed overnight like she was hoping it would have, and the waves bore witness to a faraway storm that gathered on the horizon. She fixed her gaze on Elodie and Shirin, who had gathered near the front of the crew as soon as the anchor dropped. Unsurprisingly, Elodie was busy wringing her hands. On the other hand, Shirin tried to mask her unease with boredom, though her eyes still shone a bit too brightly as she watched Kalia balance on the edge of the ship.

"How are we going to get down?" Kalia asked, raising her voice over the howling wind.

"Like this," Rahmi retorted, wrapping his arms around Kalia's waist. She hadn't been given the chance to wriggle away from him before she felt her body tip to the side, suddenly suspending her in the open air.

Kalia screamed as Rahmi laughed, and a split second of boyish joy lit up his tanned face before they careened into the water. Kalia sunk under the surface, Rahmi's hands ripped from her body, and she kicked upward until her head broke above the waves. She was incredibly grateful for the cotton breeches and tunic she wore in place of her dress, though the spare change of clothes plopped on the end of her bed the night before should have been a sufficient warning.

The salt stung her eyes as Kalia wiped the water from her lashes. Though the sea was warmer here than it had been near the prison, it still didn't stop her teeth from clacking together as she took a deep, sputtering breath.

Rahmi appeared in front of her, shaking his hair from his eyes. The sodden locks stuck to his temple, brow, and jaw. Had she not been spitting angry at being tossed from the deck of a pirate ship, she would have tucked the locks behind his ear herself.

Droplets of briny water cut a path down his nose and over the curve of his lips. Lips that had explored her body, teeth that nipped at the crook of her neck. His tongue darted out to catch the droplet as it entered the seam of his lips, and Kalia realized she was no better than the ogling men of the bordello. She cleared her throat as he reached for her, turning to swim toward the cliff face. She didn't want to feel how her skin would turn molten with a simple touch of his fingertips. And she knew that it would.

Mist rained down on them as they approached the fissure, and the rolling waves tossed her around, a beast threatening to pull her under the surface. Kalia was not a natural swimmer, quite the opposite, but Pete had taught her well enough when she was a child, and she harkened back to those lessons with every stroke of her arms or kick of her legs.

The sea rose again as Kalia clung to the top of the aperture, her fingernails digging into the wet rock, and she managed to dip inside the cliff just as Rahmi's hand planted heavily on the wall next to her own. The top of Kalia's head scraped against the ceiling of the passage as she swam deeper inside, the water rising and falling as though the passageway were a living, breathing thing. There was a scent in the air, one that she couldn't quite place, just as her knees collided with a sharp stone.

The wind whistled through breaches in the rock above them, thin shafts of light illuminating the small area. Kalia had come to a stone-made platform of sorts, one layered with a thin gloss of water. It was colder than it should have been, considering the humidity, and it only set Kalia's nerves further on edge.

"Low tide," Rahmi said gruffly, flattening his hands on the rock before them. He pushed onto the platform, water sluicing from his shoulders and down his back.

Kalia's mouth went dry as she spotted the corded muscles beneath his wet tunic. When he finally turned to face her, she was a bit too transfixed as water droplets slid through the smattering of hair on his broad chest. She *really* was no better than the men at the bordello. She briefly wondered how often Rahmi had to work the rigging or sails for his body to look...well, like that.

"I'm sure I can find a painter for you," Rahmi's voice echoed above the water. "Isn't that what you said to me?"

Kalia scowled through his smirk, ignoring his extended hand as she pushed herself onto the stone platform. She swatted at it entirely when he wrapped his fingers around her arm to assist her. Bent low to avoid knocking his forehead against the hanging rock that clung to the ceiling, Rahmi slid around to lead them through the passage.

"Try not to stare at my ass."

Kalia's scowl deepened. "Your eyes are too close, and you should consider shaving more often."

Rahmi only sent her a feral grin in return, one that, if they had not been in the midst of a creepy cave, would have set fire to Kalia's core. She tromped after him, her boots sloshing through the water, thinly layering the rock they had clambered onto.

"What did you mean when you said low tide?" Kalia finally asked after an unknown amount of time had passed. The passage twisted deeper, the crevices above them widening. Wisps of white clouds against a stark blue sky peered at them through the cracks in the rocky ceiling. She dared to look up from watching for her footing, surprised to find that he had been looking at her, too.

A slant of sunshine poured over Rahmi's face, his brown eyes glowing with the light. "The entrance and most of this passage is only accessible during low tide." He said it too calmly, something that Kalia latched onto.

She blinked. "And what happens when it isn't low tide anymore?" The casual shrug of his shoulders almost made Kalia's eye twitch. "What happens, Rahmi?" The question came out sharper than she intended.

"Not calling me captain any longer? That's a shame." Rahmi's focus markedly narrowed on her as though he were, indeed, recalling how her mouth moved when she said it. "We should move faster unless you desire to find out." His stride lengthened, forcing Kalia to quicken her steps.

The passage turned downward, the water eddying against the small stones along the path. Moss grew against the jagged rock wall, and Kalia surveyed it closely, keeping her mind away from the inevitable climb back up. Never in her life would she have thought she would voluntarily follow someone into a mysterious cave, let alone follow a man, and here she was...doing just that.

Rahmi's rumbling tone broke through, pulling her from her thoughts.

"You're from Sha'Hadra, aren't you?" Rahmi asked, leaning to the side to avoid another low-hanging rock. "Why hide in a bordello?"

Kalia gently touched the stone wall, feeling the jagged edges rasp against her palm. "I didn't hide," she said, slipping past the low-hanging rock. "It was my home."

"Was the madam your mother? Do djinn have mothers?"

The question coiled in her chest, squeezing her heart. Her mother never made her prove her worth. Her mother was kind, quiet, compassionate, and strong. The madam was never any of those things, only furthering Kalia's need to return to the desert city. "Yes, we have mothers. No, the madam wasn't mine."

Rahmi made a noise of interest at the back of his throat. "Where is yours then? Surely she wouldn't have wanted her daughter to work as whore."

Kalia didn't want to talk about her mother. She didn't want to bring the memories screaming to the forefront of her mind. She didn't want to remember her mother's body crumpled against the floor, blood bubbling from a slash in her throat. She could still see her brother's angry shouts as he tried to muscle past the guards to the neighbors who had turned them in before he was finally cut down, too.

"She's gone," Kalia said shortly, keeping the details to herself. "She's been gone a long time now."

"So you were a whore then?"

Kalia's eyes snapped up. First, she found his easy grin before lifting to meet his gaze. "What makes you say that?" She held his stare and didn't bother to look pleasant while doing it.

Unyielding cockiness rolled from him, stifling the already stale air around them. "You didn't answer my question."

"You didn't ask that question," Kalia corrected him. Being polite was an exhausting inconvenience. "You asked me about my dead mother."

Rahmi held up his hands, a huff of a laugh escaping through his nose. "Take it out on me then."

"Why do you want to know?" Kalia asked, rubbing the spot on her forehead where she had scraped it against an exposed tree root as they approached a wide archway that opened to a shaded oasis just beyond. "Do you have something against whores?" She didn't know why she was getting defensive. She had never been a whore. Nor had she gotten particularly close to any women who worked at the bordello.

"You've been on my ship for nearly six weeks now. I don't know anything about you. Call it curiosity, if you will." Rahmi pivoted toward her, a rush of humid air following his sudden shift. His feral grin had returned, bearing down on her. She refused to step back despite his insistence on being in her space. She knew it was a game to him. And she refused to let him win. "I've tasted you. I like to know about the women I know intimately."

Kalia quirked an unimpressed brow, tipping her chin up to keep her gaze planted on his. "You don't need to know anything about me other than the sound I make when I come. And you already know that." His eyes darkened, a shadow of desire boring into her. She took a moment to wonder how *he* might sound if her lips were wrapped around his cock.

Instead, she took a step back. Information was deadly. She knew that better than anyone. The more someone knew, the easier it was for them to destroy you. She had been taught that lesson at a young age and had learned it repeatedly on the streets of Sha'Hadra before it finally sunk in.

Kalia could have sworn disappointment followed in the wake of his desire as she put that much-needed space between them.

"Who are you, Kalia Salam?" Rahmi asked softly, his eyes desperately searching hers. She didn't like the tone that underlined his question. It was...gentle, a plead for vulnerability, not the unfiltered anger and roughness she had already associated with him. It wasn't *them*, and she couldn't allow for that.

Luckily, she wasn't forced to wallow in it for much longer.

There was a sharp hiss and a whack against the rock wall. Rahmi surged forward, shoving Kalia behind him. A crack sounded from beneath her boot, and she looked down, her stomach lurching in shock. She saw a broken spear lying haphazardly under the thin sheen of water trickling down the passage. Dust still fell from where it had hit the wall above her head.

"*A meal,*" a female voice hissed from the opening. "*And two of you. The fun I could have.*"

Tall and lean, the female's top half was human. Her round eyes were lined with heavy layers of kohl, and the unnatural vertical slits for pupils seemed to swallow the light streaming in from the opening in the wall behind her. Her black, silken hair was thick and tangled, sliding over her exposed breasts as she moved. *As she moved.*

Kalia's mouth fell open as the woman entered the passage. The slow glide was too smooth, and she immediately saw why. Instead of a pair of legs, the bottom half of the female was that of a giant snake. The thick trunk was broader than Rahmi's shoulders, a robust set of muscles that were built for one thing: death. Gleaming, dark scales the size of Kalia's hand covered her hips to the tip of the tail. They glimmered in the sunlight, each a beautiful purple contrasting the monstrous appearance of the creature they were attached to.

Rahmi unsheathed his blade, pointing the tip at the si'lat. "We're only here for one thing. The orb around your neck."

Indeed, a milky, white orb suspended from a leather rope was settled in the valley of her breasts. From Kalia's angle, the contents seemed to be swirling. A gurgle of water sounded from behind her, and the water streaming down the passage began to rise. It quickly surpassed the tops of her boots.

The si'lat tilted her head and grinned, showcasing a mouth full of sharp teeth. Kalia's stomach lurched when she spotted the bloody sinew stuck between two fangs in the top row. She didn't want to know what, or who, that could be.

"You're here to barter then," the female continued in a low hiss, coiling her thick tail behind her. A predator preparing to strike. The orb swayed with her breasts. "For her? She looks lovely." Droplets of green venom leaked from her gums, dripping onto her bottom lip and trailing onto her chin. "It's been so long since I've had a woman. I miss how they taste. The warmth, the beauty, the pleasure—"

Kalia sent out a blast of her power, a wave of rippling magic that carved a warning into the si'lat's mind. The si'lat stopped her slow slither forward, blinking those round eyes for the first time. A single brow arched as a gust of wind blew, ruffling her hair against her two dusky nipples. Her knuckles tightened around the second spear still clutched in her hand, each finger ending in a long talon that Kalia knew would easily open her belly with a single swipe.

"Ah," the si'lat purred, "a Voyant." Her venom came quicker, leaking in slimy streaks that dribbled onto her chest. "It's been centuries since I've had one of *you*."

Kalia remained still, her eyes darting from the si'lat to Rahmi's profile. The si'lat's smile only grew, like a cat toying with its food.

"Give me the orb," Rahmi said slowly, calm and confident. He held out his hand, palm facing up. He couldn't have expected the creature to drop the orb there, not with the way she was already feasting on Kalia with her eyes. Rahmi hadn't seemed to notice. Or, if he had, he hadn't made any moves to show it.

Despite the water rushing down the passage, hitting just above Kalia's ankles, she couldn't help the charge of relief that flooded her veins. When comparing the two, the si'lat came in dead last with her taloned fingers and venomous bite. Kalia had seen what Rahmi could do when provoked.

Rahmi lunged, the tip of his cutlass plunging toward the si'lat. The orb bounced against her chest as she slithered to avoid him, her thick tail swinging around to clip him in the back of the knees. Rahmi landed with a dense splash on his back, his face momentarily dunking under the water. He surged upward, the water now nearly Kalia's knees.

"You're stuck here with me, little dove," the si'lat said playfully. "My sisters will be ecstatic when they get home from their hunt. We've lived on what the sea has brought us for so long."

Bones floated by, rats or fish by the looks of them, and each etched with the sharp bite marks of the si'lat's fangs. The water raced into the cavern beyond the si'lat, and, for the first time, Kalia noticed the set of gills protruding from her neck. She was waiting them out, knowing they would either *need* to get past her or fight to stay alive.

Kalia released another blast of her power as Rahmi swiped his cutlass, lashing the blade through the air. The sunlight glinted off the metal, brilliant and bright as though the captain had recently sharpened it. She was sure that he had. The si'lat turned toward Kalia, her round eyes narrowed as those unnaturally long slits for pupils dilated.

"Let me taste you, little dove," the si'lat said, swiping a hand toward Rahmi. Her set of talons collided with the cutlass, and she let out a hiss of pain as one of the talons was cut clean off. Blood spurted from the end of her finger, but she didn't pay it any mind. Not when Kalia was so close. "Let me get my fill of you."

The water was past Kalia's hips, quickly approaching her waist. Rahmi's movements had slowed, the rising tide keeping him from using his legs to put power behind the blade. Kalia plunged a tendril of her magic into the si'lat's mind, sifting through the layers as the creature's subconscious thrashed and bucked beneath her grip. Kalia hooked another tendril of magic in, pinning the si'lat's mind into place.

"*There's no escape for you,*" the si'lat said, her cool voice filled with rage. As though the sounds were coming from above water, the garble of metal against talon clanged once again. "*You're mine.*"

Kalia hadn't done it since she was young and never wanted to again. But the water was well past her breasts, approaching her throat quickly. They were dead if she didn't and would most likely still be dead out of pure exhaustion even if she did, but she had to give them a chance. She dug into the si'lat's mind, finding the glowing ember of the creature's soul.

The si'lat thrashed again, but Kalia already anchored herself against it, the heat and energy of the soul scorching a path of resistance that she could feel heating her very blood. Grimacing, she grabbed onto the threads that held the soul in place and pulled. It took more effort than she remembered, possibly because the si'lat wasn't human, but Kalia finally uprooted the ember.

Kalia withdrew from the si'lat's mind as it began to blacken, the creature jerking to a standstill. With one final breath, blood gushing from a puncture wound along her ribcage from Rahmi's cutlass, the si'lat slunk beneath the surface of the water.

CHAPTER TWENTY-SIX

KALIA

"We have to go!" Rahmi yelled, holding his cutlass above his head. Blood streamed from his hairline to his jaw. Though, whether that was from the si'lat's blood dripping from his blade or an injury of his own, Kalia wasn't sure. "We're out of time!"

The tide was still rolling in with no indication that it had begun to slow. The passage back to the ship was flooded.

They were completely and utterly trapped.

Kalia whirled around, desperately gazing through the archway the si'lat had slithered through. The oasis beyond was already flooded, the water rising above the palm trees that grew in the cavern. It yawned above them, the blue sky mocking as Kalia's boots finally left the rock floor. She pressed a hand to the ceiling, sputtering against the tide that threatened to drown her where she stood.

"This way!" Rahmi yelled. "We have to get to the si'lat's lair!"

Kalia began to swim, careful not to knock her head against the jagged stone above her. The water covered the wide archway now, the slats of sunlight from the cracks in the ceiling doing little to illuminate the passage. Blood swirled from the dead si'lat below her, dyeing the water a deep shade of red. "How?" Kalia yelled back, her voice rising above the thunderous roar of the sea.

Rahmi's eyes darted around before landing where his feet kicked to keep him afloat. He looked up at her, his jaw set in determination. "Do you trust me?"

"I— what?"

"You have to trust me, *ruehi*," Rahmi said. There were mere inches left in the passage, and Kalia had to angle her head to keep her mouth and nose above the water.

Her neighbor, a close family friend, had said those very words to her when he caught her using her power as a small child. *You have to trust me*. He had given her family over to the guards instead. But now...there wasn't any time. She could put her life in Rahmi's hands, or she could accept her death.

Terror flared to life inside of her, a mindless entity that she had no control over. Kalia chose not to focus on it. Instead, she centered on the flecks of amber brown in his eyes, the curve of his nose, and the curl of his wet hair. Her swallow was thick. And, finally, despite the hesitation screaming inside of her, she nodded.

Rahmi wasted no time as he grabbed her hand, tugging her toward the oasis.

"What are you—" Kalia began to ask, but she was able to suck in one final deep breath before the captain dragged her beneath the surface.

The roaring of the sea calmed to a muffle, the brine painfully stinging the minor cuts on her head from where she had scraped it against the ceiling. Swirling bubbles and salt and the current pulled her in one direction in the cavern and then the other. Still, Rahmi's hand remained tightly bound with hers.

He kicked downward, and Kalia spotted the si'lat through the rippling waters, the orb still secured around her neck. Rahmi tugged her through the cavern's opening before he turned up, hurried strokes and kicks surging them toward the glittering surface.

Kalia's boots were heavy and saturated, but she championed her legs further. Her clothes threatened to drag her down despite their thinness, but Rahmi's steady guidance kept her from sinking to the bottom. Her lungs had just begun to prickle, a heavy sensation settling onto her chest when she broke through the top of the water with a gulping gasp for fresh air.

Rahmi's breaths were heaving, his sputtering cough wet next to her. She watched as he shook the locks of loose hair from his eyes, dragging a hand down his face to clean the droplets from his lashes.

"You—you—" Kalia began, but the words failed her. He had undoubtedly saved her, just like he said he would. Something in her heart shook loose, a freeing lightness she hadn't felt in a long time.

"We have to find somewhere to rest. We can't spend all our energy keeping us afloat; the high tide lasts too long," Rahmi said, ignoring her gaze as he looked around. "There's got to be an opening, ah— there it is."

Kalia glanced in the direction of his stare. The oasis was a natural sinkhole in the limestone cliffs, where the cavern system's ceiling collapsed long ago. Curtains of stalactites hung from the edge of the opening, in stark contrast to the stone against the bright, blue sky. Greenery decorated the walls, vegetation that dipped its long vines into the water.

He had already begun to swim away from her, and she quickly followed, rippling the surface that had already started to settle.

"How long is high tide?" Kalia asked as they reached an opening in the wall where the rising tides and battering winds had carved a small cave.

Rahmi sunk beneath the water, and, with a pinch of surprise, Kalia felt his hand under the sole of her boot, pitching her out of the sea and into the cave. She quickly planted her hands onto the rock and rolled into the cave, water sluicing from her shirt and dripping into pools at her feet. Rahmi followed on her heels, dropping his cutlass onto the cave floor before pushing himself out of the tidewater.

Kalia stared out at the flooded oasis, where the sea had covered the tide pools and palm trees completely.

"Six hours or so," Rahmi finally answered, tearing off the scarf that covered his hair to wring the excess water onto the floor. "And that's if we get lucky that the si'lat's sisters don't return from their hunt in the meantime."

Kalia swallowed, glancing back at Rahmi, who had stripped his tunic over his head and laid it flat against the sliver of afternoon light that warmed the stone. Corded muscle, built from centuries of working on the sea, and sun-kissed skin covered his core. She looked away just as her mouth dried.

No, she would not do this. Her ears strained as she tried to hear any indication that the si'lat sisters swam just under the surface, quieting her still-labored breathing to listen for the swish of a scaled tail or the scrape of talons against the rock. The cavern was silent, save for the lapping of water against the cliff walls and the occasional brush of the vines against stone.

"And we better hope the si'lat sisters don't return while we're here," Rahmi's voice echoed from deeper in the cave, his tone light despite the worry that still punctuated it.

Kalia turned around to ask why, but the reason was evident as soon as her gaze dropped to what lay at Rahmi's feet. Piles of bones littered the cave, fractured skulls and dried sinew, all etched with the gouge marks that matched those terrible fangs of the si'lat. Rats and fish and birds and a few that looked uncomfortably human, each bearing the same clue that they had been subjected to a horrifically messy death.

She tasted the rising fear in the back of her throat as she took slow steps toward Rahmi, as though she couldn't help the draw of her body to his. The heat of his skin sunk into hers as she stopped next to him, staring down at the bones. She had seen piles of dead bodies before, most of them gray and mottled from days in the sun following their executions. For a brief moment, she wondered if this was all that was left of her mother and brother, both having been buried in the desert sands outside of the city walls.

"You should remove your clothing as well," Rahmi said through the silence, kicking his boots off and leaving them against the cave wall. "To dry, I mean. Once the sun sinks below the cavern's opening, the wetness against your skin will reduce your ability to maintain your body temperature. At best, you'll catch a cold."

Kalia opened her mouth to debate the truth of his statement, knowing that one didn't get sick that way, but stopped herself. He was padding away from her, his bare feet whispering against the stone floor and the muscles of his back and shoulders rolling with every step. Seeing him like this, the casual way he bent down to flip his tunic over, how he scraped his hair from his brow...it was intimate.

She suddenly felt at odds with herself, witnessing something that she shouldn't be and unable to tear herself away. She inhaled a breath, allowing it to fill her chest before slowly letting it out. Lifting her gaze from Rahmi's back, her cheeks flushed when she realized he had been watching her over his broad shoulder, his eyes shadowed with something unreadable.

"What are you thinking about, *ruehi*?" Rahmi asked softly. He slowly walked back toward her as though he were afraid spooking her would send her scurrying back into the water behind him. His feet rasped against the stone, just another reminder that he was half-dressed and looking as though he wanted the same from her.

"I'm glad you're not dead," Kalia whispered as he approached, halting just shy of a collision. "Would have been a shame to have the opportunity taken from me."

Rahmi huffed a laugh as he reached toward her, his fingers delicately grabbing the hem of her tunic. He untucked it from the waistband of her breeches, and she grew feverish from the mere graze of his fingertips against her hips. "I'm glad you're not dead, too. Would have been a shame to return to the ship without you."

Kalia's gasp hitched in her throat as his hands covered her waist, the rough callouses biting and scraping at her too-tight skin. His touch was unhurried and methodical, unyieldingly concise. Just like him. His hands inched up, pulling the hem of her shirt with them, but his eyes never left hers. Not even for a second. He was waiting— for a confirmation, for a denial, Kalia didn't know.

"You don't want this," she reminded him quietly. "I'm a mistake in the long lines of the ones you've already made."

Rahmi's hands wrapped around her back, fingers dancing along her skin. "And you were going to forget the moment it was—" He stopped, his hands motionless along her flesh. Kalia closed her eyes. She knew what he found there. He had known they were there, but she was sure he had never seen them for himself.

Kalia managed to still even further as he rounded her body, pulling the tunic further up her shoulders. She had never been more aware of her scars until that moment. She had never felt them pull at her skin so tightly, had never so badly wanted to erase those crisscrossed lines from her back. There was a reason she never let other men see her undressed. The ugly comments that followed were a knife that pierced her heart.

Rahmi's breath seemed to slow, though Kalia realized it had only gone shallow. "Who did this to you?" The question wasn't a question but a surprising command. An angry one, at that. The orders that he spouted usually ground on her. She seemed to be okay with this one.

It took a moment to clear the lump from her throat, but he never covered her. Never shied away from the truth that lay there. "The madam knew what she wanted," Kalia answered simply. "And what she wanted was a child who never talked back." She opened her eyes to stare into the oasis, the water lapping gently against the stone walls. She focused on it and willed it to calm her.

Rahmi made a noise that she couldn't discern. "Why answer to her? She— you—" He paused to sigh, and his fingertips traced the thickest one that spanned her flesh. "You're powerful, *ruehi*."

"I was young," Kalia replied, not quite allowing the bite to stray from her tone. "I was afraid of her. Of who she knew and what she could do. I was brought to the bordello to influence the men who came, to force them into choosing a woman and spending their coin. I was never— I didn't—"

Rahmi was quiet for a long minute, long enough that she had to glance over her shoulder to see if he was still standing there. His eyes were glossed, cast in shadows created by the marching sun. She was afraid to look into them, sure that she didn't want to know what was lying there—pity, sadness, or —worse yet—kindness.

She drew up the ounce of courage that remained and lifted her gaze. She found understanding, she found empathy, but she also found rage. And darkness.

"I don't look at these and see a scared child," Rahmi nearly spat, though she knew the anger wasn't directed at her. "I see resilience. I see strength. And I see a cavern of cleverness that only the survivors of this world can bear."

Then he did something Kalia never expected. He bent down and pressed his lips on every puckered scar. He kissed each one of them as though he savored the feeling of his flesh against hers, as though he could heal each one if only he kept going. Her eyes closed again, but it wasn't out of fear this time.

Rahmi's lips came free of her back, and the delicate touch of his hands evolved into something that resembled fiery need. She twisted around in his arms, winding a hand around the back of his head to pull him down toward her. Mouth met mouth. Tongue danced against tongue. Heat and pleasure and roaming hands swirled together in a sensual game that she was desperate to play with him.

Kalia knew they were emotionally incompatible on the best of days and lethally so on the worst. Yet, she was finding it harder and harder to stay away.

"Let me touch you," Rahmi murmured, his words fanning against the shell of her ear. One of his hands gripped her hair, the other slid to her lower back and pulled her against him. His hard cock pressed against her belly. "Let me taste you." The words weren't a command or an order but a plead.

Kalia said nothing as she reached between them to grip the hem of her still-soaked shirt, pulling it over her head before letting it fall to the floor with a loud *splat*. Her hands found the crook of his neck, her bare breasts scrapped against his chest. Rahmi's tongue licked a path from her ear down to the base of her throat, nipping at the hollow of her collarbones before moving down to swirl a lazy circle around her nipple.

"Please," Kalia said breathily as his fingers hooked into the waist-band of her sea-sopped breeches. She didn't even know what she was begging for, just that he would do it.

Rahmi's chuckle ghosted against her abdomen as he slowly pulled the breeches over her hips, exposing her legs to the stinging cool air. Kalia didn't care, not as her fingers threaded in his hair and not as he planted open-mouthed kisses down her thigh. He lifted one foot before the other, pulling the breeches from around her ankles and discarding them haphazardly on top of the tunic.

"Beautiful," he murmured as he looked up the length of her body, their eyes connecting between the valley of her breasts. "So fucking beautiful."

Kalia moaned as his hands moved up her legs, as his fingers slid into the slit between her thighs. By the groan he made at the back of his throat, she knew that he found her wet. Her head tipped back, her hair brushing against her shoulders. Everything was too sensitive, every-thing too tight. She nearly found herself rubbing her thighs together just for the friction.

Rahmi tugged her down as he collapsed onto his back, pulling her down until she was straddling his hips, her sex against his taut core. Gods, he felt good *now*. How would he feel in a few minutes? She was desperate to know. Sliding against the stone floor, Rahmi shifted further down until her knees bracketed his head, his mouth positioned directly below the meeting of her thighs.

His arms threaded around her waist, her breath coming in sharp pants as he spread her knees further, forcing her down onto his face. She shuddered as he blew against her and went molten when he did it again. One hand reached up to tweak her nipple between his thumb and forefinger, a predator playing with his prey. Kalia looked down at him to find his darkened eyes peering up at her.

Rahmi was male arrogance, dominant and unforgiving. And it was when his tongue first swiped against her sex, his fingers digging into the flesh of her hips to yank her closer to him, that she knew he was controlled and yet wildly raw. And, gods, it was *Rahmi*.

"Do you like how you feel when my tongue is against you?" Rahmi asked, stoking another low moan from Kalia that echoed off the stone walls. His tongue swirled again, dipping inside of her before he sucked on her clit. "When I taste you?" He groaned again, lifting his head to curl his tongue against her front wall. "Fuck, Kalia, you're delicious."

Kalia reached down to touch herself, to run her forefinger along her clit, but he grabbed her wrist with the hand that had been cupping her breast. "Do your best to make me come then," she said, quirking a brow toward him. "I won't make it so easy this time."

Rahmi's eyes flashed at the pose of her challenge, and his question came out as a growl when he asked, "Did you think about my fingers inside of you? Did you make yourself come wishing it was me?"

Kalia watched his fingers brush against her clit, play on her belly, circle her nipple. He was mapping her body, studying it to learn exactly what made her moan and mewl and grind against him. His tongue licked her again, this time slow and methodical. "Would you like it if I did?" The words tumbled out of her.

She could picture the savage smirk that curved against her sex just by the crinkle at the corners of his eyes. It sent a shock of pleasure barreling up her spine. Kalia leaned back to brace her hands against the tops of his thighs, the angle allowing her to sink further onto his mouth, keeping him from replying. From the way he devoured her, he didn't seem to mind.

The pleasure in her core built and built as she rolled her sex against his tongue, as he sucked and licked and panted against her. And it was just as that pleasure was on the verge of tipping into oblivion when he grabbed her waist and flipped them over, careful to keep her from crashing against the stone.

Rahmi's eyes flashed wide as her knees fell open, inviting and pleading. Kalia propped herself onto her elbows to watch and challenge him, but his stare remained on her. "I've thought about nothing except how you would feel," he said, slowly tugging on the strings that held his breeches in place. "For weeks now. It's driven me to the brink of madness. And still?" He paused as his breeches fell from his hips, his cock springing free. Her pulse thrummed with anticipation as he wrapped a hand around the thick shaft, pumping it twice while watching her with a predator's intent. "I'm going to hold myself back so I can ruin you. Again and again and again."

Kalia bit her lip to keep from moaning, and his gaze lifted to her face, his eyes darting around to graph the pleasure he undoubtedly found etched there. He knelt between her thighs, just enough that her hips cradled his, and traced a path through her opening with the tip of his cock.

"Don't be gentle," Kalia said, reaching forward to pinch his chin with her forefinger and thumb. "Don't be—"

A moaning cry cut off her words as Rahmi thrust into her, spreading her and filling her in a melding pinch of pleasure and pain. Her back bowed from the stone at the toe-curling feel of him. He roughly slid his length back until he was almost free of her, white-hot lust burning the depths of his brown eyes, before pistoning into her again. His mouth met hers, and Kalia tasted the saltiness on her tongue.

The kiss was taunting and primal. Kalia raised her hand to thread her fingers through his hair, tugging his head back until he moaned with his mix of pain and pleasure. She raggedly inhaled as he picked up speed, thrusting into her with steadfast and merciless rolls of his hips.

"I've done terrible things in my life," Rahmi panted when he tore his lips away from hers, reaching down to grip one hip while pressing the rough pad of his thumb against her clit. He watched where they met with rapt attention, plunging into her again and again. The gleam in his eye spurred her on and spiraled within her until it threatened to consume her whole. "But my biggest feat will be knowing that I've fucked you so well that no one else will compare. That you'll only think of me when another man is inside of you."

That pressure began to build again, harder and more intense this time. "Don't come," she said to him, feeling him thicken inside of her. "Don't think about the way I feel or—" Her jab came to a choked cry as that blistering pressure finally released, sending carnal waves crashing through every taut muscle of her body. It took minutes, perhaps even years, for her body to come down. But when she finally did, her slick body was limp and boneless, dripping sweat onto the cave floor.

"That's my good girl," Rahmi said as he stilled, his thumb still tracing lazy circles around her clit. Another wave of pleasure crested through her, stoking a moan that echoed off the stone. "Come for me, *ruehi*."

Rahmi pulled out of her, replacing his cock with his tongue, licking up the release she had glistening there. Kalia mewled, the over-sensitivity of his tongue against her, causing her to jump. She grabbed a chunk of his hair, pulling it to the point that she thought she would cause him pain. He only chuckled, his laugh fanning against her sex before he nipped her inner thigh. She could only imagine how throbbing his cock was, how he hadn't come quite yet.

"Did you think we were finished?" Rahmi asked her, flipping her onto her front. He plunged two fingers inside of her, and Kalia's eyes rolled into the back of her head. "I want you ruined. And that's where I'll have you."

CHAPTER
TWENTY-SEVEN

KALIA

"**Y**ou have a glow."

Kalia side-eyed Reshef as he came into view, leaning his elbow against the edge of the gunnel. "I've been standing in the sun for three days; of course, I have a glow."

Reshef shook his head, pivoting to plant both elbows on the gunnel as he looked out at the sea. "No, no, that's not it. It's a *glow*, not a *tan*." It was his turn to side-eye her, and she felt his gaze track from the crown of her head to the boots she had sulked over putting on that morning. "I know it's not a haircut, though you desperately could use one."

Kalia scoffed, but Reshef kept going.

"It's not new clothes, and gods know that dress has seen better days—"

"Did you walk over to insult me?" Kalia asked. Reshef had always been a bit of an asshole, but his frank honesty was what endeared her to him.

Reshef smirked, though he kept his stare firmly leveled on her as though she were a puzzle he meant to solve. His eyes briefly flicked over her shoulder before returning her to her. "Captain is at the helm today. He was at the helm yesterday, too." He narrowed his eyes, though Kalia kept her lips firmly closed. "And he keeps looking over here."

It was quiet for a moment, and Kalia locked her gaze on the sparkling sea before her. Blue as far as her eyes could see. The water lapped gently at the hull for the first time since they had returned from the si'lat's lair. She and Rahmi were lucky that the sisters hadn't returned from hunting, though Rahmi quickly grabbed the orb from the dead si'lat's corpse as they passed through the passage when the low tide came in.

Reshef suddenly straightened, his eyes trailing between her and Rahmi. "Oh. *Oh.* My, my, my." He squared his shoulders to her, a wicked smile curling his lips. "You *harlot.*"

"I don't know what you mean," Kalia said, though a little too quickly. She could already see the mischievous sparkle in Reshef's eye. And, she now knew, that sparkle meant there was nowhere for her to hide.

"I know *exactly* why you have a glow."

Kalia was desperate to get out of this conversation. "No, you don't."

"You *do* look different, but it's because you look thoroughly fucked. That's the glow—"

"Gods, kill me now."

Shouts from the crew behind them sounded as a rope from the mainmast snapped, sending two men sliding across the deck. Rahmi ordered Alaric to the helm as he flew down the wooden steps, reaching to grab the rogue, twirling rope before pulling it back into place. The sleeves of his tunic had been rolled to the elbow, exposing the thick swirls of markings that lay there. Sweat sheened a layer that glistened on his brow, tiny droplets forming that dripped down his temple.

"That man even looks like he can fuck."

Kalia hadn't realized Reshef had been watching her closely, that smirk curling even more profound with every passing moment. "*Gods*, Reshef—"

"I mean, if he can have you looking like *that* three days later—"

Kalia had undoubtedly heard enough. She turned to press a finger into his chest. "Listen up, you little shit. Keep it to yourself, or I'll cut off *your* favorite appendage and serve it to Alaric in Doc's revolting fish stew."

Reshef lifted his hands in surrender, though the smirk never lessened. "Noted, Kalia. My lips are sealed. Nothing save for the gods themselves will pull it out of me."

Kalia's shoulders relaxed, the tenseness ebbing away. She leaned against the gunnel, once more staring out at the water. The sea had almost become a peaceful sight to her, the waves reminding her of the rolling dunes surrounding Sha'Hadra. "It didn't mean anything, anyways." From how her heart thumped a traitorous beat in her chest, she knew she was only lying to herself.

And that cyclical debate she had been having with herself over the last three days kept her from pounding on his cabin door every night. Putting her hand between her thighs after she knew Shirin and Elodie had fallen asleep only gave her so much relief. Barely any, if she were being truthful.

But continuing to be wrapped up in him only complicated things further. Kalia had already stopped swapping the dried meat and fruit she had hiding in case the ship came within swimming distance of the continent. And that was alarming enough, considering Wright was still working an angle to get her to agree to destroy the *Luminaria*.

"Yeah, okay," Reshef muttered, bending down to whisper in her ear. "Tell that to your glow." He barely budged as she pushed him away, a choked laugh following on the heels of her shove. "I came to give you information. After much discussion, and by that I mean sucking Alaric's cock one time in the storage berth—"

"Really?"

"—I found your man."

Kalia licked her lips, the taste of salt a shock against her already dry tongue. "And? What else?"

Reshef slyly glanced around, and Kalia assumed it was to ensure no one was near enough to overhear them. Satisfied, he reached into his pocket and pulled out a wrapped bundle of sliced cheese and two small apples, handing one to Kalia. If anyone were looking, it would appear that they were two friends enjoying lunch on the deck.

Friends. The word pulled at something behind Kalia's navel. She didn't know the last time she could consider someone a friend. She had so little experience with the concept that she wondered if that definition even included Reshef. But it was the only word that came close enough to her admiration for the man despite his tendency to pry.

And that tendency to pry, in this case, came in handy. Kalia wanted to know more about the *Luminaria* Rahmi was hunting and even more about why Wright wanted it destroyed. She wanted to go to the source to find the middle ground between the two.

"He's being kept in the brig," Reshef said through the bite of his apple. He swallowed before continuing. "Sounds like he hasn't been out in weeks. Doc has been feeding him leftover fish stew. Honestly, I can't think of much worse than the *fresh* one, let alone—"

"I want to talk to him," Kalia cut him off. She took a bite of her apple as one of the crew came up behind them, grabbing the coil of rope that sat at her feet. Glancing over her shoulder, she spotted Rahmi climbing the rope ladder fixed to the mainmast.

Reshef whistled low under his breath, breaking off a piece of cheese from the block and popping it into his mouth. "That's a man, I tell you what."

Kalia's head reeled back as she chewed, then swallowed. "Do I need to remind you that you were also captured and forced aboard a cursed pirate ship? Or should I set Elodie on you again to help you remember?"

"Thanks for that, by the way. Since *you* taught her to punch, she's been using *me* as target practice. And her hit isn't gentle." Reshef sighed. "There's something rather thrilling about being captured. It gets the blood flowing if you know what I mean. Has he tied you up yet? Alaric did it to me last week. It was *fantastic*—"

"We're not talking about this," Kalia said, taking a second bite of the apple. "I think we should go down there now. Alaric is at the helm. Rahmi is otherwise engaged. We won't be missed."

Reshef tossed his apple's core into the sea, quickly losing it in the ship's wake. He broke off a piece of cheese and handed it over to Kalia before breaking off a second. "If we're caught talking to him, we will also be thrown down there."

Kalia quirked a brow. "Does that mean you aren't going to come? I thought being on the ship was *thrilling*."

Reshef bristled, casting her a long look. "Of course, I'm coming. Don't be ridiculous. Like I would leave my best friend to enter the brig alone."

Unlike the hundreds of times before, Kalia didn't correct him when he said the term *best friend*. As though he knew he was wearing her down, Reshef sent the sea a nod of satisfaction, his devilish smirk softening into a small, warm smile.

Kalia had not returned to the brig since she was first brought onto the ship. She had forgotten the rotten stink that seemed to seep into the walls, the stale air that didn't allow any movement, and the lack of light aside from the dimly lit lanterns that lined the hallway. Even the water slapping against the keel was muffled, though some of it managed to leak down the bulwark like small rivers.

Reshef crossed the threshold first, using the flint stone to spark a flame against the lantern bolted to the wall. Kalia followed in after him, glancing around the iron-clad cells until her gaze landed on the one man locked inside.

Karim blinked against the sudden deluge of light. And, though the lantern didn't cast him in the best light, she knew he still looked sickly. His skin, once the same tone as hers, was pallid and ashen. His brown eyes sunk heavily into his sockets, creating large, dark circles that only contributed to his ill-appearance. His legs trembled as he stood up, but his wary gaze landed on the loaf of bread in Kalia's hand. His eyes flashed back up to meet hers.

"It's not moldy," Karim commented, nodding toward the bread. His voice cracked with every word as though he hadn't needed to speak in a long while. "Must mean you want something."

Kalia moved to place the loaf into Karim's hand as he stretched through the iron bars, but Reshef stopped her with a quick clasp of her wrist.

"Information," Reshef said. He tore off a piece of the bread and placed it in Karim's palm in a gesture of good faith. "The more you tell us, the more you get."

Karim scowled at the bread, lifting it into his mouth a second later. A groan escaped between his parted lips. "It's been weeks since I've had a fresh loaf of bread." He stuck his hand between the iron and let his wrist rest against the crossbar. "What do you want to know?"

Kalia cleared her throat as she stepped forward, letting her gaze slide over the bucket perched in the corner of the cell before gliding to the thin, hole-ridden blanket neatly folded on a crudely made wooden bench. "The *Luminaria*. Why did you want it?"

"I didn't want it. I wanted the gold," Karim corrected her. He swept a greasy lock of hair from his face, where it melded with stomach-clenching ease to the rest of his dirty hair. "The captain of the ship I hired wanted it."

Next to her, Reshef was leaning a shoulder against the cell door. He clicked his tongue against his teeth, and Kalia could picture the roll of his eyes, which undoubtedly followed. "Semantics. Why were you hunting it?"

Karim wriggled his fingers in a gesture toward the loaf of bread, and, with a deep sigh, Kalia plopped another piece into his hand. "Captain Nasir Al-Mahdi was a mercenary hired by the king to retrieve the gemstone. Our paths crossed unwittingly when we hired him to take us there. My colleagues and I...we just wanted the treasure that was rumored to lay inside."

"Why did the king want it?" Reshef asked.

Karim gestured toward the loaf of bread again. He tossed the piece Kalia handed him into his mouth before answering. "Probably the same reason your captain wants it. To break a curse. To have access to immortality without the constraints of the gods." He shook his head.

"It's a waste, though. The *Luminaria* can only be activated by a djinn. One of my colleagues discovered that on the way to the caves. We never told Captain Al-Mahdi."

"Luckily for us," Reshef retorted as he tilted his head toward Kalia. He zipped the black stone back and forth on the chain hung around his neck.

Karim stilled, lifting his eyes toward Kalia for the first time in minutes. "You're a djinn?"

"That's certainly what they say," Kalia muttered. She cleared her throat. "Where are your colleagues? You mentioned hiring the ship with them." She pre-emptively placed a piece of bread in Karim's hand, knowing he wouldn't bother answering without it.

"Dead. Ghouls."

Reshef's brow shot toward his hairline, wrinkling the skin near his forehead. "Ghouls? You can't expect us to believe—"

"They came out of the ground," Karim interjected. A vacant shadow passed over his eyes as though he had momentarily gone somewhere else.

Kalia took the opportunity to pierce through the first few layers of his mind, connecting that bridge with ease. He either wanted her to see or was too tired to fight back. She saw the ruby gemstone glittering on a pedestal surrounded by black water. She watched as the room flooded, how magic at the threshold kept it all inside the spare room, and how Karim managed to escape, only to see his colleagues be eaten alive by gray, rotting bodies.

She pulled out of his mind, and he collapsed against the iron bars, struggling to hold himself up.

"Your colleagues didn't just die," Kalia amended, her lip curling in disgust as she stared down at him. The pity and empathy she had once felt for him vanished instantly, leaving repulsion in its wake. "You left them there to be eaten alive."

Reshef snapped his head to Kalia before snapping it back to Karim as though he were watching a very intense match. In his silence, footsteps pounded down the stairs in the distance. Someone was coming.

"I had my reasons for doing what I did," Karim retorted as he sank onto the wooden bench behind him. It groaned in protest at the sudden introduction of his weight. "Reasons you will never fully understand."

"I understand completely," Kalia shot back, inhaling a breath through her nose that she deeply regretted in the next moment. The sour scents of his unwashed body and the waste bucket were nearly too much. "You're a coward. You stole the map back. You left your colleagues to die—"

"And what if I did?" Karim shouted, his hands splaying wide. A maniacal laugh burst out of him as the lantern's flame began to flicker. It accentuated his wide, wild eyes. "I'm here, and they're given over to Samael." He stumbled forward, clutching the iron bars so hard his knuckles whitened. "And I'll still be here when you lead us back to the treasure. I'll be wealthy. I'll buy the whole fucking kingdom. I'll purchase every whore in the city. I'll—"

Reshef put a hand at her lower back, leading her toward the brig's entrance. "Come on, Kalia. We don't need to listen to him." He lifted his other hand to pinch the lantern's wick, snuffing out the flame. It left Karim in the damp darkness, his shouts following them into the hallway. "What a raving lunatic."

"He's been alone in the dark for too long," Kalia replied, taking a few steps ahead of Reshef to keep him from stepping on the heels of her boots. But she stopped just as she found the illuminated doorway at the top of the staircase, brilliantly white amidst the black that swallowed them. "Do you truly think it would take a djinn to unlock the *Luminaria*?"

Reshef scrubbed a hand down his face, scratching at the stubble growing on the underside of his chin. "Hard to say. If the king wants it...if the captain wants it...we might battle for who gets it in the end."

The narrow passage was pressing in on her. Kalia felt as though she wasn't getting enough air into her lungs. She tried to swallow, but that only enhanced the feeling that she was smothered.

"Kalia?"

She tried to temper back the overwhelming sensation of dread that sat like a boulder in her gut. "Reshef. I need to ask you something. It's very important."

He must have heard the seriousness in her tone because his shoulders straightened before he answered her. "Go on."

Kalia took another breath, one that was far too shallow and one that threatened to set her heartbeat off to an uncomfortable race. She bit her lower lip, wondering for a long minute how to get the words out. Finally, she settled on honesty. "Reshef, do you know what a djinn is?"

Reshef's head flinched back, and what little she could see from his gaze grew distant. "What do you mean *what is a djinn*?" he asked in response, confusion sweeping over his features. "Aren't you the..." He trailed off and understanding sunk heavy lines onto his face. "Oh, gods. You aren't a djinn."

It wasn't a question.

Kalia blew out the breath she hadn't realized she was holding and wrapped her arms around her waist.

"Gods, Kalia, *you aren't a djinn*!" Reshef whisper-shouted. He threaded his fingers together and placed his palms on the crown of his head. "He's going to kill you for this. You can forget whatever relationship you and him have right now. The moment he finds out..."

Reshef didn't need to say *his* name.

"I know," Kalia retorted. She could have sworn her chest was on the verge of caving in. "I don't know what to do."

Reshef lifted his hand to his necklace, fingering the black stone tethered there. "We are going to figure this out, I swear it." Though he attempted to sound confident, Kalia still heard the apprehension underlining his tone. "We'll figure this out together. We—we'll figure this out. It's what friends do for one another."

Kalia felt Reshef circle his arms around her shoulders, tugging her into a tight hug that pricked tears to the corners of her eyes. For the first time in a long time, Kalia believed someone had her back. A weight lifted from her shoulders and, despite the situation she had found herself in, she felt unexplainably light.

CHAPTER
TWENTY-EIGHT

RAHMI

The extra cask of *fion* had somehow made its way up the quarter-deck, where the men eagerly cracked it open. Steins and mugs were held under the ever-flowing stream of alcohol, raucous laughter echoing over the dark waters that surrounded them.

Using the NightWatcher to estimate the location of the lunar cycle in coordination with the map Rahmi had taken from Karim, Wright drew up a secondary map with his best guess as to where the archipelago might appear. And, according to Wright, they were mere days away.

Rahmi had known Wright for decades. He knew that Wright's best guess was a near absolute.

It was cause for celebration, one that rarely came on board The Mark of Malice and one that Rahmi's crew desperately needed—one that *he* desperately needed.

Rahmi could almost taste the freedom and could already smell the stalls in Sha'Hadra that he hadn't been able to visit for three hundred years. He wondered if they looked the same or had changed in the last few centuries. He imagined the sun baking down on the red-clay houses, the brightly colored tarps flapping in the desert breeze. He thought of the vendors shouting to the customers, urging them to peek at their shares.

Then, Rahmi thought of Kalia. He imagined her in a blue dress, so similar to the red one she always chose to wear. He watched in his mind as she bent over a barrel of dried spices, smelling the herbs at the behest of the shop owner perched behind his stock. Surprisingly, he even imagined walking next to her, casually having his hand on her hip, kissing her forehead at any given interval, and burying his nose in her hair.

"Captain!" a voice shouted, drawing Rahmi away from his thoughts. "Take a drink, won't ya? It's about time you joined in!"

Rahmi found a bottle being thrust into his hands, and the cork popped off.

"Take a drink, sir! It's all thanks to you and the djinn. We'll be free of our debts soon enough."

Rahmi took a sip, the crew surrounding him drunkenly crying out joyfully. He looked at their faces, each one brightened by the moonlight. Crinkled eyes, heads tipped toward the night sky, easy breaths, relaxed shoulders. Was this how every day could look? Pardoned from his curse, wandering the sea? He took another sip, one that turned into a pulling gulp.

"Where have you two been?" a singsong voice rang out over the men's low chatter. Elodie skipped over to Kalia and Reshef, both of whom emerged from the lower deck near the ship's bow. "You've been gone for *ages* and missed dinner and everything."

Shirin followed with a bowl of fish stew settled in her palms. "It's probably cold by now. I thought I would set some aside for you in case the men finish it all."

Reshef grabbed the bowl first, taking a long swig from the rim before wiping his mouth with the back of his hand. "You're a star, the both of you." It was Shirin's turn to blush, something that didn't happen often, though that didn't catch Rahmi's attention.

No. The look of sheer emotion on Kalia's face ranged from overwhelming sadness to uncertainty to longing. It was a softness that only enhanced her natural beauty, a softness that momentarily wiped away the years of torment that usually notched a line in her brow. Rahmi had the sudden urge to make his way over to her, one that he had to quash.

"Captain!" Alaric said, jogging over to mizzenmast, where Rahmi had casually leaned. "Captain, I—" He stopped, narrowing his one visible eye at Rahmi. "I don't like that look on your face."

The quartermaster knew every expression that passed over Rahmi's features, even those so subtle he was sure he was the only person who would notice.

"It's nothing, Alaric," Rahmi said, taking another sip of the *fion* that Thomas had left in his hands. He hooked a thumb into the hilt of the cutlass, tearing his gaze away from Kalia, who had finally taken a hesitant sip of the fish stew. "What did you need?"

Alaric wasn't buying it. "Are you having second thoughts?" The question was sharp, worded as though it were a dagger flashed as a promise for retribution. At Rahmi's hesitancy, Alaric gaped. "We're *days away* from finding the *Luminaria*. You— you can't seriously be considering quitting?"

If Rahmi were honest with himself, he hated indecision more than anything. He hated insecurity. He hated foolish, wishy-washy behaviors of any kind. And yet, he had found himself face to face with it more often than he hadn't since Kalia came aboard his ship. She had somehow managed to re-center his universe and place a new perspective on his narrowed lens of life.

"What would you do, Alaric? If you weren't immortal? If you had the choice to start a family, sail the seas, or drink yourself to death in a tavern? What would your life look like?"

Alaric stepped back, staring at Rahmi like the captain had grown a second head. "Why does it—"

"Tell me," Rahmi commanded, taking another sip of the *fion*. "Be truthful. What would it be?"

Alaric opened his mouth, furrowed his brow, then closed it again. "I—," he started. He turned to look out at the sea, where Rahmi could only see the small white crests atop the waves, each shining under the light from the moon above. "This is all I know."

Rahmi handed the *fion* to Alaric, who took a hearty swig following his confession. "Aren't you curious to know how it feels to be mortal? To sail the seas because we choose to, not because we must collect souls? Or to have the honor of aging with a partner, to grow with them over a lifetime?"

Alaric cleared his throat, and Rahmi watched as his quartermaster's eyes turned toward Reshef, who had thrown his head back in laughter at something Elodie had said. Even Kalia's lips formed a slight grin. He was suddenly desperate to know what was said to make her smile.

"I think I would like that," Rahmi went on, slicing through the steady silence that had settled over him and Alaric.

Alaric frowned as he handed the bottle back to Rahmi. "She's a djinn, captain," he said quietly. Rahmi felt his gaze bore into the side of his face. "You don't know if you can have those things with her."

Or, more importantly, if Kalia even wanted those things. That part was left unsaid.

Cora had sidled up near the group of four, a sneer plastered on her face. Rahmi straightened as Cora leaned in toward Elodie, hissing something that made the laugh slide from Elodie's lips. Cora had always been mean, a defensive wall that recalled a childhood filled with petty squabbles and parents who were uninvolved on a good day but too involved on a bad one. He had spoken to her at length about it and had tried to get down to the root of her guilt to allow her to heal.

And yet, Core still had the propensity to target those she deemed weaker than her. She went for Shirin once and never did it again. Elodie, on the other hand…Elodie had grown in the decades she and Rahmi had been meeting to work through her pain. She had bloomed from a wilted flower into something far more beautiful, though that growth seemed to hit a wall, even in their weekly chats, not until Kalia.

Rahmi made to walk over, stuffing the bottle back into Alaric's hands, who briefly fumbled with it. His footsteps slowed as Shirin stepped forward and then quickened again. Kalia stepped before them, her arms crossed tightly over her chest. Nothing good could come from this. Rahmi was sure of it.

As though on cue, Kalia's eyes narrowed, her vision growing hazy. Cora's pupils widened. Shirin had turned to place a comforting arm around Elodie's shoulders. Luckily for him, it didn't seem that Cora had rallied any other crew to her side, the other men and women still eagerly downing pints of *fion*. Somewhere on the opposite side of the crowd, a fiddle whined as it began to play.

Shirin took a step back as Rahmi approached, dragging Elodie with her. From the red rim of her eyes, he deduced that Elodie was on the verge of crying. He lifted a hand, ready to tap Kalia on the shoulder when she withdrew from Cora's mind.

Cora shook her head, her face slackening as her eyes roved the deck under her feet before lifting to look at Kalia.

"You need to leave her alone," Kalia said with a falsely sweet, close-lipped smile. "No one is going to be on your side if all you do is bully those around you." Cora opened her mouth to speak, but Kalia shook her head. "We don't need to hear your excuses. I *saw* your excuses." She leaned further to whisper so low that Rahmi almost missed it. "Mommy being mean to you is only a justification for so long. It's time to grow up."

Cora set her jaw so tightly that the grind of her teeth could be heard over the stomping feet that danced on the other side of the quarterdeck. "You had no right—"

"You just haven't met someone willing to stand toe-to-toe with you. That person will always be me. And I'll gladly teach you that lesson as long as I'm on this ship."

"Those memories are private," Cora shot back. She turned toward Rahmi, expectation written on her raised brows. "Are you going to allow her to do this?"

Rahmi sighed, clasping a gentle hand on Kalia's forearm, which she immediately tore from his grip. "Cora, this is something that we've talked about. You can't—"

"It's *wrong,* captain," Cora interjected as she placed her hands firmly on her hips. "Not to mention *illegal.*" She faced Kalia once more. "I could have your head for this. All I need is a single guard, and you will be gone. If I got one message to the palace, I could—"

It didn't take long for Rahmi to notice the fist balled at Kalia's side, the tightness of her eyes, or how her smile turned brittle at the edges. He wrapped his arms around Kalia's chest, pinning her wrists to her side before lifting her feet from the deck.

"Get off me, get off—" Kalia attempted to scramble forward but only managed to elbow Rahmi in the throat.

He let out a choked cough, though he kept his grip tight on her, whisking her away. Kalia needed space from Cora, enough that she wouldn't be able to break Cora's mind wide open and rip her soul away from her body, which she seemed on the verge of doing. He knew how quickly Kalia's mind formed plans for revenge and had been on the receiving end of them himself. But from how her eyes flashed and that dark shadow passed over her face, Cora had hit on something much deeper.

Rahmi marched them through the dimly lit office, finally setting her down in his private quarters. He shut the door with a *snap,* standing guard to keep Kalia from storming back to the deck.

"Let me out," Kalia said softly, her voice filled with calm malice that, had he been a lesser man, would have chilled him to his core. "Now."

Rahmi shook his head, leaning against the door. He reached behind him and turned the brass key before removing it from the lock, swiftly pocketing it at the front of his tunic. "You're going to kill her."

"Of *course* I'm going to kill her," Kalia snarled in reply, accentuating each word as though he were a particular brand of idiot. She paced in front of him,

She was clearly fighting a roaring battle within herself, the fire that raged evident in the stiffness of her shoulders and the curl of her fingers into fists. Her attention narrowed on him, and Rahmi had just enough time to slam down a barrier before her feral and angry power blasted toward him.

It scraped, clawed, and screamed against Rahmi's mind, threatening to shred him to ribbons if he relented for even the briefest of seconds. And just as quickly as it came, her power withdrew. Kalia collapsed to the floor, a single sob shaking her shoulders. She took a shuddering breath that Rahmi was sure meant to calm her, only for Kalia to fold over herself as the tears.

Rahmi pushed himself off the door and crossed the room, kneeling close enough to her to feel her tremors. "You can tell me, *ruehi*," he said quietly. "If you can't tell me, you can tell your friends."

"I don't have friends," Kalia shot back between sobs, only for the tears to take over again. She shook her head, lowering it to rest her brow against the cool, wooden floor. "I can't have friends."

"Why?"

She took another breath, lifting her head from the ground. Her green eyes were already puffy, and tears streaked down her cheeks. "It's too dangerous, *I'm* too dangerous."

Rahmi nodded slowly, twisting to change his position from kneeling to sitting. He drew his knees up, resting his forearms on them. "Does it have to do with what happened to your family?" He was empty and helpless at how quickly the fear seemed to cling to her, how she struggled to find herself in the sea of guilt she waded through.

And when Rahmi thought she wouldn't answer, Kalia finally whispered, "Yes."

They were quiet for a long while. Waves of grief and guilt continued to flow from her, pulling Rahmi into their depths. He reached forward, wiping her cheek with a gentle caress of his finger. She didn't curve away from him, though he half-expected her to, instead leaning into his touch.

"Will you tell me about it?" Rahmi asked, snaking his hand around to wipe her other cheek before letting it rest in the crook of her neck. He let his thumb rub gently along the top of her shoulder, painting figure-eights along her skin.

Kalia took another shaky breath, lifting her hand to swipe the back of it beneath her chin to stop the tears from continuing to drip onto her chest. "I was young when it happened. We had a neighbor, a good friend of my mother's. He— he felt my power one afternoon. I— I didn't know..."

Rahmi listened as she told him all of it, bile rising in the back of his throat with every detail that spilled out of her. Magic didn't run in her family, so no one knew how to look for it. The neighbor alerted the palace guards when he thought Kalia's family was sleeping that night. How the palace guards stormed the house, attacking Kalia's mother when she begged for mercy. How her brother screamed that it was him who had the powers to protect his sister, and how he was killed when he tried to get to their mother.

How Kalia's mother was then run through with a sword as she tried to fight for her son. Kalia slipped into hiding under the floorboards of their home out of pure terror.

Fury tore through Rahmi as he heard how her family's blood dripped on her for the rest of the night as she sat, stunned and scared, in her hiding spot. The blood had long dried before someone came to check on them, a different and unknowing neighbor screaming to the guards for help. Those same guards laughed when they arrived, having torn the family apart the night before.

"The girl," the betraying neighbor had repeatedly said, " What about the girl?"

"There was no girl," the guards replied. "Take the bodies, bury them in the desert. Give them a traitor's funeral."

Rahmi held her hand in his as she stared at the worn, red rug near his bed. She didn't seem to have tears left to cry, her gaze flat and haunted. But she kept talking, kept telling the story even though the celebration was still in full swing just meters away.

Kalia had crawled from the space under the floorboards after the bodies had been taken, dried blood in her hair and streaked down her face. She spent the next five years hustling the streets of Sha'Hadra, running from the guards and keeping to herself. She knew what happened when the children didn't keep to themselves.

"The madam found me soon after that," she finished, her voice cracking and her lips so dry they were nearly flaking. "I used my power on her to try and steal money. She took me away, threatening to call the guards if I didn't let her. It's my fault they're dead." She whispered the last words, barely heard above the ship's creaking and the roaring laughter around them.

Rahmi's stomach dropped to his boots, and there was heaviness in his limbs that hadn't been there before. "That's not true," he responded, firmly enough that she looked up and blinked. "Your family was murdered by a petulant king who decided the magic of a child was a threat to him. It was not your fault. None of it was. Trust me on that, *ruehi.*"

Kalia's eyes dropped to her lap, where their fingers were still threaded together. She placed her other free hand on top of his, patting it twice. "I learned long ago that trust was never meant to be given, not even when you think it should be."

Rahmi sighed through his nose, moving his hand from her neck to pinch her chin and force her to look at him. "Then I will spend the rest of your time on this ship *earning* it."

Her gaze searched his own, and Rahmi found himself doing the same. He didn't know the last time his heart thumped against his chest just from the simple look of a woman. He couldn't recall if it had ever happened. Here he was, pinned in place beneath a pair of green eyes. He was sure he had never seen a color so beautiful before.

Kalia opened her mouth before closing it again, a thought seemingly on the tip of her tongue. "I'm sorry for the sea urchin in your chair," Kalia finally murmured, those fucking eyes dipping to stare at his lips.

Rahmi huffed a laugh. When had they leaned toward each other? The loose locks of her hair fluttered with his breath. Her hand moved up his forearm, her fingers tracing the markings he bore. He felt her heat, could see the flecks of amber within the green, the faint freckles along her nose.

"I should say that I'm sorry for dragging you aboard my ship," Rahmi responded, his fingers leaving her chin to tuck one of those locks behind her ear. "But I would be lying to you. And I just promised to earn your trust."

Kalia's chuckle was breathy, yet it still thundered against Rahmi's ears. He wanted to hear it again and again. He wanted to find out how to make her laugh, see what would make her smile—anything, everything.

Her lips parted as they leaned closer, their breath mingling in the inch between them. Rahmi watched as her eyes slid closed, anticipating the kiss that was meant to come.

That was until a resounding *boom* sounded from the deck, jolting them apart. Rahmi stood quickly, pulling the key from the pocket of his tunic, and hurriedly unlocked the door. "Stay here," he ordered, ripping open the door before running across the threshold.

CHAPTER TWENTY-NINE

KALIA

L *ike fuck she was staying behind.*

Kalia raced out on Rahmi's heels, so close that she could feel the phantom breeze that tore from him as he ran. She was almost thankful for the interruption. The kiss would have been life-changing, soul-altering. She already knew it. Somewhere along the way, somewhere in their hatred of one another, she had begun to appreciate his steady leadership. And that appreciation evolved into a tentative understanding of one another, which then took on a life of its own.

She didn't know what it meant now, and she certainly didn't know what would come after that kiss. She was still meant to disembark the ship, and he was meant to carry on as a cursed captain, sailing the Aeglecian Sea for far longer than she would even be alive.

And Wright Thackeray...gods, the whole fucking thing had turned into a knotted, complicated mess. Rahmi was pledging to spend the rest of her time on the ship earning her trust, and she contemplated working against him. That didn't even touch on the issue that she *wasn't a djinn.*

Rahmi would certainly find out, one way or another, through Wright, through her inability to free the Luminaria. And she had almost told him. It was on the verge of slipping out before she had apologized for the sea urchin instead. She needed to tell him; she couldn't wait any longer.

Even though she knew it would break her heart. And possibly end her life.

Rahmi's thundering footsteps came to a screeching halt, and Kalia nearly ran headlong into his back. She expected an attack, perhaps another ship firing on *The Mark of Malice*, men scurrying around the deck to their places at the cannons. From Rahmi's reaction in his private cabin, she believed he thought the same thing.

Instead, they found Elodie trembling, her hands balled into fists at her side as she stood over Cora, a murderous glare on her pale face. At her feet was a piece of metal rigging that had come loose from above, the rope still coiled inside. Cora's eye was already blackening, blood trickling from a split above her brow.

"I am *not* worthless," Elodie shouted, her face contorting from a glare into one of rage that Kalia hadn't seen on her before. Until now, she wasn't sure that sweet, innocent Elodie had it in her. Even if she had been using Reshef as target practice. "*You* are the one who is worthless."

Despite her position against the deck, Cora scoffed. "*I'm* worthless? You think *I'm* worthless?"

"Yes," Elodie retorted with a curt nod that bobbled the blonde bun on her head. She drew the wool shawl around her shoulders, though Kalia had a distinct feeling it wasn't due to the chill. "Because I am more than the guilt I harbor for killing my abusive husband. And despite his death coming at my hands, I am *worth* ridding myself of the pain and the anguish that he caused me. *You* have been on this ship for longer than I have, and *you* have more to learn."

Kalia took it back. She knew that sweet, innocent Elodie had it in her all along.

Cora had the decency to look abashed as she swiped her sleeve across the injury, wincing when the fabric touched the cut. Shirin placed a comforting hand on Elodie's forearm, who sucked in a breath as though she were coming up for air. The crew stopped dancing; even the fiddle whined to a stop as Cora and Elodie stared at one another.

Elodie reached a hand down, still offering it to Cora despite how cruel she had always been. Cora hesitated for a moment. Her eyes darted between Elodie's pale face and the hand. Swallowing thickly, Cora took it, and Elodie braced to help the woman get to her feet. They said nothing to one another. Cora turned on the toes of her boots and slunk away, disappearing into the depths of the crowd.

The fiddle strung to life once more, pulling the attention away from the scene near the back of the crowd. Alaric, who had needled his way to the new cask of *fion*, slammed his stein against the spout. The crew cheered as the alcohol began to pour again, steins and mugs fighting their way under the steady stream.

"I'm proud of you, El. It takes courage to stand up for yourself," Shirin said, shaking Elodie's arm. She looked at the woman like a proud mother, her tawny face bright and beaming. "How did it feel?"

Elodie swiped away the tears that formed in the corners of her eyes. "Hard. Good. Like a weight has simultaneously been lifted and placed." She paused to rub her sternum as though she could wipe away the feeling if she tried hard enough. She glanced around, startled when she spotted Kalia and Rahmi. "I'm sorry, captain. I know the rules of the ship—"

Rahmi held up his hands, shaking his head. "We've had these conversations for a long time now, Elodie. Are you ready?"

Elodie's eyes widened as Shirin's hand slipped from her arm, slackening at her side. "Ready for what?" Elodie asked though it came out as a whisper.

Kalia stepped forward to place herself between Rahmi and Elodie, but Shirin pulled her to the side.

"Wait," Shirin said, her own eyes pricking with tears. "This is a good thing, I promise."

I promise. The words hung heavy above Kalia, but she waited nonetheless. She needed to give them a chance— for her and her mother's sake. Her family didn't step between her and the palace guards so that she could live her life alone and afraid. It was *time.*

"You asked me once what my guilt was," Kalia said, looking at Shirin. "My mother and brother died at the hands of the palace guards hunting me." She looked away to watch Elodie and Rahmi, but not without first catching Shirin's gaping stare.

Kalia felt that stare on the side of her face but was sure she wouldn't be able to hold in her grief any longer if she made eye contact with Shirin again. Kalia hadn't expected the comforting hand Shirin placed on her forearm, similar to the one she had given Elodie. Kalia inhaled as Shirin squeezed her hand, a silent promise for support, something that Kalia hadn't experienced in twenty years.

Elodie's eyes were bright and focused, and she shivered as she stepped closer to Rahmi. "Captain, I want to petition my release from *The Mark of Malice.*"

Kalia froze. She hadn't seen anyone petition their release with Rahmi yet, but she knew what would come next. She had heard the stories. The crewmembers who thought they were ready, the men who were given over to Liddros instead. She sent a side-long look over to Reshef, whose broad smile reached from ear to ear. He wasn't zipping the black stone along the necklace, a tell for his anxiety.

"Why did you come aboard my ship, Elodie?" Rahmi asked, biting his lip to keep from smiling.

Kalia knew how fond of Elodie he was and how they met once weekly to discuss her guilt. *Killing her abusive husband*, Kalia had no idea.

Elodie tipped her chin higher toward the night sky, pushing back her shoulders as she straightened her back. Strength, peace, and, most importantly, confidence—that's what she portrayed at that moment. She was no longer a battered woman running from the ghost of her dead husband but a woman ready to take back the reins of her life.

"I was young when I got married to my husband, and he began drinking soon after. When he had too much, he would find me in the kitchen and put his hands on me—" Elodie began to falter lightly, but the steady nod from Rahmi kept her pushing forward. "One night, I was cooking supper, and he stumbled into the house. He was incensed that it wasn't done and came to take it out on me. He began to hit me and slapped me to the ground. What he didn't realize was that I had a knife in my hand, and the blade pierced his heart. He— he died instantly."

"What happened next?" Rahmi asked. "How did you end up here?"

Elodie took in a deep, trembling breath. "I fled my town, knowing that I would be blamed for his death despite my neighbors knowing how he treated me. I used the coin from his pockets to barter passage onto a ship destined for the capital city. I was ready to make a new life. But that ship went down in a storm, and that's where you found me."

Rahmi nodded his head, and when he spoke next, he raised his voice above the peals of laughter brought on by the crew behind him. "Tell me why I should release you from your duty to this ship."

This was it. Kalia sucked in a breath that smelled like wood wax and fresh brine, the scents so strong that they seemed to coat her tongue as she held that air in her chest. As though the mere act of breathing would keep Elodie from forming the right words. Elodie, to her credit, only blinked.

"I realize I'll hold a version of my grief forever, captain." Elodie turned to smile softly at Shirin and Kalia. Shirin tightened her grip on Kalia's arm, this time seeking comfort from a companion. Kalia wound her arm around Shirin's, hooking their elbows together. Elodie squared her shoulders to face Rahmi. "But that doesn't mean I'm any less worthy of receiving love, nor am I any less worthy of giving it. I've learned that...with the help of my friends."

Kalia's heart cracked open at that, the feeling so filling that she was sure her chest would burst open. She anxiously awaited Rahmi's decision. Surely he wouldn't...surely he couldn't...

But Rahmi smiled as he reached out and took Elodie's hand. "I'm proud of you. I'm proud of you for taking the time to learn who you are on this ship. I release you from your debt." One of the markings on his forearm glowed against his skin, growing brighter until Kalia shielded her eyes against it.

The taste of ether replaced the brine, a crackling zing that could have been lightning about to strike in a sea storm or the beginnings of snowfall on a cold winter day. The warm breeze blew around them, swirling faster and faster around Elodie until her hair pulled from her bun, and she struggled to hold down the woolen skirts that flared at her knees.

Then, just as Rahmi's marking fizzled away, everything stopped. Elodie clutched at her chest, swiping a hand into her hair and down to her belly.

"I—I'm free," Elodie said, a breathy laugh bubbling up from her throat. "I'm free!" She spun toward Reshef, who took her in his arms and pulled her into a tight embrace that she returned with ease.

"Do you want to go back to the continent?" Rahmi asked as Elodie threw her arms around him next. He hesitated momentarily before relaxing enough to pat her on her head. "You don't need to stay here any longer," he said.

Elodie took a step back, shaking her head. "I still have something to do here, captain. I need to help my friends break their curses, too." She snuck one arm around Kalia's waist and the other around Shirin's. "If that's okay with them, of course."

Kalia thought a rock had lodged in her throat, one that she had trouble swallowing past. It had been twenty years—twenty years of being hunted by the guards, beaten on the streets, and hated by the madam. And, in that moment, she realized that she had never wanted something so badly.

To be accepted.

To be chosen.

To not be alone.

Kalia didn't realize that Rahmi had been watching her until she lifted her gaze, their stares colliding just as Alaric came by with two steins filled to the brim, *fion* spilling over the edge. A handmade drum had joined the fiddle, the men dancing and stomping on the deck, loud enough that it drowned out the sound of the wind in the sails. Alaric tripped on the rigging that still lay on the ground, both steins of *fion* tumbling out of his hands. Rahmi rolled his eyes, grasping his quartermaster under the arm and hauling him to his feet.

"Come on, you three," Reshef said, walking behind Elodie to herd the women toward the stairwell that led to the lower deck. "Let's celebrate somewhere we aren't going to be dragged unwillingly to the dance floor."

"I thought you would have liked to dance," Shirin said slyly, tossing a smirk over her shoulder at Reshef.

Reshef reached over to tap her on the nose. "I would. But going to dance right now while Alaric is stumbling drunk on the deck means that I would have to take care of him when he inevitably passes out somewhere unsavory. And I don't feel like ending my night following him around with an empty bucket for his vomit."

Elodie laughed, leaning to place her head on Kalia's shoulders. "I hope you don't mind me sticking around for a bit longer," she said, her doe eyes looking up at Kalia through her lashes. "It still means three of us in that tiny closet."

Kalia shook her head, dislodging the lump in her throat long enough to say, "I don't mind. It makes me feel like I have...friends." She said the word as though it were foreign to her, her tongue knotting against it.

Shirin and Elodie stopped walking. Elodie picked her head up from Kalia's shoulder. They glanced at one another, and Kalia felt that worming twist of anxiety behind her navel. Had she misread their relationship? Had she looked into something that wasn't truly there?

"It isn't *like* you have friends," Elodie said slowly, cocking her head as she studied every inch of Kalia's face. "You *have* friends. We care for you. Deeply."

"I've never...I spent so much time alone..." Kalia began with uncertainty, but Reshef cut her off.

"You've never been alone when you're with us, Kalia. Friendship is the guiding light in a storm, leading you to a safe harbor when you need it the most," he said. "All we ever wanted from you...was *you*."

CHAPTER THIRTY

KALIA

S hirin was snoring in her bed, safely tucked in Reshef's hip pocket. It was comical seeing them paired together, Shirin's long legs threaded together with Reshef's in a platonic battle of who would win most of the mattress. Elodie was lying flat on her stomach, a half-opened bottle of *fion* barely clutched by the hand dangling over the side of her bed.

Kalia was afraid to go to sleep. Worried that she would wake up and it would all be a dream. That she would be back in the bordello watching Cranford Reed abuse the women who worked there. She realized she had been reaching out to them in her way and pleading for connection and love all along.

Or she had just learned how to read the signs. She wondered how many people she had missed out on and how many she passed by who would have given her the chance if she had only reached out with her hand in return.

It all made Kalia think of Pete—sweet, steady Pete and his apothecary—the one place she had felt safe. Pete had been a friend, a good one. She wondered what he would think of her now. She thought of his smiling face, his warm hand squeezing her own. Pete would be proud of her that she knew.

The sound of boots tapping in the hallway outside the door pulled Kalia from her thoughts. She stared at the gap in the threshold, where a shadow passed. The footsteps stopped, then started up again, the shadow sliding by again. Kalia narrowed her eyes, quietly slinking out of bed. The floor was cold against her bare feet, shockingly so, but she muffled her yelp of surprise as she grabbed the knife Shirin always placed on the small table nearest the door.

Placing a hand on the brass key, Kalia winced as the lock's mechanism clicked once, the sound like a gunshot in the silence of the night. Reshef groaned, flipping onto his other side and pulling the blanket with him. Shirin snored in response.

The footsteps stopped again as Kalia cracked open the door and slid through, sticking to the dark wall of the passage as she went. It was a man; she could tell as much by the curse he whispered and the broad build of his shoulders. She clutched the knife's handle, readying to use it the next time he returned to the door. And her chance was coming closer...just a little bit closer...

"*Gods*, Kalia, what the *fuck*!" The man whispered as she swung the knife upward, catching the tunic with the tip of the utensil. There was a long *riiiiiip* sound as the fabric tore in two.

"Rahmi?" Kalia hissed, letting the knife hang at her side. "What are you *doing* down here?"

"Looking for a new shirt now," he replied, plucking at the gaping hole at the front of his tunic. "Why are you out here with a knife?"

Kalia swung it around in a vague gesture, her brow quirked with impatience. "Pirate ship. Strange noises outside of our door. What the fuck do you think I'm doing out here?" That much should have been clear.

"I just...this was a mistake," Rahmi said, shaking his head as he backed away from her.

Before Kalia knew what she was doing, before she even had the chance to take it back, her hand shot forward and clasped tightly around his wrist. "Rahmi," she said softly, murmuring his name like it was a prayer offered to the gods. "Why are you here?"

Rahmi looked like he was fighting a losing battle. His brown eyes, darker than usual in the dimly lit passage, roved over her face. He drank her in, unapologetically so, and she found herself meeting the intensity of his gaze. Somehow, she found herself mirrored through him. She saw him, all of him.

And the prospect of him seeing all of her terrified her to her very core. It was like a cresting wave from a battering storm that threatened to sweep her away. She would get lost in him, he would consume her entirely, and she would never recover.

He reached into his pocket, retrieving something he held tightly in his fist. He looked at it for a heartbeat before holding it out to Kalia. She lifted it toward the lantern that swung meters down the passage, just enough light in the hallway to make out the beautiful carving of a horse head.

Rahmi had detailed it down to the tiny, expertly placed notches that made up the mane, the gentle curves of the eyes, and the concave crooks for nostrils. Kalia ran her thumb over the muzzle, the wood so perfectly shaved and sanded that it was smooth against her skin.

"You were carving this on our way to the prison." Kalia's gaze lifted to meet his, her entire body stiffening. "I remember watching you."

Rahm nodded his head, though his eyes dropped to her shoulders. "Yes. It was the horse of my family when I was a child. I don't finish the carvings often, but this one...this one I finished for you."

The gentle kindness radiating from him at that moment was far too much for her. He was supposed to be rigid and unyielding, jagged and broken—like her, like them.

"I won't accept this," Kalia retorted, extending her hand to return it to him. *Can't accept this*, is what she meant to say. She couldn't take it because she didn't deserve to receive it.

Something that resembled shock entered his eyes, followed by fury in its wake. He was angry. She could see it simmering within him. Yes, *that* she deserved.

"You've come this far," Rahmi seethed, the sound sinking in her flesh. "Your mother, your brother. Everything you've done to stay alive. And now you're going to wipe away all of it? You started as nothing to me, as the bane of my existence, and you became *everything*—"

Kalia was still holding out the carving, but Rahmi refused to take it. "You can't be with me, Rahmi—"

"Why?" he cut in sharply, crossing his arms over his chest. Another act of defiance. "Everything I've done leading up to this moment, everywhere I've been, every single second...all of it has led me to you. Why won't you allow yourself to be happy, *ruehi*?"

"Because I don't deserve to!" Kalia yelled at him, the words slipping before she could swallow them back down. Her eyes burned again, the tears threatening to spill over. She hadn't shed so many of them in nearly twenty years. "Because, despite your curse, you remained a good fucking person. You— you help those aboard your ship to move past their guilt. To heal and grow and find new meaning in their lives. And what have I done? Used party tricks to gain an advantage over others, hidden magic that I knew would never trace back to me."

Magic that betrayed him, lied to him, would be no help to him, and she was still a coward because she couldn't tell him. She couldn't bear to see the hurt that would undoubtedly etch into every line of his face when he realized that his curse was just that...and there was nothing he could have done to stop it. And she knew the whole time.

Kalia didn't stop the tears that flowed, the heat of them like a salve for her broken soul. "So take your fucking horse back, Rahmi. I can't—I won't—"

Silence sank like a rock in a river between them, filling every gap and every space. It promised to drag her down with it, and she hoped that it would drown her in the process.

But Rahmi stood before her, his panting breaths lifting his chest and shoulders. He didn't speak, not as he reached forward to fold her fingers closed against the horse carving, not as he stepped forward to close the gap, and not as he wrapped his arm around her waist to tug her closer to him. He wiped away the tears on her cheeks and tucked her hair behind her ear with his other hand.

Finally, he kissed her cheeks, jaw, and lips. She closed her eyes, allowing his love to fill the cracks in her soul that had been torn open so long ago.

"You're mine," Rahmi said, pulling back just enough that he was only inches from her. Her eyes opened at the gruff command in his tone. "Do you understand?"

"Yes," Kalia whispered back. She lifted a hand to place it on his chest, feeling the thunderous beat of it against her palm. It hammered away at the cold exterior surrounding her, breaking through decades of pain and suffering to reveal the softness that still thrived beneath.

"You think you don't deserve me, *ruehi*, but you broke me. You shattered me into a million pieces." Rahmi's confession left her breathless. "And then you remade me into something even more than I could have imagined."

Rahmi's lips met hers, and for all Kalia knew, the rest of the ship faded into the background. He kissed her, tongue against tongue, as they unapologetically claimed one another. She pressed against him, and his responding growl only fueled her further.

They didn't make it back to his private quarters. They barely even made it down the dimly lit hallway. Rahmi tugged her into a darkened room filled with empty crates and casks, his mouth devouring hers every step of the way. The kiss broke long enough for her dress to come over her head and for his tunic to land in a forgotten pile at their feet.

Then they were naked, and she was on the ground, her bare back flat against the wooden deck, and the dip of her hips cradled him. What had once been fiery and rough surrendered to tenderness. His fingers dipped between her thighs to feel her wetness before wrapping his hand around his cock to guide him to her. And his kiss deepened as he slid in.

Kalia moaned against his mouth at the fullness of him inside of her, at her erratically beating heart that was determined to chip away any iciness that remained there.

"I want to see you, *ruehi*," Rahmi said as he broke away from her, pulling out nearly to the tip before thrusting back in. "Let me see you."

The only light in the storage berth streamed in from the hallway, but that didn't stop her from finding the warmth of his gaze. Seeing the heat that lay there, heat that was only for her. She saw in the depths of them as he yielded to her and gifted her the control he so tightly clung to.

"You're mine," Kalia murmured as he thrust into her again, the motion careening them back against the floor. Once wrapped in fortified steel, the exterior of her shielded spirit broke free.

"Yes," Rahmi replied hoarsely, the fourth thrust leisurely yet unrestrained. "No man will ever have you again. Only me."

"Only you." Kalia threaded her arms around his neck, pulling him back to kiss him. Again and again, their tongues danced in a way that she wished would last forever.

Rahmi kept moving, and Kalia met him thrust for thrust. She opened that bridge to him, connecting their minds. And he let her. They both let all that stood within them lay there: life, a new beginning, lust, fire, passion, love, forgiveness—all of it that had hindered them, that had scarred them, that had stopped them. She allowed him to see it all, and he allowed her to feel it.

"Say it one more time," Rahmi pleaded against her mouth, curling his hips to brush against her front wall. "Please, *gods*, say it again." He buried himself within her, a groan slipping from his chest.

"You're mine," Kalia said again, her back bowed off the floor. "And I am yours."

At her own words, at the feeling of *him* within her, her release cannoned through her. Rahmi clasped her nipple between his teeth, his tongue flicking around her as she clamped down on him. She moaned at the feeling— his body on her, inside of her, their minds bridged together. It didn't matter that he was a cursed captain and she was a thief who worked at a bordello.

There was only him and her.

Rahmi roared as he came, echoing off the crates and casks around them. The sound was ethereal, and Kalia was determined to hear it again and again. He remained inside of her, neither of them wanting to end that connection, and he dipped his head to kiss her again.

He and her. Her and him.

The words were a mantra that she wanted to repeat forever. She tried to use them to erase everything that had happened, to use them as a foundation to build everything that was meant to come.

That fire sparked to life again as he thickened inside of her, and Kalia tightened her thighs around his hips to flip them around. She sank onto Rahmi's considerable length as she straddled him, taking him deeply as he tipped his head back, his eyes closed in carnal glory. She snapped her hips down, moving faster and faster until they were a mess of sweat and release.

It could have been hours or days or months before they finally collapsed next to one another, their souls fused with a bond that Kalia knew couldn't be broken.

"Stay with me," Rahmi murmured as he turned to tuck her into his side. "Not just tonight. But with me, when this is all over. On my ship, on the continent, wherever we decide to go. Promise to stay with me."

"Yes," Kalia replied, her response so quiet that she wasn't sure he heard her. And she knew that it was a promise that she would move mountains, raze forests, cross oceans to keep.

CHAPTER THIRTY-ONE

RAHMI

Rahmi awoke feeling whole for the first time in centuries, warmth radiating through him. It took him very little time to remember where he was or why. Kalia was still in his arms, tucked under the blanket he had found overnight in a pile of discarded linens in the corner of the storage berth. The dim light from the hallway was only marginally brighter from the sun that streamed down the staircase in the distance.

The crew tinkered above them, the sound of sails unfurling and yelling amongst the men muffled between the decks.

He soaked it in all in: the feeling of her steady breaths against his bare chest, her hair draped across his shoulder, his fingers on her back. He was sure that nothing had ever been this perfect, was sure that nothing could be this perfect again. He reminisced on the way she rode him, stealing every ounce of control that he so tightly held onto.

And Rahmi let her have it. *Gods*, he wished he could have given it to her sooner. It would have saved them time and, in his case, physical pain. He chuckled at the memory of the sea urchin in his seat, and Kalia stirred at the rumbling of his chest against her cheek.

Her sleepy, satiated smile carved away at his heart, softening something in him that he didn't realize had hardened. His hands stroked down her back, drawing idle patterns along the freckles that dotted her skin.

"*Ruehi*," Rahmi muttered, tenderly kissing the top of her head. She still smelled like cinnamon, and he inhaled, committing the smell to his mind for when he was at the helm of his ship. He already regretted the time he would need to spend away from her.

"You call me *ruehi*. What does that mean?" Kalia asked, stretching her hands above her head. Her breasts brushed against the side of his torso, and damn if his cock didn't harden at the sight of it. She curled her hands back to her front, shifting her head to rest on his shoulder.

Rahmi tipped his chin down to look at her, his brown eyes meeting her green ones through her thick lashes. He sighed, running a hand down the curve of her spine. "In my native tongue, it translates as my soul."

Kalia stilled in his arms, though she never looked away from him. "You've called me that from the beginning."

Rahmi lifted a hand to place behind his head, the muscles of his core and shoulders pulling with the movement. She let a finger trail down the grooves of his muscled abdomen, and he shuddered at the lightness of her touch. "And from the beginning, I knew who you were."

Her hand wrapped around his cock at the words. It wasn't long after that Rahmi found himself thrusting inside of her once more, his hand placed over her mouth to dull her loud moans.

When they finally collapsed next to one another, a heap of sweat and panting breaths, Rahmi kissed her hard on the lips before rolling over to grab his breeches. He stood, reveling in Kalia's approving stare as he tugged them on. His tunic followed.

"I have to go to the helm," Rahmi said, extending a hand to help her. She took it, letting the blanket drop to her feet as she stood. "But remember what I said. You stay with me now. In my bed." He bent down to run his tongue along the shell of her ear, and he smiled at the shudder that racked her body. "I fear you've created a monster out of me and—" He trailed off to slide a finger between her legs, sucking her release from the tip of it. "—Tasting you is something I can no longer start my day without."

Kalia swallowed, and from the fire that swept through her gaze, Rahmi had to hold himself back from bending her over the nearest cask, fucking her until she was limp and spent. His mouth collided with hers again, and she bit his lower lip. Rahmi read the promise she planted there, a promise that he looked forward to cashing in as soon as he could step away from his duties to the crew.

Rahmi barely made it away from Kalia, needing to take a series of calming breaths as soon as he walked into the passage to cool the raging hard-on that tented the front of his pants. He knew he would never get enough of her. He climbed the staircase outside the crew's berth, where the hammocks swung in tune with the ship's rocking, and emerged on the deck.

The sun shone against the bright morning sky, so in opposition with the darkness of the lower decks that he was forced to squint. The ship was already carving through the sea, the wind billowing through the sails as it picked up speed toward the archipelago that he knew they would reach by tomorrow night at the latest.

They had from the map and knew they were extremely close to the tip of the hidden archipelago.

Even the scent of the ocean was sweeter, the brine evolving into a taste of freedom that he hadn't thought he would ever get to.

"Captain," Alaric shouted as he clambered over a coil of ropes against the quarterdeck. "I set the compass with Wright according to the overnight reading of the NightWatcher. I tried to find you this morning, but—"

"Very good," Rahmi interjected. He wanted to see the readings and desperately wanted to wash the sheen of sweat that blanketed his body. A change of clothes was warranted, too. "I'll be back. Keep the crew at full sail."

"Aye, sir," Alaric said, nodding his head curtly. He pivoted on the toes of his boots, stalking back to the nearest mast with sharp taps of his heels against the deck. His shout to the men working the sail was lost to a sudden gust of wind that ruffled Rahmi's tunic and sent a cold shiver down his back.

Rahmi walked down the passage that lay beneath the stern deck. He made to slip straight through his office, his sight briefly landing on the stack of parchment scribbled with overnight readings of the NightWatcher when his footsteps stopped.

"I felt a soul slide through my grasp last night. The blonde one," Liddros said casually as he leaned against the wall, one ankle hooked over the other. "With Devlin being out of commission and the steady stream of souls I still acquire from Jace, I deduced it to be you." His stone-colored eyes darkened as they pinned Rahmi in place. "Why?"

"She earned it," Rahmi responded stiffly. "What are you doing aboard my ship?"

Liddros's humorless smirk sent a bolt of alarm scraping along his tense muscles. "*Your* ship? I loaned you this ship. Let's not get things out of line, captain." He pushed himself from the wall, stalking toward the desk. He bent his head over the pile of parchment.

Rahmi bristled. "What are you doing aboard the ship that was *lent* to me?" He wasn't about to keep the bite of scorn out of his voice, and Liddros glanced up at him at the sound of it.

"Careful, captain." There was a threat behind his stare, a ringing promise that Rahmi had no interest in learning the details of.

"The souls I send you far outweigh the souls that I release," Rahmi said, doubling back to shut the door to the office, cutting off the morning scrabbles of the crew. The last thing he needed was for Alaric to waltz in while the God of the Sea was here. "Why does this one matter?"

"They all matter," Liddros said through gritted teeth, his eyes flashing. "But, if you must know, the king requires more and more souls to remain young. And still..." He trailed off to quietly sigh, shifting on his feet. The painting of discomfort. "His health is failing."

Rahmi quirked a brow. "Isn't that a good thing? Doesn't that mean your bond to him will be broken, and you'll be free?"

"If only it were that easy. Unless we can find a way to break the bond between him and me, my life will be surrendered when he dies."

Rahmi prided himself on being an intelligent man—at least, he was far more intelligent than most. But he still felt as though he were being pulled in different directions by this conversation. "But you're a god..."

"I'm far more than that," Liddros mumbled. With the haze to his eyes, it seemed to be more to himself. He shook his head, coming back to the present. "And I made bargains that I thought I could remove myself from. Yet, here I am, which brings us to the reason for my visit. What do you know of the *Luminaria*?"

Rahmi leaned a hip against the back of the armchair, and his arms crossed over his chest. "A bit more than our last discussion. It is being sought out by another captain, who was hired to find it for the king." Liddros snorted at that. "But I could interpret the map with a lunar device a former crew member had. We pinpointed the location of the islands. We should arrive there tomorrow."

Liddros nodded. "And our deal? Is it still your wish to be free of your curse?"

Rahmi opened and closed his mouth, tipping his head to the side. Liddros raised his brows at Rahmi's obvious hesitation, but the captain didn't know what to say. His goals had shifted, to be sure. Would it be possible to be free of it entirely? To live as a mortal man? To have a life beyond this ship and the confines of the sea?

"I see you've met your match," Liddros said, a smirk growing. "Interesting. Devlin's hesitation was similar when he finally met Fenna. Tell me, captain, are you willing to change for her?"

Rahmi could say with absolute certainty that he was. "Once she assists us in finding the *Luminaria*, I expect to pursue her—"

A notch formed between Liddros's risen brows. "Only a djinn can activate the *Luminaria*."

Rahmi nodded slowly as though he were waiting for Liddros to catch up. "Yes, I'm well aware. Kalia is the djinn. She's going to—"

Liddros interrupted him again, and this time Rahmi sighed in frustration. "You don't have a djinn aboard my ship."

Rahmi opened and closed his mouth, searching Liddros's face for any hint that he was joking. Rahmi *knew* Kalia was a djinn. He had *seen* her magic. He had experienced it for himself... "No, she's a djinn. She told us herself. I've felt her in here." He tapped his temple with the tip of his finger, but Liddros was already shaking his head.

"That isn't how the magic of a djinn works. And if there were a djinn aboard your ship, I would know. Their power calls to my power; I could feel it." Liddros hung his head, dipping his chin toward his chest. "You don't have a djinn, do you, captain?"

Rahmi's mind was reeling, and he was grappling with the knowledge that, perhaps, Kalia hadn't been as honest with him as he thought. Rage and anger boiled through his veins, lighting him on fire in the worst possible way. And, even worse, it was threaded with an undertone of betrayal. He had bared his soul to her and had thought she had done the same. "If she's not a djinn, then what is she?"

Liddros shrugged a shoulder, though the edges of his frame had already begun to fade. Rahmi didn't wait to see the God of the Sea disappear; he was already hurtling out of his office.

CHAPTER THIRTY-TWO

KALIA

K alia smiled as she reached into the crate of potatoes, chopping each before scooping the pieces into the large pot. Doc was busy stirring. The galley was hot and humid, thanks to the kindling flame and the rising steam that filled the room. She bit her lower lip as she worked, keeping her head down so as not to attract the attention of Elodie, Shirin, or Reshef.

After Rahmi left the storage berth, it hadn't taken long to prepare for the day. She snuck across the hallway toward the shared room, which was, thankfully, empty when she entered it. A quick wash-up in the basin of fresh water and a clean pair of clothes were all she needed before she bustled down to the galley.

"Kalia wasn't in her bed this morning," Elodie said in a singsong voice, lifting her eyes to level Kalia with a playful stare.

"I wonder where she could have been," Shirin responded flatly, though the smirk on her face while she kneaded the dough under the heels of her palms said otherwise. "There isn't a chance she was with...the captain?"

Elodie gasped, and Doc jumped at its sudden sharpness. He turned to glare at her over his shoulder, though he kept the wooden spoon rotating around the pot. "She does have that aura about her," she said passively, returning to the pile of carrots she dutifully peeled and chopped. "A *satisfied* one, don't you think?"

Shirin barked a laugh at Elodie, shaking her head. Reshef's eyes glimmered as he leaned back to pluck an apple from the crate nearest Doc, who took the spoon out of the pot long enough to whack Reshef in the wrist with it. "I think we all know she was with the captain," Reshef continued as the apple thumped back into place. He glowered at Doc's back. "I think we also know what he sounds like when he—"

"Reshef," Kalia snapped, though the arcing irritation that had once been there didn't even simmer. She laughed instead, pursing her lips into a tight line. "Have some decency."

Reshef stood from his seat around the table, bending down to whisper into Kalia's ear as he passed. "Then find a further room next time." He snagged along the furthest counters, ripping the closed lid off a crate in the far corner. He removed an apple and took a subsequent bite before the galley cook could remove his spoon from the pot again. Reshef merely shrugged at Doc's snarl. "He must have a magical cock from the way you were praying to the gods last night."

Elodie choked as Shirin let out an uncharacteristic squeal. Doc's back stiffened, but he said nothing, keeping his stare pinned on the bubbling stew before him.

Kalia didn't bother to be coy about it, though she spotted Elodie's burning cheeks as she spun around in her chair. Kalia placed her forearm on the headrest, resting her chin on the back of her hand. "Sounds a bit like jealousy. Is your face turning green? Has Alaric not made you see the gods yet?"

Reshef's smirk deepened. "We both know I don't kiss and tell." He threw a hand to his chest, letting it rest dramatically over his heart. "That is private, you naughty girl."

Kalia laughed again while she turned to pick up the knife, returning to the half-chopped potato in front of her. "Take that into consideration the next time you decide to—" She didn't get to finish. The door to the galley swung open, knocking heavily against the wall behind it.

Elodie shrieked as Shirin jumped, and Doc's wooden spoon flung from his hand to land with a clatter near Reshef's feet. But Kalia wasn't paying attention to any of that. No, her gaze had shifted to the doorway, where Rahmi's wide frame was taking up the threshold.

And he looked downright *murderous*.

Kalia opened her mouth to speak, but Rahmi had already crossed the galley, his boots striking the deck in loud *thwacks*. Before Kalia could say anything, Rahmi removed the dagger from his belt, thrusting the tip of the blade into her throat.

"Captain!" Elodie cried out, standing from her seat so abruptly that the table shifted, sending a few potatoes onto the floor.

Rahmi ignored her, never removing Kalia from his line of sight. "What are you?" he growled, leaning so close to her face that she could see her reflection in his pupils. He leered, nostrils flared wide. Kalia tried to push him away, but he tightened his hold on her head. "What are you?" he repeated, shaking her a bit.

"Captain, you're scaring—"

"Hush, Elodie." Rahmi's voice was sharp, and while he usually apologized when he spoke to her in any unfriendly way, he didn't even bother sending her a side-long sweep.

Kalia saw red with his tone, and she leaned forward, ignoring the bite of the blade against her neck. "Do not talk to her like that. You have no right—"

"I have every right. I am the captain of this ship," Rahmi growled. "And I'm going to ask you one final fucking time. *What. Are. You*?"

Worms could have replaced Kalia's insides with how much they squirmed within her. He knew. Somehow, someway, he knew. "Did Wright Thackeray tell you?" she asked, her jaw clenched so tightly that she felt her teeth grind together. That stupid weasel. She just needed more *time*.

Rahmi's gaze searched her own, the corners of his lips downturned. "No, Wright didn't tell me. He never—" Kalia knew the moment realization struck. "Wright knows, doesn't he? He knows that you aren't a djinn."

Kalia felt Elodie and Shirin's stares bore into her face, and she didn't need to look at them to verify it. She saw Reshef zip the black stone along the chain from the corner of her eye. His body was tense and coiled as though readying to leap between them at any moment.

"Yes," Kalia whispered. "Wright knows."

She would have taken him screaming at her. *Gods*, she would have preferred that Rahmi slit her throat with that damn dagger. She would have taken anything over the shocked, deeply hurt look that cut lines on his face. The huff of breath that fluttered her hair. The way his shoulders crumpled as he sagged in on himself.

Elodie let out a soft, barely audible gasp over the stew, which had begun to boil over the pot's rim. Even Doc was no longer paying attention to it, instead peering over his shoulder at the scene behind him.

"How?" Rahmi asked, his voice hoarse. "When?"

Kalia swallowed thickly. She had never felt smaller. "Since the prison. He knew immediately. He recognized my magic. Rahmi, please—" She reached out to clasp her hand around his taut forearm, but he moved away from her, his back banging against the crates of filleted fish on the counter behind him.

"Do not touch me," Rahmi said, his whole body vibrating with intensity. "You will not touch me again."

Silence filled the room, the only sound being the fizzle of stew as the liquid dripped into the roiling flame below. To his credit, Reshef had managed to pull an innocent look of surprise onto his face, though the guilt-stricken press of his lips marred it. From how Elodie kept darting her gaze over to him, Kalia had a sinking feeling that the woman was slowly putting together his involvement.

"I wanted to tell you," Kalia started again, sending him a pleading stare. She felt the stinging prick of tears behind her eyes, ones that she knew she deserved but didn't want to fall. "Please, Rahmi, I *never* wanted to hurt you. Not anymore, not after—" She wanted him to press that blade back to her throat, something that would tell her his unyielding confidence was still intact.

His pained expression iced over, replaced by one so cold that she knew she had lost him forever. "I should have known not to get involved with you. I did know. But I should have known better than to accept the word of a swindler from a brothel."

Kalia's stomach sank to her feet, and she prayed that the sea would wash through the galley and swallow her whole. The room shuddered as if she had manifested it herself, though Rahmi's stare remained fixed on hers. Elodie and Shirin glanced at one another, their faces paling.

"Doc."

"Aye, captain?" The galley cook answered immediately, turning on his heels to finally face them. He took a moment to wipe the sweat from his hairline before tucking the handkerchief back into his pocket.

"See to it that our newest prisoner is taken to the brig."

The thought of being returned to the underbelly of the ship seized at her chest in a way that Kalia didn't expect. She stood from her seat, readying to flee the galley before the pot-bellied cook could grab her, but the ship shuddered again.

This time, the dull ringing of a bell pierced the room and shouts reverberated from above—shouts that Kalia couldn't make out, but ones she knew didn't signify anything good. Boots clattered against the deck above her, the back-and-forth running evident from her spot beneath them.

"All men to the guns!" Alaric's voice finally shrieked through the chaos. "Fire at the ready, boys!"

Elodie whimpered as Rahmi flew from the galley, not bothering to look back a final time.

CHAPTER THIRTY-THREE

RAHMI

Rahmi pushed aside the betrayal and anger that threatened to boil him alive, instead focusing on the *gongs* from the crow nest's bell. Every ring spurred him onward, settling in his chest. He used them like a mantra as he flew up the steps, taking two at a time before emerging onto the quarterdeck.

A gray haze of smoke now obscured the morning sun, and the burning smell of used gunpowder had overtaken the fresh scent of the sea. Thanks to Alaric, three men to a gun were already set, and they were busy refilling the cannon with ammunition and gunpowder before striking the flint with the stones they always carried.

Booms ricocheted off the waves that lapped at the keel, the calm of water below in opposition to the battle that had begun to rage. Another cannon fired, rocking the ship to the right as the men flocked to the gun to reload it. The cannonball arced through the air, stopping with a loud splash just short of the ship that had come into view.

The mercenary ship's sails were at full tilt, and it carved through the sea with ease as it rounded the island's bend. The ship had been hidden by the rolling hills and palm trees that made up the sprawling beach, something that Rahmi should have expected. His anger toward Kalia only roared again. If it weren't for her...

He shook his head, forcing the thoughts out of his head. He still smelled her on him, that cinnamon scent that had begun infiltrating his dreams. He had been so *fucking* stupid.

Even from a distance, Rahmi could see the mercenary's crew scurrying along the deck. He hurdled up the stairs to the helm in a flash, taking the wheel from Thomas. "Full sail, bring her about!" Rahmi yelled down to the quarterdeck, where a group of men immediately began to turn the rudder. It would take a lot of work, but they might stand a chance if he could get a better angle of the guns.

A *boom* echoed from the mercenary ship, quickly closing the gap between them, and Rahmi's veins flooded with adrenaline when he felt the cannonball embed into the stern of *The Mark of Malice*. Wood splintered, and the force of the wreck forced Rahmi forward, but he kept a tight hold on the helm. "Come on...come on..." he muttered, keeping the wheel pinned with his body. Sure enough, despite the hole that was undoubtedly somewhere beneath him, the bow of the ship had slowly begun to turn.

But it wasn't enough.

The mercenary ship was much smaller and narrowly made, making it easier to carve through the waters toward them. Another gun flared to life, and, this time, the cannonball blasted through the gunnel near the front of the ship. A squeal of surprise and a blood-curdling scream of pain followed in its wake. Rahmi cinched his lips together, trying to keep his focus on turning the ship and not on the blood that flowed with ease from the blown-off leg of his crew member down below.

"Load guns!" Alaric bellowed through the carnage. "Loud guns, boys!"

"Quick!" a familiar voice shouted from the staircase leading to the lower decks. "Elodie, Shirin, help me!"

Rahmi felt his stomach drop to his boots as Kalia's head popped out, her dark brown locks glistening despite the haze. Another cannon blasted, this one from his ship, and Rahmi watched as Kalia nearly collided with the end of the barrel. "*Kalia*!" he yelled, but the sudden uptick in noise and chaos on the deck made it impossible for her to hear.

"Are you mad?" Rahmi saw Alaric scream over to her, intercepting her path mid-way to the man, who had turned a pallid shade of white with his blood loss. "You're going to get yourself and the others killed!"

"I'm going to take him below!" Kalia yelled back, her calm voice rising over the cannon fire. "We can try and stop the bleeding. We can—"

"Samael has already taken him beyond," Alaric responded, gesturing wildly over his shoulder. "There is nothing more you can do."

The ship rocked again as another iron ball blasted a path through the decks below. Kalia stumbled, reaching for the gunnel as she tried to keep her balance, but Rahmi's gaze was already being pulled elsewhere. He scanned the sea, watching in horror as twelve men swung the gap between the two ships, landing with their cutlasses drawn.

Sulfur and metal were thick on the wind, black smoke hanging at the horizon, but that didn't stop more men from gliding over the gap. Rahmi swore as another set of cannonballs whistled through the air, paying no mind to the men who had just boarded *The Mark of Malice*. One of the iron balls went long, flying across the deck and landing in the sea just beyond his ship. But the second one slammed into the mizzenmast, showering the crew below with wood splinters.

The mast wobbled and swayed. For a brief moment, Rahmi thought it would anchor back into place with the assistance of the rigging. But the ropes groaned as they stretched, finally snapping one by one as the mast fell back, back, back and came to a crashing stop over the side of the ship. Sails, rope, and metal rigging floated in the waters below, wrenching Rahmi's efforts to turn *The Mark of Malice* to an abrupt stop.

Rahmi hauled himself away from the helm while yanking his cutlass from the sheath with a *zing* of metal against leather. "Fire! Fire at will!" he yelled as he entered the quarterdeck's wreckage. The crew worked to load the cannons that could still be used, sending blast after blast that rocked the ship. The metallic scent of blood filled the air, and Rahmi didn't want to think about how much of it was from his men.

Rahmi raised his cutlass and cut down a mercenary member who had attempted to charge him. The devastating stroke split the man's throat damn near in half, blood spewing from his flesh as he dropped to the deck. Scrambling fingers were soaked in red, and he died with a gurgle a moment later.

But Rahmi had already moved on.

Man after man was slain by his blade, a trail of bodies piling up behind him. Rahmi didn't stop. He *couldn't* stop. His eyes were set on Kalia, even through the pistol shot that whizzed uncomfortably close to him, even through the smoke that choked his lungs. He kept moving.

"We're being overrun!" Alaric called over as soon as Rahmi was close enough. His face was covered in soot and streaked with lines of sweat that looked like thick scars. "The guns at the bow have been disabled. The fall of the mizzenmast took out another quarter of the remaining ones." Alaric paused to thrust his dagger into a passing man's eye socket, the blade punching through the back of his skull. He yanked it free with the same stroke.

"Who are these men?" Rahmi asked, pushing back the locks of his hair with a swipe of his wrist. "Do we know—"

Rahmi paused when his gaze glided over to a man standing on the gunnel, balanced with the ease of a much younger man. He held onto the rigging with one hand, a sword held tightly in his other, as he swept his stare over the mayhem of the quarterdeck. Resolution spilled from him, and Rahmi recognized the immovable and merciless stance as his own mirrored back to him. Violent rage bolted down his space at the sight of the man so casually standing on the gunnel of his ship.

His fucking ship.

Their eyes finally connected, and time stretched before stopping entirely. The man's lips curled into a cruel smile as he hopped down from the gunnel, the hollow *thunk* of his boots against the deck immediately swallowed by the surging battle.

The man expertly navigated the surrounding duels, only raising his blade to slice through a fallen sail that dared to stand in his way. As he drew closer, cutting through the billows of smoke that poured from the ship's underbelly, Rahmi noticed the jagged scar that ran from his hairline, bifurcating his brow before coming to a stark end just below his eye. He was lucky the globe was still intact, though a fogginess had settled over the pupil that indicated to Rahmi he didn't have all of his vision.

It didn't lower Rahm's guard even a tinge.

"I knew I was looking for a ship," the man said as he approached. He stopped just shy of Rahmi's reach, and the thought made Rahmi smirk. "I didn't think that ship would be the infamous *Mark of Malice.*"

Rahmi took a step forward, though the man didn't flinch away. "I'm afraid I don't know your name."

The man bowed deeply, mockingly sweeping his tricorn hat from his head. That jagged scar extended up his scalp, no hair growing where a blade had once split him open. "Captain Nasir Al-Mahdi, though your reputation proceeds you, of course. Captain Rahmi Abada."

Rahmi wasn't impressed, and he set his face into a gaze of neutrality. "What are you doing aboard my ship, Nasir Al-Mahdi?" He didn't bother using the captain's given title, and the disrespect had not gone unnoticed by the way the man bristled.

"You have something of mine," Nasir said through gritted teeth, his tone no longer honey-sweet. "And I want it back."

Rahmi turned to look at Alaric, who merely shrugged. They were good at playing dumb when the situation called for it and had done it together on many occasions. Another cannon fired, and the iron ball lodged within Nasir's ship. From how his eyes twitched toward the noise, Rahmi knew he was fighting the urge to look.

"I'm not sure what of yours we could have," Alaric said, scratching the underside of his chin. "Captain?"

Rahmi clicked his tongue against his teeth, slowly shaking his head. Despite the situation they had found themselves in, toying with Nasir was still great fun. "Nothing is coming to mind. However, we have an excellent assortment of skirts that may suit you. Karim is down in the brig, and he might be able to give you a hand."

Nasir's eyes flashed, a shadow passing through them that was gone the next instant. "Very fun, Rahmi." It seemed he was done with the pleasantries. "You have misread your position. I have dismantled your ship, and you have nowhere to go. I will find Karim. My men have already gone below deck."

"That is quite the predicament, captain," Alaric said over the fray of clashing blades, resting his hand on the pommel of his sheathed dagger. The action was not lost on Nasir.

"Yes, quite." Rahmi rubbed his jaw. "Though, I'm not sure if the arrogance is warranted, truth be told." He took another step forward. "See, you're still *on* my ship. And to survive, you need to get *off* my ship. But to do *that*, you need to get through me. And I'm not feeling generous, seeing what you've done to her."

Nasir's smile grew brittle at the edges as it froze into place. "As you wish, *captain*." He swung his sword forward, but Rahmi was quicker. The devastating clash rang up Rahmi's arm, rattling his bones.

Nasir spun on the toes of his boots, undeterred by the failure of his first hit, and sliced the sword down. Rahmi deflected it with ease, letting his cutlass dangle at his side. Letting his relaxed stance wind up Nasir into making a lethal mistake, a cannon roared to life again, and Rahmi felt his ship shudder just as Nasir thrust his blade at Rahmi's belly.

Rahmi leaned to the side to avoid the strike, but something else made his blood go cold.

"The keel!" a voice shouted from the bow. "The keel has been breached!"

Fuck. Fuck. Fuck. A keel breach was nearly always fatal. If they could patch the hole quickly enough, they could keep *The Mark of Malice* from sinking into the abyss. Rahmi jutted his chin toward the bow, and Alaric nodded at the gesture. His quartermaster disappeared into the smoke, shouting orders for tar and old sails.

"You're done, captain," Nasir snarled, his unblinking stare threatening to gut Rahmi if he was given the chance. "Surrender now, and I just might let you live."

Rahmi had certainly had enough now. He arced his cutlass through the narrow space between them, catching Nasir in the chest. The tip of his blade carved a line from nipple to collarbone, Rahmi's promise of retribution. He was going to kill Nasir. Destroy him. Bloody him beyond recognition.

When he was done, he would sip *fion* while using Nasir's body as a footrest.

Nasir began to move to the left, attempting to circle Rahmi, and that was when he took his chance. Rahmi lunged, forcing Nasir on the defensive as he sent blow after blow to the mercenary captain. Swipes and thrusts and strikes flew through the air. Rahmi poured his anger into every hit.

For his curse. *Strike*. For his ebbing freedom. *Zing*. For Kalia's fucking betrayal. *Clash*.

His arm muscles burned, but Rahmi still didn't stop. It was everything Nasir could do to remain on his feet, his eyes wide with the knowledge that Rahmi was the predator and he was the prey. And when Nasir finally went down, tripping over a coil of rope that had fallen from the broken mizzenmast, when Rahmi had pressed the tip of his cutlass into the spot just above Nasir's heart, that's when Rahmi heard the shout.

"She's there!" Karim bellowed, his voice a shock over the clatters that still rang out around them. "The djinn! We need her!"

Kalia's scream was gut-wrenching, filled with a terror so profound that Rahmi felt his very soul clench. Despite everything, despite what she had done...he was faced with the realization that he still *fucking* loved her.

Rahmi loved her. And how horrible was that?

But Nasir pounced on Rahmi's hesitation, knocking the cutlass to the side. Nasir swung his foot upward, catching Rahmi in the back of the knee, sending him tumbling onto the deck with an *oof* of harsh exhalation. Rahmi took a deep, wheezing inhale to try and fill his lungs with the air that had been knocked from him, but stars had begun to dapple at the corners of his vision.

"The djinn?" Nasir laughed as he clambered to a stand, swaying momentarily as he got his footing. "*The djinn*?" He tossed his head back, letting out a barking laugh that fueled Rahmi into action.

If only he could get some air.

"I'm going to have so much fun," Nasir said, bending down to pick up his sword where it had fallen onto the deck. "I'm going to gut her and spill every last drop of her blood if that's what it takes to get me the *Luminaria*. And you're going to watch every second."

The sword's hilt collided with the side of Rahmi's head, and everything went black.

CHAPTER THIRTY-FOUR

RAHMI

"They can't be *gone*," a female voice said, waking Rahmi from his stupor. "*The Mark of Malice*? Gone?"

Rahmi's eyes cracked open, and his vision blurred as he struggled to focus against the pounding headache that radiated down the back of his neck. He blinked at the ceiling, where a golden light was dancing against the wood. Where was he? He groaned, lifting his head from the hard floor beneath him to take a look around.

He was in a cell, that was for sure. He recognized the iron bars and the locks on each door. Though this set of cells was smaller than the ones on his ship, the room was a touch wider. It smelled cleaner, too. Newer. The stench of mildew and boggy, stale water hadn't yet penetrated the ship's depths. He blinked again, widening his eyes despite the threat of his head bursting. It couldn't do that, could it? He had never been knocked out before.

"I'm so sorry, my love," a male voice answered, the gentleness of it damn near devastating. "It took on two more firings from the guns. It sunk soon after."

"Elodie and Shirin?"

The male voice didn't answer, but a soft sob followed.

Rahmi groaned again as he pushed himself up. He hooked his elbows around his bent knees, shaking his head one final time to rid himself of the fogginess that had settled over his mind. He swallowed, looking around again. Reshef was in the cell across from his own, his eyes bright despite the dim lantern light. Somehow, in a few hours, the boyish charm had hardened into something that Rahmi couldn't quite put his finger on. And he certainly didn't have the clarity to figure it out.

Glancing to his left, Rahmi spotted Kalia with her back against the keel. Water dripped from above, landing in a puddle that had begun to form at her feet. *The Mark of Malice* had left her share of scars. That much could be said for her.

"Alaric?" Rahmi whispered, his voice hoarse against the dryness of his throat. "Thomas? Searles?"

Reshef lifted his head, surprise noted on his face. "Captain, you're awake."

"Despite my better judgment." Rahmi lifted his hand to probe at the sore lump on his temple. "How long was I out?"

Reshef shrugged. "Long enough to know that I'm *starving* and no one has brought us a single moldy piece of bread yet." He leaned a shoulder against the crossbar with an irritated huff. "I would even take Doc's fish stew."

Over the *whoosh* of the water that rushed past them just on the other side of the keel, Rahmi heard Kalia shuffle closer to him. There was a *clang* of metal against metal, and Rahmi looked over just in time to see Kalia wrap her hand around one of the iron bars that split their cells. Black stone cuffs were locked around her wrists, the heavy chains resting on her lap.

"It's obsidian," Reshef went on, presumably at the knitted brow as Rahmi locked his gaze on the cuffs. "The stone blocks the use of magic and absorbs it right on up."

Kalia sent him a shaky smile. "I couldn't get into your mind to see what you were thinking, even if I wanted to." She swallowed, lifting her free hand to showcase the cuff in better light. "They popped these on the moment I was on their ship, though it was already too late for a few of them. I was cut off from my power immediately."

From the pleading, hopeful stare she sent him, Rahmi knew she was determining how he would respond. He looked away from her. His ship and crew were gone, and all that was left was *her*. And for how long? Newfound rage threatened to burn him alive and he clenched his jaw to bite back the scathing response he was itching to hurdle at her.

Rahmi wanted her to feel his pain, betrayal, and every ounce of his anger. He caught sight of her out of the corner of his eye, and a sudden pressure in his chest held him back. He felt exposed, filleted to the very bone. He was desperate to hit something, that primal urge roaring to life inside of him.

"You don't want to know what I'm thinking," Rahmi said instead, reveling briefly in how her smile slipped from her mouth. Then he was filled with a vast well of shame because who does that to the person they love?

But Kalia had. She had twisted him around her finger so tightly that there wasn't a way to disentangle him from her. And when Captain Nasir Al-Mahdi inevitably tore her apart, it was going to shred him, too. Rahmi only hoped that the pain would end him, though he knew that it wouldn't.

"What of the rest of the crew?" Rahmi asked, returning his attention to Reshef. "Did anyone make it out alive?"

Reshef slowly shook his head, his eyes only brightening. "None that I saw, though I followed our fake djinn as soon as I saw her being dragged aboard this ship." There was a creak as hollowed footsteps crossed the deck above them. "Truly, Kalia, your propensity for being nabbed has been a never-ending thorn in my side."

Kalia huffed an involuntary laugh, though it sobered when Rahmi glared back at her.

"Wright Thackeray was in my ear promising to assist me with finding the *Luminaria*, and this whole time, he knew that you were no help to us?" Rahmi shot at her. Kalia's head dipped to her chest as though she withered under his stare. It was oil on the fire of his anger. "You, of all of them? The talks we had and the honesty I was forced to come to terms with. Honesty that *you* forced me to come to terms with. Why?"

Kalia's lower lip curved into her mouth with the sharp inhale she took in. "Wright promised to get me off the ship, but I didn't agree to it, Rahmi. I swear it. He wanted to destroy the gemstone when we got to the island."

"I promised to get you off the ship!" Rahmi bellowed, finally losing his temper. She shrunk back from him, but it didn't deter him this time. "I told you that I would do everything to get you back to the continent as long as you helped me. And you took that deal knowing there wasn't a way forward!"

"I hoped we would get there, but the *Luminaria* was just a myth! Or—or I could do something with my powers," Kalia retorted. "Rahmi, please, I might still be able to help you. I still have magic. You've felt it. Wright—"

"If that man is lucky, Samael took him beyond where I can reach him," Rahmi growled, pushing as far away from her cell as the small space let him. He couldn't stand to be near her, couldn't stand to feel the gaping hole that had been blown through his heart. "Because if I find him, I'm ripping him apart with my bare hands. And then I'm giving him directly to Liddros."

Just like the rest of his crew. While they couldn't die while they were aboard his ship, he knew with absolute certainty that Liddros would take them given the chance, especially if it was to save his skin. Especially since Rahmi had no idea how long he had been off his ship. Regardless of how this ended, his time was ticking to a close.

Rahmi glanced down at the markings that had taken up residence on his skin, each dark swirl matching the souls he had taken aboard *The Mark of Malice.* Despite the light from the candle, which was quickly dimming as the wax shortened, he saw that each mark was still intact.

A cruel joke? Possibly. Liddros had always been one to toy with his captains, frequently leaving subliminal messages carved in stone and sending them on a wild chase that only ended when he saw it fit to be ended—the boredom of an immortal being. But Rahmi glanced down at his markings again and couldn't help the glimmer of hope that flared in his chest.

"Rahmi," Kalia said softly, but he only shook his head.

"They're gone, Kalia," Rahmi responded, not lifting his eyes away from the markings. "The ship, the crew, all of it. Gone. The three of us remain, and had you been honest with me in the beginning as I was with you, things may be different now."

"A lover's quarrel?" The voice made Kalia and Rahmi start, and he shifted his gaze from his forearm to the door, where Nasir was flanked by two men, each holding a coil of rope. "I would have thought you two would have been enjoying your final moments together." His pointed chin jutted toward Kalia's cell, and the two men entered the brig, one of them grabbing the iron keys from the far wall.

"One of my men found these in your office," Nasir went on, tucking a hand into his pocket to pull up a folded stack of parchment—the coordinates from the NightWatcher.

Kalia tried to scoot as far back as possible, but her shoulders hit the wall in record time. "No, no, no," she pleaded as the men bent down to grab her under each arm, hauling her to her feet. She kicked and thrashed but was ultimately no match for the bulk of the men that tied her up.

The sight of her in chains and tied with even more rope was like being pierced with a dull knife. Rahmi shot to his feet just as she was marched out of her cell, pressing his face against the cool iron bars to better look at Nasir.

"She's not a djinn," Rahmi said quickly, hoping the sudden confession would buy them time. "She told me herself. She'll be no use to you."

Kalia's shoulders stiffened, her back going ramrod straight as the two men paused at the door. Nasir cocked his head to the side, staring down at Kalia with a hint of amusement. For a fleeting moment, Rahmi thought Nasir was considering it. He even took a series of steps around Kalia, his clunking footsteps coming to a halt just out of reach in front of Rami's cell.

"Do you expect me to believe that?" Nasir asked. "You can't possibly think I would fall for that, not after I told you my plans for her." He leaned in just enough that Rahmi saw Reshef glaring at the captain's back. "I'll be sure to bring you her head, *captain*. Maybe you can find a way for it to still suck your cock when it's removed from her body."

Rami lunged, swiping his hand at Nasir and barely catching the mercenary captain's tunic with the tips of his fingers. He didn't know when he had started bellowing. He just knew that his throat was raw when Nasir turned on his heel and ordered Kalia to be taken away.

The cell's iron bars rattled with every violent thrust of his shoulder. Rahmi slammed into them. If he had pulled harder and pushed faster, he could have escaped this cell.

But Kalia was already gone, and the lantern had snuffed out— as though the universe knew that a light was already on its way to being extinguished.

Rahmi sat on the floor with his head in his hands. He had failed and done so miserably enough that Kalia would be dead by now. It hadn't been long since the mercenary ship anchored, though time moved differently in the dark. He hadn't warmed to the concept of being indecisive; it was one of the things he hated most, but when it came to Kalia...she broke and rebuilt something in him—revived a piece of him that had been dead for an eternity.

And now she was gone.

"What is the plan, captain?" Reshef asked, his voice splitting through the abyss like a crack of gunfire. Rahmi could have sworn he was playing with that stupid fucking necklace, the *zing* of stone against silver apparent even here. "How do we get her back?"

How could the man possibly ask him that? It was all boyish dreams to think they had a way out of this. "We don't, Reshef," Rahmi responded. His voice sounded so tired and beaten down...even to his ears. He couldn't imagine what it sounded like to others. "There is nothing we can do."

"I don't believe that," Reshef retorted, a stubbornness infiltrating every ounce of his tone. "I can't believe you don't have a *plan*—"

"What do you want from me?" Rahmi growled, lifting his head to glare daggers toward Reshef's cell. "We are stuck here, locked in a fucking cage—" He kicked out a leg in frustration, the sole of his boot slamming against the door. "—All while the woman I love is out there, and she can't even defend herself because of those gods-damned cuffs!"

A dim glow flared from Reshef's cell, two small circles that gave a soft gold light. Rahmi blinked and the glow was gone, as though his over-active mind had imagined it.

But it was Reshef's following words that had him furrowing his brow. "Such a *human* excuse." The two circles flared again, brighter this time, and Rahmi realized that the glow was coming directly from Reshef's eyes. They illuminated the man's handsome face, casting his high cheekbones and harsh jawline in sharp relief. "Obsidian is a funny little thing. The smallest amount can bring any magic-wielder to their knees, but if one learns how to navigate its composition...how to sneak minuscule amounts of magic through its minerals..."

A spark of fear pulsed against his throat at the sudden sinister tone, and that spark blazed to find a life of its own when the brig was washed in a bath of warm light—light that came directly from the candle that had been extinguished only seconds before. Rahmi's wide-eyed stare flicked over to Reshef, who leaned casually against the cell doors.

Reshef picked at his cuticles as the lock of his door slid open with a loud *click* that echoed into the hallway. He pushed it open with a swipe of his hand, sauntering forward to stand in front of Rahmi's cell. Gone were the naïve charm, youthful smirks, and juvenile arrogance that only a man in their early twenties could have. In their place was a calculating stare filled with an ancient fury that cooled every vein in Rahmi's body.

"I was hidden for centuries, imprisoned in this body with only a necklace to keep me safe. That is until that woman came around."

Reshef crossed his arms over his chest. "She was so...determined to be alone. And that took me by surprise, if I were to be honest, considering the lengths she'll go to protect those around her. I was desperate to know her and to understand the concept that made humans *human*. It's funny. I had no interest in it until her."

Reshef reached up and wrapped his hand around the silver chain of his necklace, yanking it from around his throat and tossing it into the corner of the brig. The room was filled with wicked power—fierce, biting, scrutinizing, and old—so very old.

"What are you?" Rahmi managed to croak through the magic that choked him, the phantom fog so dense that he struggled to breathe around it.

That boyish smirk pulled on Reshef's lips once more, though there was an edge to it that hadn't been there before. "Wickedness, captain. I'm anger, wickedness, and death, a god to you mortals. You can feel it. The difference between Kalia and I is how our magic works. He squatted down to eye-level with Rahmi. "I may not be able to pierce through that mind of yours, but I know what you must be thinking—"

Rahmi pushed himself to stand, a feat of sheer force with the swirl of Reshef's power around him, and he staggered to the bars of his cell. "I think she doesn't deserve what he's going to do to her."

Reshef watched him for a long moment, the sharpness of his eyes boring into Rahmi's very soul. It peeled him apart, layer by layer, but he never looked away. He never stood down from the djinn that was still crouched in front of him.

"Deserve," Reshef began, rolling around the word as though it were foreign on his tongue. "What do we deserve? Did you deserve to become captain? Did she deserve to be stripped from her homeland and brought to a brothel as a child? Did she deserve you to take her to task for lying to you all these months? Do you deserve the *Luminaria*?"

"Did you deserve for her to go in your place, knowing what will become of her?" Rahmi spat at him. *What may have already become of her?* They were wasting precious time that could be spent finding her.

Reshef looked delighted, his face opening with that arrogant charm Rahmi had come to know him by. "Now you're getting it. But here's the thing, captain." He stood, leaning a shoulder against the bars again. "In our short time together, Kalia taught me it isn't about what we *deserve*. It all falls back on the simple principle that love is what unites us if only we freely open ourselves to it. It connects us in a way that pure entitlement for friendships and partners could only hope to. Kalia embodies love because she had to inspect and understand it before giving it away. And isn't that the most beautiful thing of all? She *chose* to give it to you, not because you deserved it, but because she *understood* what that choice meant."

The door to the cell slid open, sending Rahmi stumbling forward. Reshef caught him with a ghostly hand around his upper arm, and a cutlass appeared in Rahmi's fist. The metal glinted against the blazing light from the lantern, sending bright patches to dance against the ceiling.

"And Kalia is a Voyant, you dumb *ahl'ahmach*. Don't underestimate her. If she had truly wanted, she could have ripped your soul from your body before you had the chance to blink."

Ramhi couldn't help but grin at Reshef using his native tongue to call him an asshole. He had been one. It wasn't unfounded. "Where do you think she is?"

"There is only one place Nasir would have taken her. My people once called it the Cave of Wonders. And it's where I planted the *Luminaria* over a thousand years ago."

CHAPTER THIRTY-FIVE

KALIA

K arim was shaking like a leaf, the trembles racking his body so severely that Kalia felt them as they sat next to one another. And it was all she could do not to roll her eyes or hiss an unpleasant *are you fucking kidding me* to him. He was the one, after all, who had pointed her out, who had assisted in stealing the documents that Nasir held so tightly in his hand as he navigated the archipelagos that appeared at the apex of the crescent moon, who had continued to seek out the *Luminaria* even knowing what lay at the end of the tunnel.

Despite the situation Kalia found herself in, imprisoned on a rowboat, her hands shackled with a rock that her magic couldn't penetrate through, she was adamantly more irritated than afraid. She always knew she would meet a sticky end, and she had known it since the first time the madam whipped her for speaking out of turn. But if this was indeed to be her death, she was just pissed that it had to be next to this jittery piece of shit.

"Karim, you're shaking the whole fucking boat," a man who Kalia had learned was Nasir's quartermaster said through gritted teeth. At least someone said it. She wanted to thank him.

"S-sorry," Karim replied, clamping his hands between his knees. The move only managed to stifle the trembling enough that the boat wasn't threatening to tip. "It's the ad-adrenaline. Gets me g-going."

This time, Kalia did roll her eyes. Though the explanation seemed to appease the quartermaster, she knew by Karim's ashen face, wide eyes, and flared nostrils that his quivering had as much to do with adrenaline as she had any connection to being a djinn.

Which is to say, absolutely none.

"How far?" Nasir snapped from the front of the rowboat, turning his milky eye to glare at them over his shoulder. "We don't have much time, and I want this done *tonight*."

Karim's trembling only increased, and Kalia clicked her tongue against her teeth in agitation. If Nasir heard her, he ignored it.

"I-I recognize th-that stone formation over there," Karim said, pointing a shaking finger toward a tall, oddly shaped rock in the distance. The dull light from the moon cascaded over it, casting a long shadow that seemed to reach across the surface of the sea toward them. "G-go past that, and the sh-shore leading to the cave is there."

Nasir squared his shoulders to the front of the boat, not bothering to acknowledge what Karim had said, but Kalia still caught the greedy gleam in his working eye. She took a moment to look around, skating her gaze over the waters. It was oddly calm, unsettlingly so. No fish darted below, no crabs skirted along the rocks that lined each small island they rowed past. There was no breeze, no birds, no ruffling of palm leaves atop the trees.

Kalia harkened it to the stillness of the prison's surroundings and even briefly dipped her eyes to the sea, half-expecting to spot a nasnas floating just beneath the surface. The water was a liquid mirror that they glided through, reflecting the spackle of stars from above.

She didn't know how long it took them to row toward the rock formation, only that the shadow of the stone had elongated in the time it took to get there. The waters became choppier as they rounded the bend of the rock, the small rowboat tossed around by the rolling waves. Eerier still, there was no wind biting at her cheeks, no rustle of her clothing. It was as though the sea had a mind of its own, refusing passage to anyone looking to enter the cave.

Kalia held on to the side of the boat, worried that she would be tossed overboard. The four men holding the oars steady were thrown into a battle with the waves, sweat coating their faces as they struggled to row. But Nasir...it was as though he didn't notice the sudden shift around them. His focus was narrowed on the rocky shore, where the salty waters battered the stone into a smoothness that Kalia knew would be slick.

As they inched closer, Karim had begun to mumble under his breath. A prayer to Liddros, a prayer to any deity who might hear him, a prayer for his mother. He cycled through each one, his eyes squeezed shut, and his hands clamped tightly in his lap. If Karim hadn't led them here himself, Kalia would have thought he made the whole thing up. There wasn't a chance this dim-witted fool got to the *Luminaria*, let alone being the only one of his colleagues to survive.

Yet here they were— sidling up to the shore thanks to Karim's guidance through the archipelagos. Nasir clambered onto the rock first, and the boat held fast against the bobbing waves. His footing was sure, and it was no trouble for him to ignore the other seven people who needed to come ashore. The quartermaster was next, though his boots slid against the wet rock, and he had the decency to hold out his hand to assure Kalia made it off the boat.

The swell crashed around her, *booms* like thunder echoing around the mouth of the cave, and the mist spraying them coated her in a film of salt and cold water. "I don't think so," Kalia said with a saccharine smile, an unsaid *you inbred cretin* pinned to the end of it.

The quartermaster huffed with a dissatisfied sigh as he stepped aside, the most polite answer she was sure she would get, and Kalia scrambled ashore with an ease that surprised even her. As Karim stumbled to the front of the boat, tripping over an oar that one of the men had wedged into place, she turned to study the yawning entrance before her.

It was set back nearly one hundred paces from the sea, jagged rocks that hung like sharp teeth lodged into the upper curve. And while Kalia knew it was silly to think, she could have sworn the two mounds of stone that sat atop the entrance were turned to watch them. She didn't know what she pictured when Karim had told her and Reshef of the cave, but this was far more horrible than she could have ever imagined. Something sinister slumbered there, something ancient and unforgiving.

The wet wind tossed Kalia's hair over her shoulder, pulling strands loose from her braid. A shout pierced through the roar. She whirled around, her mouth falling open when she saw that one of the remaining men had lost his balance while trying to climb from the boat. The sea dipped again, and the man with it smacked his head on the smooth rock in front of him. He slumped to the side, blood flowing like a red river between his eyes before he tipped over the side of the boat and sunk into the oncoming swell.

He didn't resurface, and the booming spray of the waves washed away the remaining stain of red against the stone. The last of him trickled into the water as though he was never there.

Kalia could feel the tenseness of the group, the hard swallows of the men still in the boat, and Karim's gaping stare.

"Basset," Nasir sighed in frustration, his nostrils flared as he pinned his quartermaster with a stare. "You'll row on the return."

"Yes, captain," the quartermaster, Basset, replied with a curt nod, though he had a stiffness to his shoulders that hadn't been there a moment ago.

Decidedly pleased with the quick reply of his quartermaster, Nasir stalked toward the entrance of the cave, gesturing them all to follow with a simple flick of his wrist. Kalia was yanked forward, unaware until that moment that Basset had grasped the length of her chains. She lurched, stepping into a tidepool that was shallow enough for the water to bathe just the toe of her boot.

Kalia straightened immediately, staunchly ignoring the jeering men that had finally made it to shore behind her. She used their chortling as fuel to stoke the fire in her belly, readying to rally her anger the moment the shackles were removed. They *had* to remove them, right? She even briefly considered who she would target first: Nasir or Karim.

While Nasir was decidedly worse than Karim, Kalia had grown tired of Karim's whining. As Nasir stormed toward the cave's entrance with an air of unadulterated arrogance, Karim began to tremble, if possible, even more.

The cave loomed before her, an abyss that seemed to swallow any flare of light from the moon. Kalia took a breath to calm her nerves, the pattern of her heartbeat so heavy that she could feel it in the tips of her fingers. Before her, Nasir halted in his path to retrieve a torch and a flint rock from the bag he had slung over his shoulder. It took a series of strikes for the flame to flare, but still, it didn't do any good against the lifeless dark that stood in steep contrast to the starry night sky.

"Karim," Nasir snapped, tucking the flint rock into the pocket of his coat before dumping the bag into a puddle at his feet. "Come. You'll lead us."

Karim opened his mouth, looking as though he would rather not thank you very much, but he clamped it shut in the next moment. His feet dragged forward as he moved, taking the torch from Nasir as soon as he got close enough. "Some of the passages are narrow. It's best to stay close."

Silence stretched between the group, now one short, as they moved through the cave. Water dripped into the passage, lichen the only living thing Kalia had spotted. But as she moved further in, the clip of her footfalls spurred on by the tug at her shackles, that intense feeling of being watched never eased. It kept her on edge, kept her head swiveling from one side of the passage to the other, half-expecting something to be lurking in the shadows. Even Basset seemed restless, evident by the curl of his fingers around her chains and how his eyes darted every which way.

Come to me, come see me...

Kalia froze, her scalp prickling as an iciness slid down her spine. At first, she thought she was the only one to hear the voice. It was beckoning, haunting..., and cunning. But when Basset didn't pull at her chains, she glanced up to see that he, too, had stopped.

"What was that?" one of the men behind her asked in a hushed voice that still managed to root in the stone walls around them.

"We're close," Karim noted. The torch's flame flickered as though on a phantom wind, and she could make out the pale tinge on the back of his neck. She wondered if he was still trembling, though by the way the shadows danced on the ceiling, she realized that he was. Nasir, however, trembled for a far different reason. "N-not far now."

They walked further on, the jagged stone walls clipping Kalia's shoulders when she wandered too close to avoid the puddles at her feet. The denseness of the cave was off-putting; even the air she breathed was a touch too stale, too heavy. She wondered what could reside down here. Then she thought she probably didn't want to know. There were no animal bones, no scat, no tiny scrambling of paws against the floor as they walked.

"Here," Karim breathed, holding the torch high above his head. In the dim light, Kalia saw a carving of a serpent around a staff. It seemed to sway with the flame, the body coiling—ready to strike. "I recognize this from the last time."

Nasir shoved ahead of him, snatching the torch from Karim's hand to inspect the serpent further. His eyes didn't stray from the carving as he asked, "And how does it open? How do we get in?"

Karim audibly gulped. "Blood."

The men behind Kalia shuffled as though suddenly uncomfortable with where they had found themselves while Nasir paused. His head tilted thoughtfully, and Kalia certainly didn't like the way his eyes narrowed. She could almost see his mind working, speculation buried on his cruel face.

"Do you remember, Karim," Nasir started, "how I promised to track you to the end of the world if you betrayed me?"

Though his voice was soft, Kalia's gut twisted at the inflection. Karim, it seemed, had yet to catch on.

"Yes, captain," Karim replied, nodding his head. "I do."

It happened so suddenly that Kalia barely had time to blink. One moment, Nasir was gazing up at the carved serpent; the next, he had pivoted on the heels of his boots, the sparkle of metal in the light of the flame oddly sharp. Karim gasped, the sound throaty and primal before he glanced down to stare wide-eyed at his belly.

Right where Nasir had lodged his sword.

"Thank you for bringing me here," Nasir said. He wrenched the sword from Karim's gut, who fell to his knees with a nauseating *smack* of bone against the rock. "I've found a final use for you, after all."

Karim gaped like a fish out of water, red-tinged drool dripping from the side of his mouth in long, thick strands. He collapsed to his side, his breathing still quickened and shallow. It wouldn't be for long.

Nasir bent down, cupping his hand against the wound to collect a palmful of blood streaming from Karim's belly. The flow slowed before stopping entirely, and Karim finally died with his wide eyes still plastered to the ceiling. Nasir stood, paying no mind to the man he had slain, and slapped his hand against the serpent with a sickening *thwack*.

For a moment, no one moved. Time stopped. Heavy breaths filled the air, underscored by the steady *drip, drip, drip* of Karim's blood into the puddle he had fallen in.

Then a cold swept in, one so frigid that Kalia was sure her lungs would freeze inside of her chest. It tightened her skin, burned her throat, and watered her eyes. It was piercing and never-ending, unnatural and jarring. The torch's flame snuffed out, plunging them into a never-ending darkness that threatened to swallow her whole if the cold didn't do it first.

Then, the cave began to shake. Shouts of shock echoed from behind her as the men shuffled closer to the wall. There was a *smack* and a groan, and Kalia imagined that one of them had cracked their forehead against the stone. They deserved it. The heavy scent of minerals rose around her, and ground rock that had been pulverized was raining down from the loose stones above them. Kalia coughed as she inhaled it, the sudden barrage of chill and dust nearly sending her to her knees.

It all stopped just as instantly as it had started. Sniffles, coughing, and panting filled the abyss again, only this time, there was a grinding of rock on rock. A door slid open, bathing a sliver of pale moonlight into the passage.

They were in.

"*Godsdamn,*" one of the men said in awe, and Kalia couldn't help but agree.

She had never seen so much treasure in her whole fucking life. Piles of gold bars and silver coins, chalices embossed with rubies and sapphires. Necklaces that were too heavy to be worn, and gemstones the size of her fist. It was all scattered amongst the chamber, a hall so large that she was sure the palace's throne room could fit inside of it.

Not that Kalia had ever seen the palace's throne room, but she couldn't imagine it was bigger than this.

The men surged forward, whooping and laughing as they dove into the riches. Basset had placed a gold crown atop his head and had begun to stuff the pockets of his breeches full of coins and gemstones. One of the other men careened straight into a pile, laying on top of it as he hugged the treasure into his chest.

The madam would be resentful if she knew where Kalia was now, and she took a moment to bask in that very thought, imagining the indignant press of the madam's lips and the heated flash to her eyes. All the madam ever wanted was to be filthy rich. Kalia could buy her freedom and more with this, could live without fear of retaliation or being tracked down. It was all right here. Everything she ever wanted was within reach.

But that thought gave way to one more sinister, and Kalia's stomach clenched when it roared to the front of her mind. Karim had said his colleagues died here, how they had never made it out of this chamber alive. But as she swept her gaze over the jewels that lined the pools of water, the mounds of pearls, the gaudy rings...one particular detail stuck out.

There were no bodies, bones, or skeletons to be seen. As though Kalia was seeing it all in a new light, the piles of treasure suddenly looked too put together, too perfectly scattered. Something was wrong, horribly wrong. The instinct that had kept her alive all of these years kicked to life, and she had the urge to run as fast as she could from the chamber.

But Nasir, who had been the only man not to be distracted by what lay inside, fixed his eyes on the doorway that had been carved in the opposite wall. Kalia felt a tug on her chains as he marched toward it. She didn't know when he had taken hold of them, but she had missed that exchange entirely.

They passed Basset, his breeches dangerously close to sliding down his backside from the sheer weight of the coins overflowing his pockets. They passed the other three men, all of whom she didn't bother to learn their names. Each of them was buried in the piles of jewels so tall that she was sure they towered over Rahmi.

Her heart squeezed. He hadn't even looked at her as she was being taken away, though she heard his screams as she rounded the corner out of the brig. She wouldn't get the chance to apologize. She knew that now. All she could hope for was that, somehow, Rahmi got away...that he was far, far away from this vile place.

The final chamber was markedly smaller than the first and split into two peninsulas surrounded by a basin of eerily calm water. It didn't even ripple; it merely reflected the single shaft of moonlight that spilled in from above. A narrow walkway spanned the two capes. And just beyond that, on a jagged stone pedestal, stood a red gemstone.

The *Luminaria* was stunning. It bore no chips or markings to indicate that it was flawed. It was perfectly shaped with rounded edges that came to slim points, and Kalia wanted nothing to do with it.

"I'm not going to help you," she said, squaring her shoulders to face Nasir. "It's not meant for you."

Nasir rounded on her, his jaw set tight. "You will help me, djinn." He placed a hand on the pommel of his sword, the blade still stained red with Karim's blood. "Or you will not make it out of this cave."

Kalia spat at him, the gob of saliva settling on the curve of his cheekbone. Nasir stared at her for a long minute, tension threading the gap between them, before he lifted his hand from the pommel and swiped it off with one finger.

"Was that out of defiance, or has no one taught you *manners*, girl?"

Kalia smirked, amusement sparking in the recesses of her chest. "Take off these shackles and find out."

Nasir contemplated her as he lowered his hand back to the pommel, and she watched with satisfaction how his finger tapped against the hilt. Irritation. She recognized the tightness of his shoulders and the slight pinch of his brow. And, for that moment, she thought she had won.

But there was an ugly twist to Nasir's mouth, and he stood a little taller as he peered down at her. "Rahmi is still in my brig. You refuse to get me the *Luminaria*, and I will drag you back to the ship and kill him in front of you. The choice is yours, little djinn. I would make it quick."

CHAPTER THIRTY-SIX

RAHMI

Rahmi cut down the first man he came across quickly, the surprised yelp swallowed by a surge of power that left his hair on end. Reshef was hot on his heels, silencing the pitiful cries of the sailor. But that wasn't all Reshef did, and Rahmi watched in horror as the sailor turned an unnatural shade of puce. His eyes bulged, his veins darkened, and a web of black cascaded from his throat before he keeled over.

"Was that necessary?" Rahmi asked, wiping the blood from his cutlass on the back of the man's tunic. "I had him just fine."

Reshef cracked his knuckles, stretching his neck back and forth as though he were readying for a back-alley fight. "I've hidden myself for a thousand years, captain. My magic is begging to be released."

Rahmi made a noise of frustration at the back of his throat, mostly centered on the realization that Reshef's power could have come in handy a time or two before this point. "How many of you are there, then? Liddros said—"

"Liddros knows three of my kind are remaining in his realm," Reshef growled. He moved through the corridor with inhuman elegance, and Rahmi briefly wondered how he hadn't seen it before. "And he's been hunting us for centuries. What he doesn't know is that I'm the fourth. While his powers are muted, they are still existent. We must hurry if we want to beat the king to the Luminaria before Liddros finds me."

Rahmi raced after Reshef, taking the stairs two at a time to keep up. He sliced through a second man, then a third, but the djinn was already a step ahead. Waves of power crested over them, terrible winds that left a taste of wild ether on his tongue. Rahmi landed at the top of the staircase, his stomach lurching at the sight before him.

Bodies dropped where they had been standing, *fion* glugging from an open cask and the steins rolling across the lower deck with every gentle rock of the ship. Able men in their prime, nearly a dozen of them...

"Are they dead?" Rahmi asked, glancing back at Reshef, who had begun to take the second set of stairs that led to the quarterdeck. He could already smell the brine cutting through the sour scent of the lower berths.

Reshef paused, one hand on the railing and one foot on the above step. "Is that a problem?"

It was decidedly *not* a problem, but Rahmi wanted a chance to exact his revenge, too. These men had dragged him aboard this ship, had sunk *The Mark of Malice*, and had taken Kalia to where only the gods knew. He dared not voice it at the risk of sounding absurd, but Reshef's lips carved upward in a way that made Rahmi regret the thought.

"Are you jealous, captain?" A childlike insincerity to his voice made Rahmi want to throttle him, djinn or not. "Should I have saved some for you?"

"No," Rahmi replied adamantly, gesturing vaguely toward the stairs. "Have your fun, I suppose."

Reshef barked a laugh. "I will allow you the *thrill* of rescuing our dear friend, Kalia. That way, you can be the pirate in stained breeches for her. Do we have a deal?"

Rahmi clenched his teeth. "How thoughtful of you."

Reshef said nothing else as he barreled up the staircase, not bothering to be quiet. A harrowing twist clamped down in Rahmi's gut when he remembered that he had once put a knife to this man's throat and had threatened to bleed him like a stuck pig. He glanced back at the dozen men Reshef had ended with a mere thought. How far would he have let Rahmi go before turning him into a pile of bone dust?

Shouts echoed from the deck, snapping Rahmi out of his thoughts. His boots pounded against the wooden steps as he ascended the quarterdeck, and he entered the melee with his cutlass tightly clutched. Not that he needed it, as Reshef certainly had it handled on his own.

Pistol shots rang out, lead bullets whizzing through the air toward the djinn. But with an unneeded flourish of his hands, the bullets transformed into rose petals, each lazily wafting toward the deck. The sailor who had fired the pistol glanced over to Rahmi, blinking, from where he stood near the gunnel. In the next moment, and another crest of power, all that remained was a pile of hard-worn clothes, a tiger cub nestled on top.

On and on it went. Cutlasses into brass cymbals, the holder suddenly transformed into a small monkey wearing a vest. A dagger into a sandglass, shattering as soon as it hit the ground. Coils of rope into a line of sausage links that comically throttled a sailor on the run.

Another man into a parrot, indignant squawks blaring from his beak as he marched around the deck. A third man into a flying carpet, where it zoomed around the sails, shaking its corner tassels as though they were tiny fists.

Rahmi settled onto a crate to watch the chaos, laying the cutlass across his lap. Reshef inched closer and closer to the ship's bow, a smile plastered on his boyishly handsome face. There was nothing for Rahmi to do but wait. And, while Rahmi preferred to be in the battle, Reshef had an unmistakable flare for ridiculousness...and a thousand years' worth of ideas to prove it.

When the smoke settled and the crew of *The Midnight Mariner* had been turned into a host of animals and objects, Reshef came to stand in front of Rahmi. An apple appeared in his palm, and he took a calm bite. He leaned an elbow on the gunnel and stared out at the sea.

"You left me to do all of the heavy lifting," Reshef said with the air of someone who had worked particularly hard. A second bite from the apple, the crunch loud against the quiet of the night. "Could have used your help out there."

Rahmi rolled his eyes, leaning back against the wall. "I didn't want to get turned into some aquatic creature by mistake. Was that one a lizard?"

Reshef furrowed his brow. "Which one?"

"Mid-deck. Portly. Holes in the toes of his boots."

"Ah, no. That's an olm, a cave-dwelling salamander. I saw them in another realm before I got stuck here. It's a common misconception."

"I'll take your word for it."

Reshef took another bite of his apple as Rahmi tipped his head back to look up at the sky. A star shot across, bright despite the light from the crescent moon. The waters were calm and peaceful, allowing him to collect his thoughts and secure a plan to find Kalia. He was interrupted by a sudden squawk from the parrot, his talons clicking against the deck as he marched over, red feathers ruffling.

"Well, if you're done resting, we should go release the others from the lower deck," Reshef sighed, tossing his apple into the sea.

Rahmi shot up from the crate, catching the cutlass by the leather-wrapped hilt. "They've been down there the entire time? Who was rescued? I thought they all *died*."

"Please," Reshef said, pushing himself away from the gunnel and sauntering toward the bow. He stepped over the squawking parrot, who did a quick about-face and marched after him. "You're upsetting Iago."

Rahmi guessed Iago was the aptly-named bird, but he breezed past it as he followed Reshef. "How did they survive?"

"Most of them were captured when the ship began to sink," Reshef said as he grabbed a lantern from the mast and bounced down the stairs. I wouldn't know who is here and who isn't, but I felt them aboard this ship when I removed my necklace. I thought keeping them out of the fray would be better."

Rahmi grumbled a curse under his breath, suddenly feeling less beholden to the djinn. "You could have said something." With every step, the air began to stale and sour again.

"You're right, I could have," Reshef answered simply. He took a right, then a left, then walked down a long passage lined with rooms that, at one time, had been meant as cabins for the rich to rent on their voyages. Now, they were filled with expensive clothes, old sails, crates of food, and casks that seemed to be for *fion*. "Hello, my love."

Alaric, as were Elodie and Shirin, were there, their soot-covered faces peering through the darkness at them. Thomas, Elric, Bart, William, Searles, Cora, and many more bolted to the wall with sets of rusted shackles. They weren't obsidian, but the iron was rusted enough that Rahmi knew it would be a job to free them all.

That was until Reshef blinked, and the shackles fell away, disintegrating into piles of metal shavings. Alaric gaped as he turned over his hands, staring at his wrists. His eye patch had been removed, the socket in plain view. Elodie squealed in surprise while she rubbed her forearms, reddened by how tightly the shackles had been locked around her. Even stoic Shirin made a noise out of the back of her throat.

Elodie was the first to stand, the first to make her way over to Reshef, sliding her arms around his waist to give him a big squeeze. "I *knew* you were different. I could *feel* it!" She pulled away before he could return the hug and shouldered past him to stand in front of Rahmi. "The captain took Kalia." It wasn't a question.

"Yes," Rahmi replied, swallowing thickly when he realized how much time had passed.

"And we're going after her," Elodie stated. It was not up for debate.

"Yes." Rahmi looked down at her. "And it's going to be dangerous," he added, silently hoping it would deter her.

It didn't.

"I know, but she deserves to be rescued."

Rahmi couldn't help but smile at her wording. Reshef gave him a conspiratorial wink over his shoulder. "Then we should probably get going, shouldn't we?"

"The path through the archipelagos is going to be too narrow to sail this ship," Alaric said from the helm, his one eye pressed against the looking glass. "It's deceivingly wide at the front, though it's probably meant to be. We'll run aground if we try."

Rahmi's crew had quickly gotten over the flying carpet, the squawking parrot, the painted turtle, the olm, and the horde of other animals and objects the sailors had been turned into. By the healthy distance they kept away, he could tell who was most comfortable with Reshef, Elodie and Shirin for example, and who wasn't. The djinn didn't seem to mind one way or the other as long as Alaric stayed by his side.

And from how Alaric had grabbed the back of Reshef's head and pulled him in for a devouring kiss, it sure didn't seem like it would be an issue.

"Rowing is going to take too long," Rahmi said in agreement, running a frustrated hand through his hair. "They've been gone for hours now, I assume." The primal need to hit something flared to life inside him again, but he tempered it as Elodie climbed the steps, cooing at the tiger cub she had snatched off the deck.

"Captain, what's the word for *prince* in your native language?" she asked, adjusting her arms around the cub. It looked disgruntled, and Rahmi wondered how much of the sailor was still in there.

"*Ameer*," Rahmi answered at once, though he narrowed his eyes on the woman a heartbeat later. "Why?"

"My little Ameer," Elodie cooed again, scratching between the tiger cub's ears.

"Elodie, you can't *name* the tiger," Rahmi said exasperatedly as Alaric dutifully looked away. "Twenty minutes ago, it was a *human*."

"And now it's a tiger," Elodie said happily, as though she didn't see what the ethical dilemma was. "My tiger."

"And what will you *do* with the tiger when we figure out how to get to the cave?"

Elodie looked at him as though he were something particularly disgusting on the underside of her boot. "It's a tiger, captain. It'll be fine on its own."

He didn't have the patience for this. He began to turn to glare at Alaric, who was struggling to contain his amusement, but Shirin and Reshef climbed up the steps at that moment.

"The *Luminaria* is a conduit of power that the djinn are bound to," Reshef explained to Shirin, who was listening with rapt attention. "With it, someone without magic can control the djinn still on the continent."

"So why can't you take control of it?" Shirin asked as she paused near the top step. "Keep it with you so others can't get to it?"

Reshef shook his head. "It doesn't work that way. The four of us used our magic to bind the stone to the chamber. It would take all four of us to remove it. Only those that our magic deems worthy can."

"So there's a chance that Kalia can't get it out," Shirin said, a hopeful glint filling her eye. "There's a chance that the *Luminaria* is safe."

"Yes, but if she can," Reshef pressed on, "then who has direct access to it? Captain Nasir? The king? We have almost limitless power. We've been hunted for centuries. What do you think the king would do with my magic if he got ahold of it?"

Shirin went a bit pale as she nodded, though she perked up considerably when she noticed the tiger cub cradled in Elodie's arms.

"His name is Ameer," Elodie said, the tone of a proud mother, as Shirin bounded up the rest of the steps to play with the cub's tail.

"You cannot keep the tiger," Rahmi ground out, tilting his head back to gaze in profound irritation at the stars. "It has to go."

"What are you going to do? Drown it?" Elodie asked with enough sass that Rahmi's head snapped back into place. "*It was a human less than twenty minutes ago.*"

This time, Alaric snickered. Rahmi felt a vein pulse in his forehead and even imagined throwing the tiger cub and Elodie off the ship's side. "None of this is helpful," Rahmi barked. He was at his limit. "Kalia is out there. This ship is too large to get through. We don't have time to row. We will lose access to the archipelago in a matter of hours. Are there any other suggestions?" That didn't even come close to the issue that *The Mark of Malice* had been sunk, and his life was soon to be forfeit. He just needed to see Kalia safe first.

The group quieted, and for a long minute, the only sounds were his crew on the quarterdeck and the squawking of that stupid fucking parrot. Rahmi unsheathed his dagger, stalking toward the steps to remove its head from its body, but Reshef stepped in front of him.

"If we can't sail there, captain," Reshef said, "then we'll fly there."

Before Rahmi could challenge him on the notion of that absolutely ridiculous idea, Reshef lifted his fingers to his mouth and whistled so loudly that Rahmi heard ringing in his ears. It took only a short time for his unasked question to be answered.

The flying carpet zoomed around the main sail, coming to a halt in front of Reshef as though it were a dog called by its master. Reshef patted the worn-looking purple fabric and turned to send Rahmi a smug smile.

"This—this is—" Rahmi spluttered. "You can't be serious."

"As serious as you were a moment ago when you went to behead Iago," Reshef retorted. The carpet waved a single golden tassel at Rahmi. "This is going to be the quickest way. I can promise you that."

"This one carpet can't hold all of us. Three at the most? We don't have the room," Rahmi countered.

Reshef made a noise of agreement at the back of his throat before he turned to face the quarterdeck. "You, you, you, you, you, you, and...hmm...you." He pointed at different animals around the deck, including the olm, and each changed form, popping into different patterned flying carpets. The fleet of carpets zoomed around before coming to a halt near the stern. Each bobbed in the air, waiting for a command.

"Come on, captain," Reshef said, squaring his shoulders to face Rahmi. He hopped onto the purple carpet, turning to offer a hand to Rahmi. The mischievous gleam in his eye made Rahmi uneasy. "Do you trust me?"

Rahmi huffed an irritated sigh, and something tightened in his chest at the thought of flying. But Kalia's life was in balance, as was the *Luminaria's*, and what choice did he have? At that moment, he had never understood her better. His brave *ruehi*. "Fine, but I'm getting my own fucking carpet. No way I'm riding with you."

CHAPTER THIRTY-SEVEN

KALIA

Kalia laughed out loud, tossing her head back. "You can't kill him. He's an immortal cursed captain. And, trust me, I've tried." A few times, but that she didn't add. "It's an empty threat."

Nasir closed the space between them with a single step forward, though Kalia held her ground. He loomed over her, his condescending stare glaring down his nose at her. "There's long been a rumor, little djinn, that the cursed captain can pass on their immortality if you cut out his heart. Is that something you're willing to bet on? I would certainly *love* to find out if it's true."

Kalia never took her eyes from the captain, though they narrowed considerably. "You're lying."

Nasir's chin flicked toward the *Luminaria* behind her. "You can find out, or you can get me that gemstone. The choice is yours." Kalia went silent as her fingers tightened into fists, and Nasir smirked at the sight of it. "Tick-tock, let's go."

Kalia spun away from him, facing the *Luminaria* head-on. What was once seemingly beautiful and untouched only looked unsightly now. She hated that gemstone for what it did to Rahmi, to the king, for what it was doing to her. The first step forward was full of hesitation, but the moon's cool light lit her path along the small bridge that connected the peninsulas.

She crept over it, peering down into the inky, black water surrounding her. It was like glass, and she saw the bright-eyed girl she knew so well in that reflection. Hair pulled loose from the braid, skin paler than it should have been, eyes filled with feminine rage. And that's what she fixated on, that rage.

Kalia half-expected the *Luminaria* to grow teeth and bite her as she approached it, but the glinting red gemstone just sat there. Now that she was up close, she could spot tiny scratch marks on the surface. It wasn't perfect. Somehow, the thought gave her comfort.

Do you believe yourself worthy? A phantom voice breathed against the shell of her ear. She recognized the cadence as the same voice they had all heard outside the chamber. Kalia swallowed as she lifted her hand to hover above the gemstone, her hand basking it in shadow. The chains of her shackles clanked against the pedestal.

No, Kalia whispered in return, though she didn't say the words out loud. Somehow, she knew that she didn't need to*, but she had to—for the man I love.*

Her fingers wrapped around the gem— warmer than she expected— and lifted it from the stone. For a moment, nothing happened. The air was unnaturally cold in her lungs. If she were to believe Karim, if what he said came next—

A shriek filled the chamber just beyond the *Luminaria*'s small room, and Kalia felt her stomach drop to her feet. At the same time, the water surrounding the peninsulas bubbled and roared to life, quickly overtaking the bridge and the edges of the capes, washing over her boots. It rose and rose, like a being that had taken on a life of its own. It was at her calves as she sloshed toward where the bridge had been and was above her knees when she reached the other side.

"Come on!" Nasir shouted at her, his eyes wide with fear. "Hurry up, girl! Come on!"

The water was up to her hips, bubbling and roiling not even beginning to slow. She knew it would drown her, but she held on tightly to the Luminaria. She could have sworn a ghostly hand wrapped around her fist to keep the gemstone in place. Shockingly, Karim had been right. The water never left the chamber, only slapped against an invisible barrier like a wall had been erected there.

It was at her waist now, but Kalia kept pressing forward. She was feet away, inches even, and finally passed the chamber's threshold. A powerful gust of wind roared in her ears and forced her to her knees. It was...pleased. How could a wind be pleased? It stopped as quickly as it started.

"I'll take that now."

Nasir stood before her, water dripping down his tunic and frock coat, and his hand was extended toward her. Expectant and vigilant. When Kalia's eyes darted past him to assess the crossing to the cave, Nasir unsheathed his blade with one smooth tug.

"Do not think about—"

In an instant, Kalia thrust her shackles forward, catching the tip of his blade in one of the links of her chains. She twisted her wrists, forcefully yanking the sword from his hands. She couldn't catch it, and it fell to the sand at her knees. Nasir's bewilderment might buy her a couple of extra seconds. Pushing forward, she shot to her feet and shouldered past the captain, breaking out in a run with the gemstone still tightly clutched in her hand. She pushed her legs faster and faster, willing them to save her.

Nasir recovered quickly, and Kalia could hear his thundering footsteps as he powered after her. Her skirt was sodden and heavy, bunching at her ankles. It slowed her down, and the sudden pressure of his hand on her shoulder made her yelp. Her knees hit the ground again, pain and nausea radiating through her, and she tried to scramble away from him. A heavy boot settled on her lower back, and Kalia cried out as he shoved her head into the sand, a mouthful of it coating her tongue. Her chains dug into her ribs, threatening to wedge into places she didn't have any interest in them being.

"I could leave you in this gods-forsaken place," Nasir grunted out as he damn near laid on top of her to pin her into place. She felt his hot breath on the back of her neck. "I could leave you to these *things*, where they would eat you alive."

Out of desperation, Kalia glanced up. Basset was fighting a pair of ghouls with a single gold chalice, the crown askew on his head. The ghouls' long claws swiped at him, and he jumped out of the way just in time. Another one of the men hadn't been so lucky, and three ghouls were bent over to feast on his belly. The other two oar men were nowhere to be found. Either they had gotten lucky enough to make it out of the chamber, or the cache of coins had buried their bodies during their struggle for survival.

Kalia thrashed again, wriggling her hips to try and throw Nasir off balance, but she only managed to sink into the sand. His hand closed over her nose and mouth, the palm of his hand still wet from a salty mixture of water and sweat. She tried to take in a breath, but he only tightened it against her. Her fingernails scratched at the back of his hand, hard enough that she knew she was making him bleed, but he only chuckled.

"You will give me that stone. One way or the other, little djinn. Even if I have to pry it from your dead hands."

Her vision blackened, but she willed herself to remain present. There was a roaring in her ears that had nothing to do with that phantom wind, and stars speckled at the sides of her vision. She was light-headed, her mind foggy, but she still fought. She still...she still...

Kalia felt her fingers unfurl and felt the warmth of the gemstone slide from her palm. Nasir removed his hand from her face immediately, and she took in a choking gasp that she couldn't get down fast enough. She gulped at the air, not caring that she still had sand on her tongue or that a ghoul suddenly realized she was lying there.

Nasir removed his foot from her back and stood straight up. He let out a chuckle that turned into a celebratory laugh, the sound sliding unpleasantly down her gut. "Finally!" he cried out, and she saw him raise the gemstone into the air from the corner of her eye. "I can feel it: the power, the magic."

Kalia rose to her knees, fighting the urge to crumple back to the sand. She had failed. She hadn't been strong enough to keep the *Luminaria* from him. And now... "What next, then?" she sneered at him. "Sail back to the king? Let him have complete control of this continent?"

Nasir sighed, moving to squat next to her. He held the gemstone up in the space between them, mockingly showing it off, daring her to make a move for it. "Fuck the king," he retorted, boring his stare into her own. The moon reflected off the gemstone, bathing his thick scar in a red glow that looked astonishingly like a smatter of blood. "If he wanted this, little djinn, he should have found it himself."

He stood again, tipping his head back toward the cracked ceiling. "I call the djinn to me," he roared, twisting the gemstone around in the palm of his hand. "I order them to heed my commands."

Kalia scrambled back, scooting on her backside to push away from the ghoul that had locked its sunken eyes onto her. With every shaky step toward her, the sickeningly sweet stench of decay only became stronger. Rotten and mottled, the gray skin seemed to be holding on by the slim strings of sinew connected to the bone. *Gods*, it was grotesque, down to the claws still sported red flesh from the oar man it had killed.

She felt metal against her palm and heard the clink of her shackle against it. Feeling desperately around, she found the hilt of Nasir's sword and drew it into her hand. It was almost too heavy, but she swung it upward anyway. The edge of the blade collided with an exposed bone, the shock of it reverberating up her arm. The ghoul stumbled backward, giving her just enough space to stand—giving her just enough space to clutch the hilt with both hands and swing it one more time.

Flesh and bone ground against the sword, and with a sickening *thud*, the ghoul's head fell into the sand at her feet. Kalia let out a sigh of relief as she dropped the sword. She immediately picked up her soaked skirt to find Nasir once again. It didn't take long, as he was still in the middle of the chamber, but now he was surrounded by four humans...the djinn.

And Kalia recognized one.

"Reshef?" Her heart shuddered, threatening to stop entirely.

Reshef glanced over to her, a mask of devastation blanketing his face. "I'm sorry, my friend," he called back to her, his words brittle and wavering. "I should have told you sooner." Another djinn, a woman with flowing locks of salt-and-pepper hair, couldn't keep her eyes from him. "Your captain is coming, but I fear he will be too late."

"Hush," Nasir barked, and Reshef's lips immediately slammed shut. "You work for me now, and we have much to do." He didn't look back at Kalia; he hadn't realized yet that the *Luminaria* did not affect her. She used that to her advantage.

Creeping closer to Nasir's back, Kalia stooped down to pick up a jewel-encrusted dagger from the sand. He was so busy gleefully listing off the things he wanted, prioritizing them before changing his mind a moment later, that he didn't hear the clink of her chains. The blade looked sharp enough, and she hoped it would do the job. When she got within striking range, she lunged.

The dagger wasn't large enough to cut through his wrist, but it still managed to slice two fingers clean off. He let out a yowl of pain, the *Luminaria* tumbling to the ground. It bounced once, twice, then settled near Reshef's boots.

"No!" Nasir screamed, cradling his hand to his chest, but Kalia had already dropped the dagger.

Bounding forward, Kalia swiped the gemstone from the sand and bolted toward the exit. She ignored the ghouls, each in a different stage of decay, hobbling after her. She ignored the bellows of support from the djinn, all still rooted in place. She even ignored the pounding of Nasir's boots after her, though he was markedly slower than before.

She could seal it shut if she could get out of the chamber. And if she sealed it shut, she *just might* be able to use the *Luminaria* long enough to get the djinn out...leaving the captain and what was left of his crew trapped inside. It was a long shot, but it could work. It could—

Something solid caught Kalia in the ankle, and she tumbled forward. Sliding against a scatter of jewels, she rolled to a sudden stop against a pile of coins. She groaned as she heard Nasir scream, "*Get the ghouls! Get the ghouls!*" to the djinn standing in a circle, and pushed herself up to keep going. But Basset was there, his forearm split down to the bone, and he reached for her throat to hold her in place.

"I got her, captain! I got—"

Kalia didn't let him finish his sentence. She had grappled to her side, her fingers reaching for anything and finding a palm-sized gem. She smashed it against the side of his head, feeling his skull dent and crack in its wake. She didn't stop to ponder it as he crumpled to the sand, blood pooling from his wound. He didn't move.

She bound forward with the *Luminaria* still in her hand, but Nasir had beaten her to the chamber entrance. Eyes wild and blood steadily streaming from where his fingers had once been, he held the jewel-encrusted dagger between them.

"You will give that to me," Nasir ordered, but Kalia didn't budge. "Give it to me, little djinn."

But Kalia only smiled, only flashed her teeth at him as she shook her head. "You can't force me to do anything," she said with a biting laugh that ticked Nasir's ja. "Because I'm no djinn, I'm a Voyant."

Nasir lunged for her, swiping the blade through the air, but he was a hair too slow. There was a flash of metal against the cool, silver moonlight, and a cry of surprise bit out from the shadows.

Then Rahmi appeared, flanked by Alaric and Thomas, each with their cutlasses drawn.

For a moment, Kalia forgot that she knew how to breathe. He was *here*. She was suddenly bathed in his spicy scent, his unyielding presence managing to shrink the size of the chamber. She wanted to reach for and touch him to make sure that it wasn't a piece of her imagination come to life before her very eyes.

But she had stayed rooted for too long. Nasir grasped onto her shackles, forcing her back against his front. She felt the tip of the jewel-encrusted dagger at the column of her throat, and Rahmi froze in place.

"I would advise you to take her hands off of her," Rahmi said, the low rumble of his voice skittering across her flesh. "It's on you what happens next, but if you leave this chamber alive, it isn't going to be me that you should be worried about. Especially if she gets those shackles off."

Kalia heard Nasir's tongue glide out to lick his dry lips. "Very well, *captain*." His tone was oily sweet, taunting and cruel. "Djinn, leave the ghouls. Attack Rahmi's crew. Leave the captain and his whore to me."

CHAPTER THIRTY-EIGHT

KALIA

The chamber exploded.

Nasir dragged Kalia back as Reshef rushed forward, his gait clunky as though he were fighting the order with every cell in his body. Rahmi dove to the side, and Reshef staggered toward Alaric, his hand raised to chest height. There was a swell of power, one so terrible that Kalia wanted to fall to her knees before it blasted from Reshef. Alaric managed to lurch out of the way, but the tail of his tunic singed, filling the chamber with the smell of burning cotton.

The salt-and-pepper woman fell against Thomas, her pleas for forgiveness going unheard as she shot a crest of magic toward him. He slumped to the ground, blood pouring from between his lips.

The rest of *The Mark of Malice* crew streamed into the chamber, clogging the entrance and tripping over Thomas. But they were still no match for the magic-wielders. The third djinn, another woman with short, slicked-back curls and rosy cheeks, joined Reshef and the other woman. The wind whipped around, scattering coins and blowing sand into gritty twisters that pelted them with flying jewels and gold bars.

Then there were the ghouls. Without the power of the djinn holding them into place, the ghouls were free to roam. And they didn't seem to differentiate between djinn or human, snapping their sharp teeth and clawing at the backs of both. The only distinction was that the djinn had been ordered to leave the ghouls, a command they had to take at face value. Cutlasses slashed through the air, metal meeting the ghouls, but they still surged forward, tearing at the shoulders of the djinn and shredding them into bloody strips of flesh.

If that wasn't enough, Kalia gaped as seven flying carpets zoomed into the chamber, a rider tightly clutching onto each one. She spotted Elodie and Shirin, as well as Elric and Cobden. They threaded through the twisters of sand, slashing their cutlasses from above. Distracted by the magic carpets, the ghouls turned away from the djinn.

"Hi, Kalia!" Elodie waved as she whizzed by. We're here to rescue you!" Kalia could have sworn one of the carpet's corner tassels waved at her, too. Elodie whirled in the air, dashing back into the fray of sand, smoke, and pistol shots.

"Give that to me," Nasir gritted through his clenched jaw, using every attempt to pry Kalia's fingers, but Rahmi had gotten hold of one of the flying carpets, zooming through the melee toward them.

He hopped from the carpet, tumbling head over foot before lunging forward and shoving Nasir away from her. "Now!" he shouted, fumbling with a set of keys at his belt. The carpet surged forward, wrapping around Nasir, who screamed and thrashed angrily.

"What are you doing here?" Kalia breathed out as he took her shackles in his hands and inserted the first key from the ring into them. The key didn't turn. "How did you get out? How did you find me? Did you know Reshef is a *djinn*?"

Rahmi's smirk was devastating as he inserted a second key and then a third. "Where do you think the flying carpets came from?"

"Where *did* the flying carpets come from?"

Rahmi shook his head, lips pursed as he inserted a fourth key. "No time, *ruehi*. Do you still have the *Luminaria*?"

Kalia clenched her fingers around the stone as he inserted the fifth key. It turned. "Yes, I have it."

Rahmi nodded, unlocking the first shackle before turning to the second. "When I get these off, I'm going to order the carpet to you. Take the *Luminaria* far from here, and bring Elodie and Shirin. Some of my crew are still aboard the ship. They'll sail you back to the capital." The second shackle unlocked, the set falling into a heap of iron and obsidian at their feet.

Kalia's power roared to life, filling her in ways she hadn't known it could. She missed it when it was just out of her reach. "And you'll be right behind me?" She lifted her stare from her free wrists, connecting her gaze with his. "Right?" she asked again when he said nothing in return.

Rahmi swallowed as a shriek echoed through the chamber. "You'll seal us inside when you leave to ensure nothing gets out. *The Mark of Malice* is gone. I'm only allowed off the ship for one day every seven years. I went off once with you to get the NightWatcher. My countdown began again the moment I was removed from my ship." He lifted a hand to brace the back of her head. "It was an honor to love you, *ruehi*."

His lips crashed onto hers, meltingly sweet. For the briefest of moments, his tongue swiped against her seam, and she opened for him long enough for their tongues to dance. She loved the taste of him and didn't want it to end, but he pulled away a second later.

As though unwillingly, Rahmi whistled over his shoulder at the flying carpet, which immediately unraveled itself from Nasir. "Go. Live your life. Forget about me and all of this." He pressed his lips to her forehead just as the carpet zoomed over, coming to a halt at her hip.

"Don't make me do this, Rahmi," Kalia pleaded with him as he grasped around her waist and lifted her onto the carpet. It folded slightly against her weight but remained steady. "Come with me, please. We'll get you back to the sea. We'll—"

"It's too late for me," Rahmi cut in with a curt shake of his head. He slapped the back of the carpet as though it were the hind of a horse, and Kalia grabbed ahold of the edge just as it dashed away. When she glanced over her shoulder, Rahmi had already turned toward Nasir, his cutlass cutting and swiping.

Kalia had never felt so helpless as she looked on at the battle raging below. Alaric was unconscious, his body wedged between two piles of gold coins. Thomas hadn't moved, blood still dripping from the corner of his mouth. Elodie was fighting two ghouls who hooked their claws into her flying carpet, desperately slashing her cutlass to get them to let go. And Reshef...and Reshef...

The *Luminaria* burned heavily in her hand. "Stop," she ordered the carpet, lurching forward as it came to a sudden halt. She glanced down at the gemstone, then back to Reshef, then back to the stone. It would take all of her power; she knew that the layers of his mind were complex and untested, and she might not recover...

But Kalia had never backed down from a challenge, especially concerning those around her. She learned that her friends made up some of the best parts of her and had taught her to love the parts of herself that she thought didn't deserve it. So, without another thought, Kalia thrust all of her Voyant power toward Reshef, barreling every ounce of her magic to punch through his mind.

His body went ramrod straight, the fourth djinn looking at him with concern, and then they were on a beach. The breeze was warm and sweet, something scented of coconut and citrus in the air, softly flapping her skirt around her ankles. She had imagined the sand to be sugar-fine, nothing like the rocky coast of the capital, and she took a moment to wriggle her toes into it. She wanted to keep them in the bright sunshine and under the blue sky.

"If you're going to take me out of the battle, you're going to have to imagine a cold drink in my hand," Reshef joked, that boyish charm tugging a smile on his lips. One that Kalia didn't return. He swallowed thickly, nodding to her. "I know that you're upset with me, that finding people who were honest with you was important, but what is going on out there...it's still happening. My body is still moving, still carrying out the order of my master. You have to use it."

Kalia shook her head. "No, Reshef, I can't. I don't *want* this, I don't want you to—"

"You shouldn't have even tried to get into my mind. You're already bleeding," Reshef said, his eyes growing with unfiltered concern. Kalia lifted her hand to prod her upper lip, not surprised to see that blood had already begun to drip from her nose. "It has to be you."

"Why? Why can't it be someone else? I don't *want* to be your master, I can't—"

"Because our magic chose *you* to remove the *Luminaria*. Because fate brought you here, brought us together. And I know you wouldn't use it to harm others...but Nasir would." Reshef's tone became clipped and frantic as more blood began to pour down Kalia's face. "You have to, Kalia, please. You'll have everything you ever wanted. We can provide that for you. Please. I'm going to— I'm going to kill Alaric if you don't. I won't have a choice, and it will end me. *Please*."

For a brief moment, Kalia imagined what that might look like. She imagined the wealth she could have, the property she could own. She could buy the bordello if she wanted to, but she would have to put the madam out of business for good.

She wrenched out of Reshef's mind, her vision clearing in time to look down and see the salt-and-pepper-haired djinn had turned toward Elodie, who was still battling one of the ghouls. Her hair was loose, her face sweaty and flushed. It was clear to Kalia that she was tired by the swings of Elodie's arms and her grip on the hilt. And she certainly wouldn't last battling a ghoul *and* a djinn.

Kalia made up her mind at that moment. She turned over the gemstone in her palm, clearing her dry throat and licking her lips. "I order the djinn to me!" she cried, raising the *Luminaria*. "I order them to heed my command!"

The four djinns below stilled just as the salt-and-pepper woman's hands rose to target Elodie. The battle ceased, the sand twisters fell into piles, and even the ghouls seemed to slow. Nasir looked up at her, his mouth open in a scream that she could not hear. Even Rahmi had stopped. His cutlass hung above his head.

There was immense power that flowed through her, limitless and terrible. She *could* have everything she ever wanted. She knew that now. It was endless, that well of magic. But she knew that wasn't what she truly wanted. Being the master of four djinn would only endanger her...Elodie...Shirin...Rahmi. She knew that she had no business taking any more from them.

Rahmi.

Kalia could free him, break his curse, and they could be together. But Kalia also knew that she only had the strength to do this once, only had enough strength for one command before that terrible power swallowed her whole. And she had to take it—for Reshef, for Alaric, for her.

"Djinn, I order you to destroy the *Luminaria* and set yourselves free."

CHAPTER THIRTY-NINE

KALIA

"No!" Nasir's bellow could be heard over the chaos from ghouls and the clang of metal on metal.

Energy pulsed like a living and breathing thing around them, sending surges of wind. It again whipped the sand into a frenzy, forcing the crew to shield their eyes against the grit. Basset, who had woken amidst the battle, had been taken to his knees by Cobden with a dagger against his throat. Even the ghouls staggered away, scrabbling back on unsteady gaits.

The chamber rattled and shook, coins spilling off the large piles and plunking into the water surrounding the room's edges. Stone broke away from the ceiling above, crashing down to the sand. One of them barely missed Elodie, who was fortunate enough to zoom away in time, the ghoul having ripped his claws from the carpet's fabric. It was almost comical, the shreds of the carpet flapping behind her as she flew, but that wasn't what held Kalia's attention.

The *Luminaria* in her palm began to glow brighter until Kalia squinted against the shine. It burned her hand, the heat of it blistering her flesh, but she couldn't let it go. She winced and cried out before the gemstone blasted apart, crumbling into a red dust that coated her skin.

Two of the djinn disappeared instantly, the woman with the slicked-back curls and a man with a broad nasal bridge, but Reshef and the salt-and-pepper woman remained behind. And, with a surprised squeal that rang out against the stone walls and jewels, Reshef suddenly appeared behind Nasir.

Rahmi's eyes widened, and he stumbled back just in time for Reshef to place his hand on the crown of Nasir's head.

"*No, no, no!*" the corsair shouted, thrashing with all of his strength to tear away from Reshef's grasp. But Reshef never let go. In the blink of an eye, Nasir's skin wrinkled and tightened as though he was being mummified before their eyes. His eyes sunk back before drying out completely, and he died with a silent scream wedging his mouth open.

As Reshef released him, Nasir's corpse tumbled to the ground and disappeared in a cloud of bone dust and tattered clothing.

Everything was quiet, too quiet. Kalia glanced around to spot the ghouls...or what was left of them. The salt-and-pepper woman had removed all of their heads from their bodies, scattering them around the chamber in a flurry of violence and rotting flesh.

Kalia maneuvered the carpet down to the ground, hopping off when she was within a few feet of Reshef. The djinn's chest still heaved, his breath coming in heavy pants that lifted his shoulders. Her feet sank into the soft sand, no longer packed to the stone thanks to the twisters that whirled it around.

"Why did you do that?" Reshef asked as she stepped closer, though he never turned to look at her. His voice was hoarse and filled with an emotion she couldn't pinpoint. "You had the *Luminaria*. You could have disappeared. You could have had everything you ever wanted."

Kalia curved around to face him, ignoring the crew that shrank away from them, ignoring that even Rahmi's gaze was darting between Reshef and what remained of Captain Nasir Al-Mahdi. Instead, she reached out and took his hand in hers, squeezing it tightly. "Because *you* were worth saving, my friend."

Without warning, Reshef tugged her into a hug that crushed her against his chest. Kalia could have sworn that she felt something drip from his chin onto her scalp, but when she looked up, his cheeks were still dry, and his eyes were fixed on something behind her. Kalia pushed away, turning to look over her shoulder and spotting the salt-and-pepper woman staring at Reshef, her lips softly parted.

"Reshef?" she asked, her tone so shaky and disbelieving that his name almost came out in a whisper. "Reshef, is that truly you?"

Reshef swallowed. "Mama?"

Kalia watched as his outer façade crumbled away, as tears did well in his red-rimmed eyes, and his head shook in utter denial.

The woman rushed forward with the speed of a parent reuniting with a child, her trembling hands reaching for him. They pressed against his cheeks, swept through his hair, patted his shoulders and chest. And all the while, Reshef's eyes were shut tight, enjoying every touch, every moment.

"My son, how...*how*?" his mother asked, her gaze raking over every inch of him. "You're grown. You were just a boy when I sent you away with the Luminaria."

"Yes, I was," Reshef chuckled. His eyes opened as he sniffled, wiping his nose with the back of his hand. "The obsidian you gave me, it protected me."

"I never thought I would lay my eyes on you again," she said, pulling him into a hug that Reshef collapsed into. "My boy, my *son*." She suddenly pushed him away, her gaze sharpening into one that resembled the golden-eyed stare of an eagle. "He will know you're here now. You have to go. We all have to go. Liddros, he—"

"I have one more thing I have to do," Reshef cut in, though he took her hands in his. "Then, yes, I will go." He squared his shoulders to face Rahmi, who went suddenly still. "I could kill you, you know, for what you did."

Kalia felt the air ice in her chest, and her skin tightened against the bone as she watched hopelessly as the djinn stalked toward the man she loved.

Rahmi, to his credit, nodded his head. "I understand." He lifted his chin, pulling back his shoulders as though readying to face his death. Kalia's belly squirmed, the contents turning into an oily sludge that threatened to crawl up her throat. "It's against my nature to ask for mercy, but—" His gaze slid briefly toward the pile of dust that was Nasir.

Reshef grinned that shit-eating smile Kalia knew so well, extending his hand toward Rahmi. The captain glanced at it, hesitating briefly, before lifting his own to grasp it. She felt her entire body relax, a breath escaping through her lips that she hadn't realized she had been holding. Reshef said nothing else as he released Rahmi's hand and turned to Kalia.

"You're leaving then?" Kalia asked, taking a small step toward him. Her throat tightened, a lump forming and burning there.

Reshef's smile turned brittle at the edges as he nodded. "I must. Liddros, he...he's more than he says that he is. I have to go before he finds us again."

Kalia glanced away from him, taking in the chamber. The sand had finally settled, dusting the crew in golden orange. It stuck in their hair, their clothes, and against their skin. Thomas had been healed, and he was sitting up with the help of Shirin, who had propped him against her legs. Even Alaric had woken, and the injury to his head healed, though the dried blood remained.

"I don't want you to go," Kalia finally said, her voice cracking against the strain of her sadness: her first friend, the one who had methodically chipped away at the wall around her heart.

Reshef placed a hand on her shoulder, pulling her into a tight hug that she was desperate not to let go of. "And you'll still see me. In all of the familiar places. I'll still be here in the apples you eat and the tobacco you steal."

A sob stifled her laugh as he finally pulled away from her.

"Now, I'm not in the business of granting wishes," Reshef lightly continued, his boyish charm flaring to life. "I find the whole notion to be unbelievably absurd. But...as a thank you for what you did, I'll give you one. What do you want more than anything in this world?"

What *did* she want? Wealth? She was surrounded by it. Even a handful of these coins would be more than enough. Power? She had felt it, had dug into that well of magic, and realized that she wanted nothing more to do with it. Security? Elodie was there, as were Shirin and Rahmi...

She paused, gazing at Reshef, who looked at her expectantly. "Can you break his curse?" Her gaze glided over to meet Rahmi's, and something was shining there that she couldn't pinpoint. Something that she hadn't basked in for a long, long time. Pride. Excitement. Love. "Would you want that?"

"Before you answer that," Reshef interjected. "I cannot keep your life as it is now. I am close to limitless in my power, but I am not Liddros. If you wish to be made mortal, to have your curse lifted—"

"Yes," Rahmi answered immediately, not allowing Reshef to finish. "Yes, that's what I want. All I want is her."

Kalia's heart swelled in her chest, so much so that she thought it would burst. But Reshef only smiled and nodded his head. "So be it."

There was one final rise of power, one final crest of that phantom wind. Rahmi hissed in pain, groaning out a primal need to shout, but Kalia could only keep her eyes fixed on his markings. Each disappeared, one by one, fading and fading before only his unmarked flesh remained. Rahmi turned his arms over, staring at them in utter shock before looking up at Kalia, his eyes only for hers.

"Kalia, I—" Rahmi began, but she was already running. She leaped into his arms, not caring that the crew was watching, and kissed him. Their lips met in a tangle of tongue and teeth. A coming home. A new beginning. He pulled away long enough to whisper, "I love you, I love you, *I love you*." Each proclamation noted by another kiss. He twirled her around before setting her down.

"And I you," Kalia responded, wrapping an arm around his neck to tug him into one more embrace. She knew there would never be enough, could never be enough. And her heart, once only a hole in her chest, began to thud beneath his touch.

Behind them, Reshef had approached Alaric, that boyish charm evolving into a fragile vulnerability. "Alaric, I—"

Alaric stepped forward, taking Reshef into his arms. "You'll come back for me, aye? When all settles, and you find us somewhere safe, you'll come back for me?" His single eye studied Reshef's face, a plead etched into every line of his features.

"Yes," Reshef said, sagging with relief that slumped his shoulders. "I'll come back for you." His lips pressed against the quartermasters, a promise sealed between two who weren't meant to fall for one another and did so anyway. He stepped away from Alaric, hesitantly and wistfully, and glanced back at Kalia. He blew her one final kiss before disappearing altogether, his mother with him.

The chamber was silent as the crew looked at one another.

"What now, captain?" one of the men asked, stepping away from Basset's slumped body. Kalia didn't know when Nasir's crew had been killed in the chaos. "What do we do?"

Rahmi looked at Kalia before pulling the old parchment from his pocket. "Where did you find that?" she breathed out, watching with rapt attention as he unfolded it.

"Captain's office before we came here, nicked it off his desk," Rahmi responded with a wink and a shrug. He tore it to shreds, slowly distributing the tiny pieces around the chamber. "And to answer your question, Elric, we are still pirates after all." He opened his arms wide to gesture around the chamber. "I say we empty this hall until we cannot stuff our pockets anymore." The crew cheered, and even the magic carpets happily zoomed around. Rahmi turned back to Kalia, reaching out to tuck a strand of her hair behind an ear. "And then, we go home."

"And where's home?" Kalia asked coyly, a smirk playing on her lips.

Rahmi's brows rose as he gathered her in his arms once more. "You're my home. But...I do recall there being an escape strategy for Sha'Hadra. Maybe we should start there?"

Kalia couldn't think of a better idea than that.

CHAPTER FORTY

KALIA

Two years later

The marketplace of Sha'Hadra was unfathomably hot. The warm desert breeze fluttered the stripped fabric blanketing the street, casting the shoppers in shadows. It did little to stave away the heat, and most stall owners still fanned themselves with large leaves routinely gathered from palm-like trees that grew just outside the city limits. The melding scents of fresh flowers, dyed leathers, and barrels of ground spices were heavy on the air.

And that was what Kalia was looking for.

Shirin had become quite the prolific chef in her days since leaving *The Mark of Malice*, something she had discovered when she had access to more than Doc's fish stew. Chicken, beef, all types of vegetables...Shirin had conquered them all. And every tiny bit was helpful, considering how much they had to make to feed the children of Sha'Hadra.

Rahmi and Kalia had filled all seven flying carpets with coins, gems, and jewelry from the Cave of Wonders. With a few crew members in tow, they had slyly sold them around the capital city to pay off the madam and barter transportation back to Sha'Hadra. With the remaining coin, and there was more of it than Kalia knew she could spend in a lifetime, they bought an abandoned mansion on the out-skirts of town. Had remodeled it and turned it into a refuge for the orphaned children that lived on the streets, making it into a safe place for them to find food and shelter. To learn how to read and write, to learn trades that would serve them as they turned into adults.

It was everything Kalia wanted as a child, everything she could have hoped to bring back to her home city.

And the view of the mountainous dunes, the desert flora that pep-pered those hills, the sand meeting the horizon in a haze of golden orange...those things weren't so bad either.

"I'm going to find the flour, Kalia!" one of the children yelled out, her excited voice piercing through the low chatter of the street-goers. One of her friends followed, and they giggled as they ran off together.

"Be careful!" Kalia shouted at their retreating backs, watching as both girls' brown braids bounced against their shoulder blades, their sandals slapping against the stone. "Meet us back here as soon as you're done!"

It had taken time for Kalia to release the guilt she felt for her mother and brother's deaths, those feelings roaring to the forefront as soon as she stepped foot back in her hometown. She didn't realize how much she pushed down until she walked those familiar alleys. She struggled with how to cope for weeks, helpless and floundering. It wasn't until a young boy attempted to pickpocket Rahmi that the idea came to her, and she began to foster relationships with the orphaned youth of the city.

It took weeks, months even, of reaching out for them to begin to trust her. But Kalia kept building their trust, using that foundation her friends had taught her. Eventually, it paid off.

And she found that Rahmi enjoyed it just the same. He took some of the youth bordering on adulthood under his proverbial wing to teach them how to carve wood and make leather. His smile grew daily as he watched them excel in what he taught, and three of the older ones finally sold enough leather bags and specially made wooden furniture to fund a marketplace stall of their own. One that Rahmi helped them oversee.

"Those girls seem very devoted to you," a voice murmured behind Kalia. "Are they yours?"

Kalia turned with difficulty, the alleys of the marketplace strained with the number of tourists racing from the capital to enjoy the warm season and found herself looking into a set of stone-colored eyes. "No, they aren't mine," she replied, narrowing her eyes at him. "Why?"

The man shrugged, his muscular shoulder lifting and dropping. "I've been curious, Kalia Abada, about the life you've made with your husband since leaving *The Mark of Malice*. I found that I had some time to come and find out."

Kalia swallowed, and something pulled behind her navel as she took a step closer to the man. "How do you know my name?" she asked, her gaze roving his face. It was almost too perfect. His square-cut jaw was too sharp, his muscles too pristinely sculpted beneath his clothing, his frame too tall, and his eyes lit too brightly in the shadows. And suddenly she got the feeling that this man wasn't human.

He smirked. "I've known about you for quite some time now. Kalia Salam, now Abada of course, the destroyer of the *Luminaria* and the one who freed the djinn. Your reputation does proceed you—"

Kalia felt a hand wrap around her forearm, felt her being tugged behind the body of a wide-shouldered man. She was bathed in his scent— leather dye and spices that now replaced the brine and ship wax— and glanced around Rahmi's elbow to see that he gripped the hilt of his blade in his hand.

"What are you doing here, Liddros?" Rahmi growled, his cutlass halfway out of the sheath tied to his hip. It was one of the only things he brought to Sha'Hadra; the rest was sent to a watery grave at the bottom of the Aeglecian Sea.

Kalia gaped up at the dark-haired man who was now smirking at her husband. *Liddros*? *The God of the Sea*? He bent his head toward Kalia as though to say *in the flesh* before he slid his gaze back toward Rahmi.

"I just came to see what you've been up to since your curse was broken," Liddros said, reaching over to pinch some ground spices in the barrel next to him. He lifted it to his nose, sniffing briefly before flicking the herbs from his fingertips. "I'm always curious to see what my former captains are doing."

The shop owner eyed Liddros carefully, though he seemed to know better than to say anything. The god certainly had that air about him.

"You still have a captain on the seas," Rahmi noted, not removing his hand from the hilt of the cutlass. "Why don't you find a way to torture him? You have no business here."

Liddros's eyes flashed, though that smirk remained planted on his lips. "Jace certainly is my only captain...for now, at least."

Kalia couldn't help but read the meaning behind the statement, and an anger she hadn't felt in months swirled inside her veins. "What do you mean *for now*? Will you make more captains to find your souls for the king? That's disgusting—"

Liddros's eyes glided over to meet hers, and Kalia tempered the shudder that prickled the back of her neck. His smirk only deepened. "I've always liked you." He paused to shake a finger at her, still stained red from the spice he had pinched. "I think you're good for him. However, your propensity to speak out of turn is concerning. It would be best if you were more careful—"

"Are you threatening her?" Rahmi hissed, loud enough that a few shoppers stopped to watch the confrontation.

"Of course not," Liddros replied coolly. "And I would consider removing your hand from your cutlass before the palace guards cart you off. I would hate to see the life you've made for yourself cut short because you cannot swallow your anger."

Kalia glanced around to find two palace guards close by, each of their gazes wandering over the shoppers' heads. She flicked her glare back to Rahmi, laying her hand gently on his forearm. His ease at her touch was barely noticeable, though his hand rested on the blade's pommel rather than the hilt. Liddros seemed pleased enough.

"To answer your question, no, Kalia. I am not *making more captains*. Though it is certainly more nuanced than that." Those stone-colored eyes, so unnatural in human form, bored into her. "There are things set into motion that will change the foundations of this world. Only one captain to go."

Kalia searched his stare, not backing down from its intense scrutiny. "You led us to the *Luminaria*, didn't you? You had no intention of using it to set yourself free."

Beneath her hand, Rahmi's forearm stiffened again. "I thought you sent me to retrieve it *for* you. *For us.*"

Liddros canted his head. "Do you truly believe I could free you when I couldn't free myself? I merely planted the tools and plucked the strings of time, all the while hoping that the result would fall into my lap. And fall into my lap, it did. You both should be grateful, too. It led you to one another, did it not?"

"Kalia! Rahmi!" a high-pitched and sharp voice waded through the crowd. "We got the flour! We found it!"

Despite her burning anxiety, Kalia set a smile on her face, turning to look down at the two girls who appeared at her hip. Their cheeks were flushed, and one of the girls lifted the flour sack, a triumphant grin on her lips. "And thank the gods for you both. Shirin wouldn't know what to do without either of you."

The two girls beamed at one another.

Liddros stooped to eye-level with them, and the movement was preternaturally graceful despite his bulk. "I heard you've been a big help to Rahmi and Kalia as of late. I'm sure they are extremely grateful for you both."

"They are," one of the girls, Aisha, said with pride. "We help all the time. Shirin in the kitchen. Elodie with reading, though I'm not very good at that yet. I used to help Alaric, and he let me try on his eye patch once, but Kalia said he went to live with his *boyfriend* a few weeks ago. I met him. He was tall."

"Indeed," Liddros said, arching a single brow. "Then you will allow me to present you with something to remember an old friend by." He reached behind his back, producing two toy-sized pirate ships from thin air. Both were finely carved from a block of dark wood, and Kalia saw a name etched delicately into the side of each one: *The Hangman's Revenge*.

Both girls squealed with delight as they took the toys from Liddros. "Will it float?" Aisha asked, bobbing it through the air as though it were floating on the sea.

"I sure hope so," Liddros responded as he stood. "What kind of ship would it be if it didn't?"

"Do you think Thomas would take us to the oasis to play with them?" the second girl, Dareen, pleaded as she turned toward Rahmi. "Please, please?" Aisha also turned to look at Kalia eye level, her brown eyes wide despite the sun that peered over the edge of the stripped fabric above them.

"I guess we'll need to go home and find out," Rahmi responded with a smile. Kalia knew he could never say no to the children, especially the younger ones. It set a yearning in her chest, imagining that man with a child, their child.

Kalia turned back to Liddros, starting when she saw he had disappeared. Rahmi glanced at her, unease settled in the depths of his eyes. It mirrored her own. "Let's head home," Kalia called to Dareen and Aisha, who had run to the nearest alley entrance to play with the toy ships in their hands. "Elodie and Shirin would love to see your new things."

Both girls sprinted ahead of them, pushing through the crowd as Rahmi snaked an arm around Kalia's waist to pull her tight to his side. "What do you think that was about?" she asked, squeezing through a gap in the shoppers as they headed to the market's exit.

"I think we would be dead on this street if it were for anything other than what he voiced," Rahmi responded, finally taking his hand off the pommel of his cutlass.

"And Jace?" Kalia went on. "The third captain?"

Rahmi nodded. "And may the gods have mercy on his soul if Liddros has nothing better to do than watch him." He paused to plant a kiss on her temple. "Come on, let's go home. I'm sure the boys have tormented Searles enough in the hours we've been gone."

Kalia smiled at the thought. Searles still wasn't comfortable around the children, though he stuck around anyway to help with the ongoing renovations of the house. It helped that he began to court a local woman who had stolen his attention a few months back.

"I think the flying carpets are enough distraction that Searles had some assistance." She imagined the tassel-waving carpets with children clambered on them, laughing as they zoomed around the dunes, their toes tickling the sand. More importantly, it was safely out of sight from the guards. Even Elodie's tiger, who had grown to full size in the last year, lazed around as the children played with his tail.

Their family was patchwork and odd, filled with people who had lived for centuries and were still navigating a fresh start. It wasn't perfect, and there was still much to do, but Kalia knew that the man by her side would be the one to see them through it. To guide them through every storm, with her as the light to his darkness.

His *ruehi*. Her captain.

First, I want to thank my husband, Joe, for the never-ending support and love he has given me. Thank you for letting me cry on your shoulder, for listening to me read passages out loud, and for helping me manage my anxiety when I questioned why I was doing this every other day. You are my life partner, my dream, and my heart. I love you forever!

Thank you to my close-knit family! My parents cultivated a creativity in me that still burns brightly to this day. You let me spread my wings and chase my dreams to the tallest mountains. There isn't enough gratitude in the world for me to express. To my sisters, who inspire me and challenge me, thank you for being my first readers, for your *honest* edits and feedback, and for loving me through every stage of life. I'm so immensely proud to be your big sister!

Finally, you can't read, because you're a doggo. But soulmates come in all forms, and one of mine is in you. You, my Sadie-girl, are an old lady now, but you have been my road trip partner, running buddy, college roommate, daily rock during cancer treatments, and much more. You've sat at my feet every single day while I write these stories. One day, you'll be gone, and I'll endure a lifetime of missing you for the privilege of loving you. I stole your name so that everyone can know a piece of you forever.

Author and full-time respiratory therapist Sadie Hewitt grew up in Ann Arbor, Michigan, and is a diehard Michigan Wolverines fan. She doesn't claim a home anymore, rather chooses to travel the country with her football-fanatic husband and two feral, yet lovable, dogs. She loves to write in urban paranormal fantasy and fantasy romance, mostly about powerful women, morally gray men, found families, and a sprinkle (or pour) of magic and spice.

When she's not thinking of ways to crush her readers completely, you can find Sadie scaling mountains worldwide, catching up on her own TBR, and checking out the local coffee shops.

Don't forget to check out her latest series, The Mage, today!

Made in United States
North Haven, CT
12 April 2024

51214070R00253